"Commentaries that deal explicitly with ~~the Greek~~ ... are not common. Those that move beyond ~~word studies and basic grammar~~ are even less common. Professor Varner does what is rare: He treats lexical semantics, grammar, and syntax at both the sentence and discourse levels. Applying the nascent discipline of discourse analysis, this volume provides a careful and helpful study of the message of James that exhibits 'trust in the text' to accurately communicate James'—and God's—message to the church."

—**Rodney Decker**, professor of New Testament
Baptist Bible Seminary

"Will Varner has written an excellent volume that both introduces discourse analysis and provides useful and meaningful commentary on the book of James. He rightly shows that discourse analysis is not a thing to be feared, but rather something of direct benefit to exegetes and practitioners. Varner's introduction provides a concise and helpful articulation of his method of discourse analysis, and his analysis itself is grounded in the text throughout. I highly recommend this commentary as an exemplification of what the future of commentary writing can and should look like."

—**Stanley E. Porter**, president, dean, and professor of New Testament
McMaster Divinity College

"You've no doubt heard that the three most important things about real estate are: location, location, location. Likewise, the three most important things about biblical interpretation are: context, context, context. There are great dangers in trying to make sense of a whole sentence by a word or two, or a book by only one paragraph. Will Varner has done pioneer work in this unique commentary on James with this perspective in full focus. This volume explains the whole in view of the parts, and the parts in view of the whole. No other commentary has helped me more for understanding and preaching the book of James than this linguistic commentary. It is simply outstanding!"

—**Rick Holland**, executive pastor, Grace Community Church
Director of DMin studies
The Master's Seminary

"William Varner has done an outstanding job of taking complex ideas and presenting them in an accessible and very readable fashion. His unique commentary on James not only provides much insight into the text, but also serves as a valuable resource for helping students of Greek take their language skills to the next level."

—**Martin Culy**, associate professor of New Testament
Briercrest College and Seminary

"The field of 'Jacobean' studies has been enriched by this innovative and provocative work. A Linguistic Commentary on the Letter of James adds to the wealth of literature available to those who desire to understand this epistle. The author's discourse analysis approach sets him apart from the traditional commentaries on James. Yet he is dedicated to a methodology grounded in the grammatical realities of the text that enables an individual to 'hear' the message of James. Readers will find this a perceptive and challenging commentary filled with rich exegetical insights and informed discussions on the theme, unity, structure, and intertextuality of James. Varner recognizes the value of knowing a biblical author's literary style in solving exegetical and textual problems. Students and scholars of James will accrue rich dividends by investing in the reading of this thought-provoking, well written, and linguistically informed commentary."

—**Dr. Paul W. Felix**, associate professor of New Testament
The Master's Seminary

"Will Varner's commentary breaks new ground with a discourse analysis of the epistle of James. Varner tills the soil with innovative linguistic, syntactical, semantic, and rhetorical investigations. He also employs cutting edge work in the field, including verbal aspect theory, speech-act theory, and comparative studies of wisdom literature. The reader will reap a new understanding of the structural 'big picture' of the epistle, rooted in cogent discussions of syntactical cohesion, semantic chaining, linguistic prominence, and discourse peaking. The careful cultivation of the text yields a rich harvest of original insights."

—**Paul Hartog**, associate professor
Faith Baptist Theological Seminary

THE BOOK OF JAMES
A NEW PERSPECTIVE

WILLIAM VARNER

THE BOOK OF JAMES—A NEW PERSPECTIVE
© 2010 William Varner

Published by Kress Biblical Resources

P.O. Box 132228
The Woodlands, TX 77393
www.kressbiblical.com

ISBN 978-1-934952-12-2
Cover Design: Mario Kushner
Text Design: Valerie Moreno

DEDICATION

I wish to dedicate this commentary on James to Taylor and Lorraine Reece, retired missionaries to Japan.

"Buz" and "Rainy" were spiritually influential on me at very important times in my young Christian life. They have continued to be living models of what a couple serving the Lord should be.

More than anyone else I have known, they have lived the lives that James describes in his letter.

"But be doers of the word, and not hearers only, deceiving yourselves." (James 1:22)

"Humble yourselves before the Lord, and he will exalt you." (James 4:10)

"Behold, we consider those blessed who remained steadfast." (James 5:11)

CONTENTS

ACKNOWLEDGMENTS

I would like to thank Stanley Porter of McMaster Divinity College and Andrew Pitts of Veritas Theological Seminary for inviting me to write a commentary based on the principles of discourse analysis. Although this volume did not end up in the project they first envisioned, it was Stan's pioneering work in this field and Andrew's mastery of the approach that enabled me to finish the work.

I would also like to thank The Master's College, the Riddle Family Foundation, and the Believers Foundation for their assistance in seeing this project through to publication. A former student who is now a colleague, Abner Chou, has been a great help to me through his research on James and his other work on the NT use of the OT. Students in Intermediate Greek II have worked through the Greek text of James and I thank them for challenging me to get it right. One of them, Cliff Kvidahl, has remained at my side during his seminary days, and has become my invaluable research assistant. Students and faculty at The Master's Seminary, especially Richard Mayhue and Michael Grisanti, have been an encouragement to me as I have tried to plow new ground through this linguistic approach.

John MacArthur, President of The Master's College and Seminary, offered a valuable suggestion that greatly improved the Introduction. Former students, Aaron Gaglia and Geoff Kirkland, helped with proofreading.

My wife, Helen, has always been patient with my hectic schedule of research, teaching and preaching. Her desire that I always stress the practical application in my teaching is another indication that she is a doer of the word and not just a hearer.

WHAT YOU SHOULD EXPECT
FROM THIS COMMENTARY

I have nearly a thousand commentaries in my library and I have consulted commentaries for over forty years, so I know something about their style and purpose. In my opinion many commentaries end up being a series of word studies joined together, oftentimes with no real effort to show how all the micro-texts fit together within the larger macro-text. Furthermore, many traditional commentaries consist mainly of comments on other commentaries. This type of commentator will inform the reader about the views of other commentators on a verse, and then will tell you his or her own view. Now I am beginning to sound pretty cynical, but I don't mean to do so. I am just telling you that the commentary in your hands is not like the ones I have just described.

If you come to this commentary just to find the meaning of a single word in a verse, you will probably be disappointed. Furthermore, if you come here to find all the interpretations of each verse, you will also be disappointed. My approach is to study each verse but always to keep my eye on the Big Picture of the discourse as a whole. That is where many commentators fall short of a real analysis of the text. They will tell you a lot about the individual trees in the forest, but will often fail to describe what the forest looks like – and how those trees contribute to the appearance of the forest as a whole.

The way I try to do this is to study the entire Letter of James as a whole, utilizing the tools of an exciting new discipline called discourse analysis. The approach has been around for years, but it is just beginning to be utilized in Biblical Studies. I describe the method in the lengthy first chapter and it would really be valuable for you to work through those pages to get an idea how my approach to the text differs from other commentators. If you just cannot do that, pick up the chapter about two thirds of the way through when I start to apply discourse analysis in general terms to the text of James as a whole. You may be surprised at the degree in which we actually look at the details of the text, but as we work from the bottom up, we will never forget that we are also studying the book from the top down. This commentary will work best for you if you are studying the entire Letter of James, although I believe that it will still be valuable if you just consult a single paragraph.

You will not find in these pages a typical "Introduction" that deals with the author, the recipients, the date, and the genre of the writing. I follow the wisdom of Richard Bauckham, one of my favorite writers on James, who has suggested that these issues can only be addressed as part of the exegesis of the book. So I deal with those issues in my actual comments on the text at the appropriate places in that text. In Appendix One, "Why Have We Been Unjust to James the Just?," I do deal with the identity of James and his crucial leadership role in the early church.

If your background does not include some exposure to the Greek language, the analysis may sometimes be difficult to follow completely in all its details. I am sorry for that, but I decided early on that this commentary is not for everyone. I have tried to balance the Greek citations with English translations, but there is no way around the fact that this work leans heavily on the Greek text of James.

I am not so arrogant as to think that I have written the best commentary on James or that I believe that there is no need for those types of commentaries I criticized earlier. As a matter of fact, I recommend the commentaries of J.B. Mayor, Luke Johnson, Douglas Moo, Craig Blomberg, Ben Witherington, and Dan McCartney. Each of these is written along the lines of a traditional commentary, although they do not usually lapse into those bad habits I criticized earlier. They are each mentioned in the Bibliography and I cite them occasionally, especially Moo. McCartney's commentary was published after I finished my rough draft so I was not able to utilize it like I desired. Commentaries most useful for expositors are noted by an asterisk in the Bibliography and briefly annotated.

Exegesis should always lead to exposition. The teaching and preaching of James should be the ultimate goal for any commentary. To better facilitate that goal, I have offered in Appendix Two some homiletical suggestions on how each chapter of James can be communicated to laypeople in churches and Bible classes. These may be helpful to some readers, if only to serve as seed thoughts for further reflection.

I do believe that the commentary makes a valuable contribution to the study of James and I hope that it will help to continue the "discourse revolution" that began quite awhile ago in literary circles, but has taken longer to make an impact in the study of Biblical literature.

My life has been greatly affected by the message of James. It has opened up for me again the Wisdom literature, of which it is the prime New Testment example. It has also awakened in me an interest in the poor and the otherwise marginalized souls in the community and in the church. And it is a very strong reminder that the apostles had their feet firmly planted on the ground of earthly life when they expounded the words of eternal life. Those effects on me are my prayer requests for you as you work through this commentary.

A DISCOURSE METHOD
FOR JAMES

F or forty years I have preached and taught the Word of God with the full conviction that it is inspired and inerrant. I have lived long enough to fight "the battle for the Bible" and I can affirm that the losers in that battle are those who deny its full truthfulness in all its details. Along with that conviction has been a personal commitment to historical-grammatical hermeneutics and exegesis. My pastor and colleague, John MacArthur, likes to add a third adjective to those hyphenated words: his-torical-grammatical-*contextual* exegesis. I heartily agree with that addi-tion, and it is in light of that commitment to contextual exegesis that I introduce many readers to discourse analysis. This exegetical discipline is based on a firm conviction that a text can only be interpreted correctly in light of its context. And that includes both its surrounding context and also its far context, that is, the book as a whole. When "discourse" appears in this chapter, it is simply another term for the "entire book." I view the discourse analysis method that I will employ in analyzing James to be fully consistent with what historical-grammatical-*contextual* exegesis has always taught, but with a rigorous attention to *context*.

So then what exactly is discourse analysis? In teaching discourse analysis to students over the years, I have often remarked to them that discourse analysis is better *described* than *defined*. I also have reminded them that, in my opinion, discourse analysts have been better at apply-ing the method to actual texts than in theorizing about their work. To put it simply, when humans perceive that a discourse "makes sense" to them, it generally means that there is some theme that flows through the discourse that allows them to recognize it as cohesive rather than as a bunch of unrelated words.

This admittedly simplified statement forms the groundwork for the type of analysis which we will apply to the Letter of James. Some critics of discourse analysis argue that since this analytical method works from the "top down," it does not warrant treatment as a truly grammatical approach to language. That can be a valid criticism only if the critic has already concluded that "grammar" is limited to the clause and sentence level.[1] When we acknowledge that the meaning of individual words in a sentence cannot be confidently determined apart from their wider discourse context, then we must acknowledge that working from the top down is also a necessity. Actually, discourse analysts work both ways, i.e., from the bottom up and from the top down, in studying the discourse as a whole.[2]

For many years teachers of exegesis have stressed the importance of never taking a text out of its context. Discourse analysis is simply a way of extending that context in a rigorous manner to all the levels of a discourse. In recent years, it has been encouraging that a few handbooks on NT exegesis have begun to recognize the important role that discourse analysis plays in understanding a text.[3] In this commentary, the role of words in clauses will be rigorously examined, but it is recognized that we must view all the details of the "small" picture in light of the metastructure themes explained in the "big" picture.[4]

DISCOURSE METHODOLOGY

Lest we become too exclusively theoretical, we must ask how such an approach works in actually analyzing discourse. Jeffrey Reed mentions four guiding principles that form the general basis of the discourse analysis of NT texts.

---

[1] An example of this type of criticism can be found in the otherwise valuable grammar by D. B. Wallace, *Greek Grammar Beyond the Basics* (Grand Rapids: Zondervan, 1996), xv.

[2] "In discourse analysis one can begin at the top (the discourse) or at the bottom (the word), but one must work through all of the stages, from both directions, to provide a full analysis." S. E. Porter, *Idioms of the Greek New Testament* (2nd ed. Sheffield: Sheffield Academic, 1994), 299.

[3] See R. Erickson, *A Beginners Guide to NT Exegesis* (Downers Grove: InterVarsity Press, 2005) 80-91; and W. Egger, *How to Read the New Testament: An Introduction to Linguistic and Historico-Critical Methodology* (trans. P. Heinegg; Peabody, Mass.: Hendrickson, 1996) for brief sections on discourse analysis and text-linguistics and their application to NT exegesis. See also the relevant chapters in J. B. Green, ed., *Hearing the New Testament* (Grand Rapids: Eerdmans, 1995) and S. E. Porter, ed., *A Handbook to the Exegesis of the New Testament* (Leiden: Brill Academic, 2002).

[4] One of the most important developments in this regard is the work of OpenText.org, which is an online syntactical analysis of each book of the NT, displayed as both a clause analysis and as a word group analysis (www.opentext.org). The Logos Research Systems now includes in Logos 4.0 *The OpenText.org Syntactically Analyzed Greek New Testament* as well as a similar program, *The Lexham Syntactic Greek New Testament*. These syntactically tagged databases can be searched as well. For a thorough discussion of how these and other corpora can be utilized in discourse analysis, see M. B. O'Donnell, *Corpus Linguistics and the Greek of the New Testament* (NTM 6; Sheffield: Sheffield Phoenix, 2005).

1. Analysis of the production and interpretation of discourse

2. Analysis beyond the sentence

3. Analysis of social functions of language use

4. Analysis of cohesiveness[5]

I wish to emphasize at this point the vital role of two of these tenets with some elaboration on an additional principle, that of prominence. Together, they form the theoretical basis of my own particular method, which will then be outlined.[6]

THINKING BEYOND THE CLAUSE AND THE SENTENCE

Reed affirms what many other writers have also recognized that the first and most often mentioned tenet of discourse analysis is to examine language at a level beyond the sentence.[7] This is perhaps the most distinguishing tenet of discourse analysis. Sadly, traditional biblical exegesis, while always nodding its approval on the importance of context, has sometimes ignored this principle in practice. The analysis of words and clauses is vastly important, but their importance is constrained by the perspective of the larger discourse in which they are found. It is probably helpful to view all the linguistic elements of a text as comprising different "levels of discourse," with individual words on the bottom level and then clauses, clause complexes, sentences, paragraphs, and the entire discourse on the ascending levels, similar to a pyramid.[8]

---

[5] J. T. Reed, "Discourse Analysis," in *A Handbook to the Exegesis of the New Testament* (NTTS v. 25; ed. S. E. Porter; Leiden: Brill, 2002), 189-94. The reader is referred to the rest of this chapter for more detailed discussion of these four tenets and for further guidance on "doing discourse analysis" (194-213).

[6] For a thorough treatment of the various elements of discourse analysis and their application to NT texts, see S. E. Porter and M. B. O'Donnell, *Discourse Analysis and the New Testament* (Leiden: Brill), *forthcoming*.

[7] Reed, 190-92. "The study of larger units of language (than words and clauses) is normally called *discourse analysis*, or *text-linguistics*." D. A. Black, *Linguistics for Students of New Testament Greek* (Grand Rapids: Baker, 1995), 170.

[8] Porter coveys this analogy by the figure of a pyramid, with "word" as the base and successive levels as "phrase," "sentence," "pericope," and finally "discourse" as the cap of the pyramid. *Idioms*, 298. Longacre describes the levels from the top-down as "discourse, paragraph, sentence, clause, phrase, word and stem." R. E. Longacre, *The Grammar of Discourse* (2nd ed.; London: Plenum Press, 1996), 291-94.

As an example from the NT, discourse analysts are not content to examine the role of the genitive absolute participle at simply the clausal and sentence levels. They also ask if the author may be using this type of participle in the context beyond the sentence at the discourse level.[9] An example of this approach can be seen in Matthew's use of five genitive absolutes as an overall discourse strategy in the infancy narratives of chapters 1 and 2, as well as in the rest of the book.[10]

COHESION AND COHERENCE

The second of Reed's principles that I wish to stress is *the role of cohesiveness* in discourse. Oftentimes, the word *coherence* is also mentioned in close connection with a text's *cohesiveness. Cohesion* is a means of linking clauses and sentences into larger syntactical units while *coherence* is a semantic dimension and refers to the various ways which readers make sense of a text.

Both cohesion and coherence stress the need to see language as a dynamic interaction between speaker and listener or writer and reader. Specifically, cohesion occurs where the interpretation of some element in the discourse is dependent on that of another. Cohesion is so important that O'Donnell makes the following telling observation, "Many treatments of discourse analysis are in reality simply discussions of cohesion. In many ways it is the simplest area of discourse analysis to understand."[11] Westfall adds, "Cohesion involves the interpretation of some element in the text depending on another element. That is, 'the one presupposes the other,' or the preceding element *constrains* the meaning of the second element."[12] Discourse entities linked to each other are said to have a cohesive "tie."

There are a number of ways in which to establish the cohesion of a

---

[9] L. K. Fuller, "The 'Genitive Absolute' in New Testament/Hellenistic Greek: A Proposal for Clearer Understanding ," *JGRChJ* 3 (2006), 142-67. An intermediate grammar that recognizes this function of the genitive absolute participle is R. Young, *Intermediate New Testament Greek: A Linguistic and Exegetical Approach* (Nashville: Broadman and Holman, 1994), 159. Both the above authors draw on the research of P. and A. Healey, "Greek Circumstantial Participles: Tracking Participants and Participles in the Greek New Testament," *OPTAT* 4 (1990), 177-259.

[10] W. Varner, "A Discourse Analysis of Matthew's Nativity Narrative," *TB* 58.2 (2007):98-120.

[11] O'Donnell, *Corpus Linguistics & the Greek of the New Testament*, 156n.

[12] C. L. Westfall, *A Discourse Analysis of the Letter to the Hebrews* (LNTS 297; SNTG 11; London: T&T Clark, 2005), 31.

biblical text. *Grammatical* cohesion is evidenced in Hellenistic Greek by the agreement between subject and verb, and the agreement between nouns and adjectives. Examples of this in Greek, like in English, are so numerous they need not be mentioned. Unlike English, however, there is a closer agreement in Greek between the formal features of person with verbs and gender endings with nouns.

Lexical cohesion is the use of the same word or of similar words from the same semantic domain. Lexical repetition to form cohesion can be seen, for example, in the repetition and fronting of eighteen dative singular forms of πίστις in Hebrews 11:3-31. Sometimes, lexical cohesion can be established by "lexical chains" or "semantic chains" in a passage. This involves the repetition of the same word or words from the same semantic domain within a stretch of text. Westfall points out such a semantic chain of four different verbs (λαλέω, λέγω, ἀκούω, and συνεπιμαρτυρέω) in Hebrews 1:1-2:4, which serves to span together the subunit within the larger unit of 1:1-4:16.[13]

Relational cohesion is signaled by conjunctions and other connectives. Mark, for example, often uses εὐθύς to signal significant turning points in his narrative (1:23, 29; 6:45; 8:10; 14:43; 15:1) as well as important events within a narrative itself (9:15, 24). Matthew is well known for utilizing the adverb τότε for a similar purpose in his narrative strategy (2:7, 16, 17; 3:5, 13, 15; 4:1, 5, 19, 11, 17).[14]

Referential cohesion refers to links between an element in the immediate text and something else. For example, *anaphora* is a referential link to a prior element in the text. Greek has many resources for this function, such as the use of the relative pronoun ὅς in Phil. 2:6: ὅς ἐν μορφῇ θεοῦ ὑπάρχων ("who although he was in the form of God"), with the relative pronoun referring back to Jesus in the preceding verse. On the other hand, *cataphora* is a referential link to a following element in the text. The Greek demonstrative pronoun οὗτος can function both in an anaphoric manner and, although not as often, in a cataphoric manner. The latter cataphoric function is illustrated by James 1:27: θρησκεία καθαρὰ καὶ ἀμίαντος παρὰ τῷ θεῷ καὶ πατρὶ **αὕτη** ἐστίν, ἐπισκέπτεσθαι ὀρφανοὺς καὶ χήρας ἐν τῇ θλίψει αὐτῶν—"pure and undefiled religion before our

---

[13] Westfall, *Hebrews*, 95-98.

[14] For a thorough discussion of Matthew's use of conjunctions beyond the sentence, see S. Black, *Sentence Conjunctions in the Gospel of Matthew: Καί, Δέ, Τότε, Γάρ, Οὖν and Asyndeton in Narrative Discourse* (Sheffield: Sheffield Academic Press, 2002).

God and Father is **this**, to visit orphans and widows in their affliction." Finally, *exophora* is a referential link to some element outside the text, known to the readers. Paul's appealing to the knowledge of the Corinthians about another letter, unknown to us, that he had written to them is just such an exophoric referential link (1 Cor. 5:9).

"Cohesion, you may say, is the glue that holds a discourse together."[15] Hellenistic Greek has an abundance of resources available that can function as cohesive links in biblical text.[16]

PROMINENCE

The third feature of discourse analysis that I wish to stress as a key part of my own method is the function of linguistic *prominence*. I will attempt to formulate a broad definition of prominence and then seek to describe briefly its special cohesive and coherent functions in discourse.

Reed succinctly makes the contrast between cohesion and prominence as follows. Lexical and grammatical ties function as a *cohesion of similarity*, while prominence functions as a *cohesion of dissimilarity*.[17] In other words, an author uses language to set apart certain entities from other entities of the discourse. The reader's attention is drawn to important topics in the discourse, which are then supported by less prominent material. Thus prominence functions to set aside certain ideas as more semantically or pragmatically significant than others.

Interpreters have often noticed variation in the expected word order of individual words or clauses. When Paul places his relative clauses before his verbs in Romans 7:15, 16 and 19, 20, we can say that he lends prominence to those clauses which usually follow the verbs. It has often been noted that the Johannine phrase ἐγώ εἰμι, in which the pronoun is not required by the Greek verb, indicates prominence (e.g. John 6:48, 51).

Rather than speak of emphatic or less emphatic features, it is best to suggest a cline of prominence that could be labeled by various degrees.[18] More important than closely defined labels, however, is the

---

[15] Young, *Intermediate New Testament Greek*, 254.

[16] For further discussions of cohesive features in the Greek NT, see Young's *Intermediate New Testament Greek*, 254-55, and J. Grimes, "Signals of Discourse Structure in Koine," *SBL Seminar Papers 1975* (ed. George MacRae; Missoula, MT: SBL, 1975), 1: 151-64.

[17] Reed, *Philippians*, 385.

[18] Reed describes his own approach to discourse prominence as functioning on three levels: *background*, *theme*, and *focus*. Reed, *Philippians* 107-10, 386.

notion that some information is less prominent in the discourse and some more prominent. In the case of non-narrative text, those items with background prominence serve to support the main argument by providing explanations, conclusions, and summaries. Those items in thematic prominence provide information that is central to the author's "message." In non-narrative text, thematically prominent elements, when first appearing in a discourse, are expected to appear again. The reader can expect the rest of the discourse to be about the theme of an introductory sentence. It is also possible to make such thematic statements even more prominent, as we shall see. While background and thematic elements can appear across the discourse at all levels—clause, sentence, paragraphs, and discourse—the more focused elements often are prominent at the level of paragraph and then fall out of this level of prominence in the next.

A fruitful way of viewing the cline of prominence has been proposed by Porter, and is the approach that will be utilized in my own analysis.[19] Porter traces the discussion of prominence to the notion of *deviation from a norm*.[20] The importance of a *semantic* role for prominence cannot be overemphasized, lest this linguistic feature become simply ornamentation for artistic sake, rather than performing the function of communicating meaning more effectively. In other words, it is simply not adequate to identify prominence by noting examples of deviated syntax apart from a larger semantic framework.

Linguists have long recognized a fundamental set of two levels of grounding, generally referred to as background and foreground.[21] Foreground material embodies the more important events of a narrative or the most important steps of a procedure or the main points of an exposition. Background material includes events of lesser importance or subsidiary procedures or secondary points of exposition. Building on his earlier work on verbal aspect, Porter suggests a threefold cline of *background, foreground* and *frontground* levels of prominence.[22] "The frontground provides a narrower range of characteristic semantic features than do items of background and foreground, conveying discrete,

---

[19] Porter, *Discourse Analysis and the NT, forthcoming.*

[20] Porter, *Discourse Analysis and the NT,* forthcoming. Note resemblance to a *cohesion of dissimilarity.*

[21] Longacre distinguishes the prominence of "mainline" material in relationship to "supporting" material. *Grammar of Discourse,* 21.

[22] S. E. Porter, *Verbal Aspect in the Greek of the NT, with Reference to Tense and Mood* (SBG 1; New York: Peter Lang, 1989); Porter and O'Donnell, *Discourse Analysis and the NT, forthcoming.*

[23] Porter, *Discourse Analysis and the NT, forthcoming.*

well-defined and contoured description."[23] "The frontground elements seem to function at the level of the sub-paragraph and paragraph. Frontground elements . . . are clearly differentiated in their conceptualization and presentation from both background and foreground material. These can be referred to as discourse peaks, since they tend to jut out of the mainline, causing a 'zone of turbulence'."[24]

Much more could be said about the details of prominence, but within the constraints of this chapter, enough has been proposed to now turn to the specific question of how this approach to prominence can best be utilized in analyzing a NT discourse.

DISCOURSE PEAK AS FRONTGROUND PROMINENCE

To conclude this discussion of prominence, I would like to suggest an example of prominence that plays a large role—I would say the largest role—in focusing our attention on the main "theme" of James. This type of prominence not only is marked by certain surface features in the text, but it also conveys a semantic macro-theme or themes that can be traced throughout the text. I suggest that this concept should be viewed as an example of Porter's "frontground prominence." It is what the evangelical linguist Robert Longacre has termed the "peak" of a discourse. Longacre's often cited comment about a discourse without prominence is also appropriate here. "The very idea of discourse as a structured entity demands that some parts of discourse be more prominent than others. Otherwise, expression would be impossible. Discourse without prominence would be like pointing to a piece of black cardboard and insisting that it was a picture of black camels crossing black sands at midnight."[25]

In the second edition of his *Grammar of Discourse*, Longacre again describes this concept of peak as a "zone of turbulence."[26] This would be the ultimate example of the prominence of *dissimilarity*. Most of Longacre's discussion of peak is in the context of narrative discourse. Elsewhere, however, he does apply the function of peak to the non-narrative hortatory text of 1 John.[27] Longacre further explains the idea

---

[24] Porter, *Discourse Analysis and the NT, forthcoming*. For the expression, "zone of turbulence," see Longacre, *Grammar of Discourse*, 38.

[25] R. E. Longacre, "Discourse Peak as Zone of Turbulence," in *Beyond the Sentence: Discourse and Sentential Form* (ed. J.R. Wirth; Ann Arbor: Karoma, 1985), 83.

[26] Longacre, *Grammar of Discourse*, 38.

[27] Longacre, *Grammar of Discourse*, 49. See also "Toward an Exegesis of 1 John Based on the Discourse Analysis of the Greek Text," in *Linguistics and NT Interpretation: Essays on Discourse Analysis* (ed. D. Black; Nashville: Broadman, 1992), 271-86.

of peak as a "zone of turbulence" in the following way.

> Peak essentially is a 'zone of turbulence' in regard to the flow of the discourse in its preceding and following parts. Routine features of the storyline may be distorted or phased out at peak. Thus, the characteristic storyline tense/aspect may be substituted for by another tense/aspect. . . . Routine participant references may be disturbed. In brief, peak has features peculiar to itself and the marking of such features takes precedence over the marking of the mainline, so that the absence of certain features or even analytical difficulties can be a clue that we are at the peak of a discourse.[28]

Longacre then expands on this summary definition by offering some peculiar features of peak.[29] While most of his examples are from narrative fiction, he also recognizes that the same basic features are present in hortatory discourse, with appropriate adaptations for a different genre.

1. RHETORICAL UNDERLINING

In this feature the writer employs extra words. "It's as if you took a pencil and underlined certain lines of what you are writing."[30] Longacre illustrates this characteristic of peak by referring to the passage in 1 John (4:7-10 and 11-21) which he calls "the greatest passage in the NT on the obligatory nature of Christian love."[31] The first passage serves as the doctrinal peak with its declarative statements about the nature of love, while the second passage serves as the hortatory peak with its concentration of imperatives. This rhetorical underlining calls attention to the theme of the entire discourse—the imperative necessity of love among those who are born from God.[32]

---

[28] Longacre, *Grammar of Discourse*, 38.

[29] The following section depends heavily upon Longacre, *Grammar of Discourse*, 38-48.

[30] Longacre, *Grammar of Discourse*, 39.

[31] Longacre, "Toward an Exegesis of 1 John," 280. The recognition of both a doctrinal and a successive hortatory peak is seen also in James 3:13-18 and 4:1-10 and forms a key role in my own analysis of James.

[32] Longacre also calls attention to what he believes is the peak of the Genesis flood story. He points out rhetorical underlining in Genesis 7:17-24 where the ever-mounting, ever-abounding flood waters are described with a great deal of paraphrase and repetition. The effect is something like the speeding up of the camera at the high point of a film in order to produce a slow-moving sequence. Longacre concludes about rhetorical underlining, "It is one of the simplest and most universal devices for marking the important point not only of narration but of other sorts of discourse as well." *Grammar of Discourse*, 39.

2. CONCENTRATION OF PARTICIPANTS

Another expression for this characteristic is the *crowded stage*. In drama, most if not all of the characters appear on the stage at once at the peak of a play. A NT example of this can be found in the dramatic discourse of the Acts of the Apostles. Twice in the book, in chapter two and in chapter fifteen, all the main characters introduced thus far appear on the stage at once. It should not be missed that both of these chapters embody major events (Pentecost and the Jerusalem Council) that advance the cause of the Gospel at critical stages in its penetration of the world beginning at Jerusalem but extending to the ends of the earth (1:8). These events determined the course of the Gospel's progress from that point onward, the first involving particularly the Jewish people and the second involving particularly the Gentiles. In non-narrative text, this "concentration of participants" could include the concentration of a large number of the virtues commended or the vices condemned in the overall discourse by appearing in the peak as a list. Galatians 5:19-23, for example, contains fifteen works of the flesh and nine fruits of the Spirit listed with asyndeton. These actions are either the good fruits of Paul's gospel or the bad fruits of the "gospel" that draws a "curse" from him (1:8, 9).

3. HEIGHTENED VIVIDNESS

There may be a shift in the nominal/verbal balance or a shift in the surface structure tense. There may be a shift to a more specific person, such as a shift from the second person to the third person, or vice versa. Other devices include the use of rhetorical questions for effect (cf. James 3:13 and 4:1). This "heightened vividness" as a mark of peak can be illustrated in the Letter to Philemon. Of the five commonly accepted paragraphs, verses 17-20 clearly perform the role of peak by a definite shift in the verb structure. Allen comments on this peak in the letter.

> Up until this point, there has been no imperative used. However, here at the PEAK of the book and within the confines of only four verses, three command forms appear. The most salient of the three appears in v. 17 and gives a unique summary of the book: "Receive him (Onesimus) as you would me." Furthermore, there are no less than eleven verbs in this paragraph, and not one of them is a verbal (participle or infinitive). In the preceding paragraph of eight verses there

are only seventeen verb forms, and five of those are verbals. There is a wide range of mode shift in these four verses as well, including the use of the imperative, indicative and optative modes.[33]

Furthermore, there is a change in sentence structure to newly introduced short, staccato-like sentences and an increase in finite verb forms. The resulting rhetorical "punch" created by these heightened and vivid departures from the style of the co-text mark 17-20 as the discourse peak which also effectively embodies its semantic "message."

4. CHANGE OF PACE

Variation in the sheer length of syntactical units (clauses, sentences, paragraphs, embedded discourses) may be important. A shift to shorter sentences or a shift to longer sentences will emphasize the change of pace. A further device of changing the pace in peak is a stylistic change from the use of more conjunctions and a transition to less conjunctions and transition, or *asyndeton*. The latter section of Romans (chs. 12-15), while still embodying doctrinal tenets, has long been seen as the more ethical section of Paul's discourse. The heavily paraenetic 12:9-21 is marked by a long series of rarely used participles functioning as imperatives in 12:9-19, unconnected by conjunctions. The change of pace in this passage is exemplified by the entirely different pacing of both the previous and the following co-texts (Romans 12:1-8; 20, 21), which contain no such participles. This change of pace distinguishes 12:9-19 as the ethical peak of this section.

5. CHANGE OF VANTAGE POINT OR ORIENTATION

The readers directly addressed in the discourse may be asked to consider the behavior being commended to them by viewing it as embodied by a person. An example of this change of orientation is Hebrews 11:13-16, which appears like an interruption in the middle of the author's treatment of the faith of Abraham and Sarah in 11:8-12, 17-19. This entire pericope is itself a part of a larger pattern of eighteen exam-

---

[33] D. L. Allen, "The Discourse Structure of Philemon: A Study in Textlinguistics," in *Scribes and Scriptures* (ed. D. A. Black; Winona Lake: Eisenbrauns, 1992), 91. O'Donnell reaches a similar but more nuanced conclusion in his discourse analysis of Philemon. (O'Donnell, *Corpus Linguistics and the Greek of the New Testament*, 444-84). He recognizes the key role of the same paragraph, which he defines as verses 17-22, and states that "this is the heart of Paul's request," namely, for Onesimus to be returned to him (480).

ples of patriarchs and matriarchs who lived πίστει, "by faith" (11:4-31). In 11:13-16, however, the author elaborates on the specific nature of their faithful action and comments on the unseen reality that is the basis of their faithful deeds. That unseen and unreached reality is a city that God has prepared for them. "This discourse peak indicates that the heavenly city is one of the unseen realities that the author wished to emphasize."[34]

Viewing discourse peak as an example of frontground prominence may open the way for studying more effectively a number of NT discourses. It also seems evident that this approach has particular usefulness for solving a problem that has challenged interpreters of the Letter of James for generations—namely, the perplexing problem of the book's overall structure. In a later section of this introductory chapter, I will seek to apply this concept of peak and suggest a new approach to that question, based on the discourse structure of the letter. Before we turn to that issue there is one more important feature of discourse analysis that must be considered.

INFORMATION STRUCTURE AND FLOW

How do the elements of cohesion and prominence specifically work in the various sections of a biblical discourse such as James? And how do we decide where the beginnings of those sections occur? These questions are addressed when we examine the issues of linearization and information flow, i.e., the ways in which an author groups a discourse into "chunks" that convey the intended message in a cohesive manner resulting in a coherent message to his readers. The problem is that authors can produce only one word at a time. They then must organize these words into clauses, and these clauses into clause complexes and sentences, and these sentences into ever larger segments of text. And all of these levels must also progress in some linear fashion and meet the authors' objectives and (hopefully) the expectations of their readers. Thus a good starting point, or "theme," must be chosen at each point along the linear progression or misinterpretation may follow.

We have had occasion to quote the description of this function by Grimes. Here we quote him again, with his further expansion on what he calls "staging."

Every clause, sentence, paragraph, episode, or discourse is organized

---

[34] Westfall, *Hebrews*, 250.

around a particular element that is taken as its point of departure. It is as though the speaker presents what he wants to say from a particular perspective. I find it convenient to think in terms of how various units are STAGED for the hearer's benefits. This staging is at least partially independent of both content structure and cohesive structure. It operates at many levels of text organization.[35]

Our purpose here is not to enter into a debate about terminology, but to use the term "staging" to describe the way in which authors "stage" their argument to flow in a linear manner throughout their discourse.[36] The resulting "staged" sections of a discourse have also been referred to as "chunks" or "groups" composed of thematically related material or material marked by formal features of the grammar.[37]

How specifically do authors group or stage their discourses? Writers have described the *prominence* or *salience* or *markedness* of an author's discourse strategy.[38] Working together, an author's choice of these principles is manifested in what Longacre distinguishes as "mainline" and "supportive" material.[39] In this regard, Westfall distinguishes between "central" and "marginal" sentences according to the larger number of lexical "bonds" which central sentences share with other sentences in the paragraph or "group."[40]

Lest this theoretical discussion extend far beyond the confines of this introduction, an attempt should be made to explain how NT authors could use the resources of Hellenistic Greek to group or "chunk" their discourses and thus convey the theme in the best linear fashion. It should also be kept in mind that this is not just an exercise in uncovering the formal features of a text. This grouping procedure helps the reader to determine the author's thematic "topic" since it works at all levels from the clausal level to the discourse level. "That is, we assume that every sentence forms part of a developing, cumulative

---

[35] J. Grimes, *Thread of Discourse*, 323, and the following two chapters, 323-44.

[36] This term is also applied by Cotterell and Turner to Biblical discourse. "Discourse is characterized by *staging*, the orderly progression in a necessarily linear sequence." P. Cotterell and M. Turner, *Linguistics and Biblical Interpretation* (Downers Grove: IVP, 1989), 241.

[37] Westfall utilizes the term "chunking" to describe this function, but also refers to "grouping," a term which I prefer. Westfall, *Hebrews*, 6, 20, 28, 29. Since the familiar term "paragraph" is delineated in English text by spacing, i.e., by indenting, I will try to use the term "section" or "grouping."

[38] See the earlier discussion on cohesion and peak as frontground prominence.

[39] R.E. Longacre, *Grammar of Discourse*, 21-28.

[40] Westfall, *Hebrews*, 73.

instruction which tells us how to construct a coherent representation" of the theme of each chunk and ultimately of the entire discourse.[41] This creating of a mental representation of the entire "message" of the discourse is the result of the coherence conveyed through the cohesion and prominence communicated by the surface features of the text.[42]

Previously, we mentioned that authors use cohesive "ties" to bind together their discourses. In Hellenistic Greek we can observe grammatical, lexical, referential, and relational cohesive ties. Our concern here is how an author can group together semantically related themes by the formal and functional features of the language. Categories of choices can be made first from the *grammar* to create groups or units of thematically related information. Second, choices also can be made from the categories of lexical clusters, called grouping with *lexis*.

Important *grammatical* categories in grouping are as follows:

1. *Tense* can be used to create paragraphs or sections with an emphasis on shifts of episode (especially in narrative) or topic (especially in non-narrative). Mark's use of the so-called "historic present" may also be viewed as an episodic shift at the discourse level to bring events to greater attention of the reader by means of foreground prominence (Mark 1:12, 21, 40).[43]

2. *Mood* shifts can be used for grouping, more often in the epistles. Eph. 4-5 is especially grouped by modal choice with the use of the indicative mood of the semantically related verbs παρακαλέω, λέγω, and μαρτυρέω collocated with different infinitives of indirect discourse (περπατῆσαι, 4:1; περιπατεῖν, 4:17, e.g). Our later examination of James will indicate that his use of the imperative mood collocated with vocatives and nominatives of direct address also signal significant discourse shifts and new sections.

3. *Person and Number* in forming units is common. In the

---

[41] In the discussion that follows, I acknowledge the influence of Cynthia Westfall's thorough treatment of this subject in *A Discourse Analysis of the Letter to the Hebrews*, 36-55, as well as in an unpublished paper titled "Cohesion and Chunking in Discourse," (2006).

[42] For the importance of the reader's attaining a mental representation of a discourse through coherence, see the discussion by R. A. Dooley and S. H. Levinsohn, *Analyzing Discourse: A Manual of Basic Concepts* (Dallas: SIL International, 2001), 10-19, 21-22, 25-26, 29, 31-32.

[43] S. Porter, *Verbal Aspect in the Greek of the New Testament with Reference to Tense and Mood*, 189-98; S. Porter, *Idioms of the Greek New Testament*, 30-31, 301-02.

Apocalypse, for example, most of the material is described in the third person, singular or plural, depending on the participants. The author's shift to the first person singular of the verbs εῖδον (I saw) and ἤκουσα (I heard) clearly breaks the discourse into chunks and reveals a new topic to be considered (7:4, 9; 8:2, 13; 9:1; 13, 16, 17, e.g.).[44]

More examples of how authors group their material by categories of the grammatical system (e.g., by voice, case, conjunctions) could be cited. Enough illustrations have been given to indicate the large number of grammatical resources available to authors to utilize in organizing and grouping the segments of their discourses.

Lexical repetition and patterning are the most effective ways in which authors bring cohesion to their writing. Lexical choice is the most dominant means of cohesion in texts. These can be seen in the lexical repetition of the same word or synonymous words or in the effective use of antonymy, hyponomy, and meronymy. Chains of cohesive ties ("semantic chains") can indicate the topic of a paragraph. Some examples of the ways in which NT authors group their sections by lexis are as follows:

1. *Lexical Reiteration* can be illustrated by the familiar refrain in the Beatitudes, each of which introduces a different topic: **μακάριοι** οἱ πτωχοὶ τῷ πνεύματι, **ὅτι** αὐτῶν ἐστιν ἡ βασιλεία τῶν οὐρανῶν. **Blessed** are the poor in spirit, **for** theirs is the kingdom of heaven (Matt. 5:3). The repetition of μακάριοι and ὅτι in each succeeding beatitude (5:4-11) introduces a new ethical characteristic with an accompanying promise, but both are still bound together thematically with the others in the larger section.

2. *Semantic Chains* consist of words that are in the same semantic domain—groups of words that have associated meanings.[45] Authors often create linkage in paragraphs by utilizing words that are closely related semantically. An often overlooked example of "semantic chaining" is used by Paul in Phil.1:27-2:5, which unfortunately has been obscured by the change of chapters added much later. Paul states in 1:27 that his desire for the Philippians is that they "stand firm in **one** spirit, striving **together** with **one** soul for the faith of the

---

[44] See Westfall, *Hebrews*, 43, 44, for a complete list of these references.

[45] An attempt to organize NT vocabulary according to a word's semantic domain is J. P. Louw and E. A. Nida, *Greek-English Lexicon of the New Testament Based on Semantic Domains* (2 vols.; 2nd ed.; New York: United Bible Societies, 1989). The "Introduction" to vol. 1 (vi-xx) explains the theoretical semantic basis of the lexicon.

gospel" (ὅτι στήκετε ἐν ἑνὶ πνεύματι, μιᾷ ψυχῇ συναθλοῦντες τῇ πίστει τοῦ εὐαγγελίου). The words for "one" (ἑνὶ and μιᾷ) are accompanied by a compound word containing the prefix συν—("together"). Paul next grounds their unity in 1:30 by stating that they are experiencing the **same** conflict that he does (τὸν αὐτὸν ἀγῶνα ἔχοντες). He then calls for their continued unity in 2:2: "that you **think** the **same** thing, having the **same** love, being of the **same** soul, **thinking** the **same** thing" (ἵνα τὸ αὐτὸ φρονῆτε, τὴν αὐτὴν ἀγάπην ἔχοντες, σύμψυχοι, τὸ ἓν φρονοῦντες). He finally grounds all of his exhortations to unity by appealing to them in 2:5: τοῦτο φρονεῖτε ἐν ὑμῖν ὃ καὶ ἐν Χριστῷ Ἰησοῦ ("for **think this** [have this attitude] which was in Christ Jesus"). The semantically related words εἷς, μία, and ἕν, plus the intensive uses of αὐτος including the συν/συμ—compounds, when collocated with the **thinking** verbs (φρον—roots) together convey semantically one of the main themes of Philippians—the call to the brethren to manifest outwardly the inner unity which they have with Christ and with one another.

3. *Labelling and Lists* can be used to group a section when the list can be labelled in the context. Romans 8:35-39 contains a "pile" of semantically related entities that could be labelled as "the things that will not separate us from the love of God," a phrase repeated at the beginning and the end of the list (8:35, 39). Examples of this type of lexical repetition can be seen often in the NT, with James 3:13-17 also being an example of a list of behaviors exhibiting either wisdom from above or from below—a characteristic that lends prominence to the paragraph as the peak in the book.

Other examples of grouping by lexical repetition could be multiplied such as grouping with "figures of speech," and with "discourse markers."[46] These examples illustrate the diversity of the resources in ancient Greek for grouping in a discourse.

DISCOURSE PEAK OF THE LETTER OF JAMES

By applying the techniques of cohesion, prominence, peak, and grouping to the text of James, I propose that James 3:13-18 is the peak of his discourse. And as the peak, this crucial passage highlights the primary concerns of the author. How does James focus his spotlight on this section and give it the frontground prominence over other sections of his

[46] See Westfall, *Hebrews*, 50-55, for scriptural examples of each of these.

discourse? This section fits all the expectations for its being *dissimilar* to the rest of James' encyclical letter. It functions, in terms of frontground prominence, as the most prominent section of the book. Consider the following unique linguistic characteristics of this passage that illustrate Longacre's characteristics of "peak." Stating them again, they are: general dissimilarity from the co-text; rhetorical underlining; concentration of participants; heightened vividness; change of pace; and change of vantage point.

1.   **The section begins with a question**: Τίς σοφὸς καὶ ἐπιστήμων ἐν ὑμῖν; ("Who is a wise and undersanding person among you?"). As will be noted later, other sections of James begin with the collocation of a nominative plural in direct address with an imperative verb. The only other exception to this is 4:1-10, which also begins with a question: Πόθεν πόλεμοι καὶ πόθεν μάχαι ἐν ὑμῖν; ("From where among you do wars and battles come?"). This section is so closely related to 3:13-18 that it illustrates rather than contradicts the unique role of 3:13-18. I argue that 4:1-10 functions as the "hortatory" peak of the discourse while 3:13-18 is its "thematic" peak.

2.   **The first imperative shifts to the third person from the second person pattern of the other sections**: δειξάτω ἐκ τῆς καλῆς ἀναστροφῆς τὰ ἔργα αὐτοῦ ἐν πραΰτητι σοφίας. ("Let him show from his good behavior his good works with meekness of wisdom"). Although there are fifteen third person imperatives in James, this is the only instance when one appears at the beginning of its section in the thematic position of the clause. The others form supportive material by appearing later in the clause or the section in the rhematic position.[47]

3.   **There are vice and virtue lists marked by asyndeton**. These lists do not appear elsewhere in James. 3:15 refers to: ἐπίγειος, ψυχική, δαιμονιώδης ("earthly, sensual, devilish"). 3:17 mentions: πρῶτον μὲν ἀγνή ἐστιν, ἔπειτα, εἰρηνική, ἐπιεικής, εὐπειθής, μεστὴ ἐλέους καὶ καρπῶν ἀγαθῶν, ἀδιάκριτος, ἀνυπόκριτος ("it is first pure, then peaceable, gentle, reasonable, full of mercy and good fruits, impartial, sincere"). These lists describe polar opposite behaviors that contrast

---

[47] *Theme* and *rheme* are terms used to describe the initial position in the clause or sentence (the *theme*) and what is later stated about the theme (the *rheme*). For James' second person imperatives in thematic position, see 1:2; 16, 19; 2:1, 5; 3:1; 4:11, 13; 5:1, 7, 9. For the supportive third person imperatives in rhematic position, see 1:4, 5, 6, 7, 9, 13, 19; 4:9; 5:12, 13 (2), 14, 20.

the kind of "wisdom that does **not** descend from above" (οὐκ ἔστιν αὕτη ἡ σοφία ἄνωθεν κατερχομένη) with that behavior that exemplifies "wisdom that is from above" (ἡ δὲ ἄνωθεν σοφία). Again, in the later analysis of how this passage contributes to the structure of James, it will be noted that the polar opposite behavior it describes provides the overall theme of the discourse which can be mapped onto every separate section.[48]

4. There is a marked difference in the ratio of adjectives to other words in this section. The ratio of adjectives to other words in this section is 20%. The ratio of adjectives to other words in the rest of the book is 10%. This is consistent with the author's purpose in this peak to describe the behavior that is evidence of the wisdom that he is commending throughout the book. The large number of adjectives describes what the wise person looks like so the readers will seek to emulate the behavior of such a person.

5. There is a change of vantage point in this section. In other sections, the readers are directly addressed about their behavior. Here by way of a rhetorical question the readers are asked to consider what the behavior of a wise person is like (and an unwise person as well). In contrast, the other questions in the letter are used in the confrontational diatribes by which James challenges his readers (note the series of questions in 2:4-7 and 2:14, 16, 20, 21). While specific exemplars of behavior are held up to the readers in other sections (Abraham, Rahab, Job, Elijah), here the readers are asked generally to contemplate the example of a "wise person." Those other exemplars are living examples from Israel's sacred history of the wise person held up for emulation in this section.

6. Summary words in this section appear in significant ways elsewhere in James. The specific examples of the commended and condemned behaviors show up in supportive material in many other sections. No other section of the discourse contributes so much of its vocabulary to the other sections as 3:13-18. While this may appear to contradict the idea of dissimilarity, I remind the reader that while dissimilarity marks the surface features of James, semantic sim-

---

[48] Commentators have recognized that these polar contrasts play a major role in James' letter. See L.T. Johnson, *The Letter of James* (AB 37A; New York: Doubleday, 1995), 83, 84. Other authors who have discerned this theme as one of James' chief emphases will be cited in the commentary itself.

[49] "By their nature, summary statements unite together the information they summarize." Steven Levinsohn, *Discourse Features of New Testament Greek* (2nd ed.; Dallas: SIL International, 2000), 277. They can both end and begin sections. Here the lists both look back and look forward in the text.

ilarity and summary mark this passage. This would be similar to Longacre's "crowded stage" in which all the characters appear at crucial times.[49] Consider a sampling of some of these lexical connections with both the preceding (anaphoric) and succeeding (cataphoric) sections of the discourse. "Wisdom" (σοφία) in 3:13, 15 looks back to 1:5. "Let him show" (δειξάτω) in 3:13 echoes 2:18b. "Works" (ἔργα) in 3:13 summarizes his previous discussion in 2:14-26 (and interestingly does not appear again after its use here). The "meekness" (πραΰτητι) of 3:13 recalls its use in 1:21. The wisdom "from above" (ἄνωθεν) in 3:15, 17 echoes the gifts that come from above in 1:17. Not only does this language look back to the previous co-text, it looks forward as well. The bitter "jealousy" (ζῆλον) of 3:14 anticipates the same problem condemned in 4:2. The warning "not to boast" (κατακαυχᾶσθε) in 3:14 previews the same problem in 4:16. These lexical connections are only a sample of those that are present in this passage. Furthermore, the many additional semantic parallels have not even been mentioned and will be left for the later commentary on the passage. Enough of them have been noted to illustrate the crucial function of this section as a summary of the entire discourse.

These six examples of the uniqueness and *dissimilarity* of 3:13-18 highlight its prominent role in the discourse as a whole. There are abundant illustrations in this section of the above-mentioned characteristics of Longacre's "peak"—the rhetorical underlining, the concentration of participants, the heightened vividness, the change of pace, and the change of vantage point.

These characteristics also convey the ideational "message" that James wants readers to understand, namely, that there are two ways that they can follow: the way of heavenly wisdom or the way of earthly wisdom. This thematic peak is what controls our author's approach in the individual paragraphs of his discourse. In each of them, a moral behavior is commended and the opposite behavior is condemned. The reader is called to make a choice between these two ways. In the following section (4:1-10), James challenges his readers to become either a friend of God or his enemy in 4:4: μοιχαλίδες, οὐκ οἴδατε ὅτι ἡ φιλία τοῦ κόσμου ἔχθρα τοῦ θεοῦ ἐστιν; ὃς ἐὰν οὖν βουληθῇ φίλος εἶναι τοῦ κόσμου, ἐχθρὸς τοῦ θεοῦ καθίσταται ("Adulteresses! Do you not know that friendship with the world is enmity with God? Whoever desires to be a friend of the world makes himself an enemy of God"). This paradigm of two opposite behaviors is stamped on every paragraph/section of the discourse.

Recognizing the thematic peak of James and how it provides the overall thrust of his message enables his readers to understand why James wants them to be "perfect" (τέλειοι — 1:4). This important term, echoing the dominical statement in Matthew 5:48, is defined by the rest of 1:4 as follows: καὶ ὁλόκληροι ἐν μηδενὶ λειπόμενοι ("and entire, not lacking in anything"). Many writers have noticed the way in which James describes this perfection or "wholeness" that should characterize his readers.[50] If they try to have it both ways, then they will be guilty of "doubleness," described by the colorful and unique word δίψυχος (1:8; 4:8) — a "double-souled" or "double-minded" person. To James, the wisdom described in 3:13-18 that comes from above to those who ask God for it (1:5) will be displayed in fruitful deeds. This wisdom also will enable his readers to be whole people in their undivided devotion to the one true God who Himself has no "variation or shadow due to change" (1:17).

DISCOURSE PEAK AND THE STRUCTURE OF JAMES

For over four centuries, discussion about the structure of James' letter could be referred to as commentary on "A German Tale of Two Martins." Those two influential Germans were Martin Luther in the sixteenth century and Martin Dibelius in the twentieth century. Both could see no coherent structure in the book. While there were others who voiced exception to the views of the two Martins, their pervasive influence has certainly dominated the discussion.

Luther's comment about James being "an epistle of straw," as compared to certain other NT writings, is his most well known comment on the book.[51] There will be occasion to discuss it later in the commentary. His views about the style and structure of James, however, were equally negative. Discounting apostolic authorship, Luther concluded that the author must have been "some good, pious man, who took a few sayings from the disciples of the apostles and thus tossed them off on paper."[52]

---

[50] P. J. Hartin considers this goal as the essence of the book's teaching on the spiritual life. *A Spirituality of Perfection* (Collegeville: Liturgical, 1999). Bauckham calls perfection or wholeness "the overarching theme of the entire letter." R. Bauckham, *James* (NTR; London: Routledge, 1999), 177.

[51] Luther's expression could be more literally rendered "a right strawy epistle" (*eyn rechte stroern Epistel*). *Luther's Works* (St. Louis: Concordia, 1972), 35: 362. Hereafter referred to as *LW*.

[52] *LW*, 35: 397.

[53] M. Dibelius, *James* (rev. H. Greeven; trans. M. A. Williams; Philadelphia: Fortress, 1976), 34-38.

Furthermore, in his erudite commentary, Dibelius concluded from his form critical analysis that James contained no overall thematic or structural unity.[53] He did acknowledge that three individual treatises (2:1-13; 2:14-26; 3:1-13), which he called "the core of the writing," were coherent in their diatribal style. But the rest of the book, however, was primarily composed of loosely arranged sayings, sometimes connected by catch words, in the style of what Dibelius referred to as Jewish paraenesis.[54] Dibelius' influence on later writers is undeniable and pervasive.[55]

Among recent writers who have discerned some measure of coherence in the epistle's structure, many often stress the key role of chapter one in serving as a sort of "table of contents" for the rest of the book.[56] Others have argued more specifically that 1:19 ("be swift to hear, slow to speak, slow to anger") comprises a three point outline of chapters 2-4.[57] Despite this recent trend toward seeing greater coherence, Taylor and Guthrie recently concluded that "no consensus has emerged concerning the details of the book's organization."[58]

With so many differences about the book's structure among scholars past and present, what hope is there that we can ever discern an overarching strategy in its composition? Or, should we just conclude that there is no evident overall strategy and be satisfied with arranging by intuition James' discrete topics in a linear list? I am convinced that a discourse analysis of this book that gives attention both to how authors indicate prominence and to how they group their messages

---

[54] Dibelius, *James*, 1-10.

[55] For discussions by various writers on the literary structure and genre of James, see Johnson, *James*, 11-25; P. H. Davids, "The Epistle of James in Modern Discussion," *ANRW II* (25.5): 3621-45; M. E. Taylor, "Recent Scholarship on the Structure of James," *CBR* 3.1 (2004): 86-115.

[56] Johnson, *James*, 15; Bauckham, *James*, 68-73. Bauckham, however, along with Moo observe that the great diversity among the proposed structures for the epistle may indicate that there is no clearly discernible structure to the book. Moo opts for "an overall concern" rather than a structured theme. That concern is James' desire for spiritual "wholeness." D. J. Moo, *The Letter of James* (PNTC; Grand Rapids: Eerdmans, 2000), 44, 46.

[57] An early advocate of this approach was H. J. Cladder, "Die Anlage des Jakobusbriefes," *ZTK* 28 (1904): 37-57. More recent advocates are Z. C. Hodges, *The Epistle of James: Proven Character Through Testing* (Dallas: Grace Evangelical Society, 1994) and R. W. Wall, *Community of the Wise: The Letter of James* (NTC; Valley Forge: Trinity, 1997), 35-37.

[58] M. E. Taylor and G. H. Guthrie, "The Structure of James," *CBQ* 68.4 (2006): 681-705. For the most recent scholarly efforts in this area, see the thorough study by L. Cheung, *The Genre, Composition and Hermeneutics of the Epistle of James* (Milton Keynes: Paternoster, 2003) and M. E. Taylor, *A Text-Linguistic Investigation into the Discourse Structure of James* (LNTS 311; London: T&T Clark, 2006).

offers fresh hope that we can then uncover the structure of this little book and its ensuing overall message.

We have previously covered the topics of prominence and grouping and suggested the idea of discourse "peak" in the role of frontground prominence. We called attention to James 3:13-18 and its appeal to divine and human wisdom as polar contrasts that focuses James' call to his readers to choose the lifestyle of a "friend of God." By recognizing this thematic peak, a reader can also better develop a mental representation of the discourse. "By reducing the flow of the texts to polar opposites, dialectical discourse not only clarifies the issues; it also serves as an aid to memory."[59]

How does this overall approach view the book in its parts? I suggest that the collocation of imperative commands with nominatives of direct address (most often ἀδελφοί, "brothers") is the grammatical/cohesive tie that James utilizes to group his discourse into sections. This approach involves more than just noticing a repeated lexical device and seizing on it as a key. Each discrete section, introduced in this way, signals a new group of semantically related information as well. Occasionally, this grammatical tie functions simply as a span within a section (5:7-10) and a lexical semantic chain within that section indicates this to be the case.[60] The thematic second person imperative in each section serves as the central clause with the following indicative clauses and/or clause complexes providing support for the mainline imperatival command. There may be additional imperatives (often in the third person) that expand further the command of the central clause/sentence and are then further supported by a series of indicative clauses. The main thrust of each section, in accord with the overall theme in the discourse peak in 3:13-18, is an appeal to readers to follow the divine viewpoint ("wisdom from above") by obeying the imperatival

---

[59] K. J. Tollefson, "The Epistle of James as a Dialectical Discourse," *BTB* 27:2 (1997): 63.

[60] Evidence for this assertion will be provided in the later commentary on that section.

command that he has delivered. Consequently, his readers are exhorted
to reject any human viewpoint ("wisdom not from above") about the

Sections of James		
Section	Nominative of Address	Imperative Command/ Rhetorical Question
1:2-15	ἀδελφοί μου	πᾶσαν χαρὰν ἡγήσασθε
1:16-18	ἀδελφοί μου ἀγαπητοί	μὴ πλανᾶσθε
1:19-27	ἀδελφοί μου ἀγαπητοί	ἴστε plus ἔστω
2:1-13	ἀδελφοί μου	μὴ ἐν προσωπολημψίαις ἔχετε
2:14-26	ἀδελφοί μου	τί τὸ ὄφελος
3:1-12	ἀδελφοί μου	μὴ πολλοὶ διδάσκαλοι γίνεσθε
3:13-18	ἐν ὑμῖν THEMATIC PEAK	τίς σοφὸς καὶ ἐπιστήμων
4:1-10	ἐν ὑμῖν HORTATORY PEAK	πόθεν πόλεμοι καὶ πόθεν μάχαι 10 imperatives in 4:7-10
4:11-12	ἀδελφοί	μὴ καταλαλεῖτε ἀλλήλων
4:13-17	οἱ λέγοντες	ἄγε νῦν
5:1-6	οἱ πλούσιοι	ἄγε νῦν . . . κλαύσατε
5:7-11	ἀδελφοί	μακροθυμήσατε plus 4 imperatives
5:12-18	ἀδελφοί μου	μὴ ὀμνύετε
5:19-20	ἀδελφοί μου	γινωσκέτω

ethical demands in the section.

According to this proposal, the main sections of the book can be displayed as follows.

In this analysis, there are fourteen sections of the discourse in addition to the epistolary prescript. Each of these contributes its own unique semantic development of the main theme—namely, demonstrating behavior that accords with divine wisdom. A few comments are necessary about occasional departures from the otherwise uniform language features in each section. Three of the sections begin with a rhetorical question rather than with an imperative (2:14-26; 3:13-18; 4:1-10). The first passage (2:14-26) could be viewed as a consequential application of the section beginning in 2:1, particularly continuing the theme of partiality as applied to the poor. More will be discussed about this issue in the commentary.

Section 4:1-10 begins with a question and immediately follows the *thematic* peak of the discourse (3:13-18). Commentators have noted that there are many verbal similarities in these passages and often take them as two sections of the same unit.[61] I suggest that 4:1-10 is a sub-unit of 3:13-4:10 and should also be considered the *hortatory* peak of the discourse. This is evidenced in the "zone of turbulence" created by the concentration of ten imperatives in 4:7-10.

This explanation of the linearization of James pays attention to the special way that he indicates frontground prominence by the use of peak. It also notes the ways that he uses the grammatical resources of his language to group his discourse to most effectively communicate the details of the theme embodied in his peak. With this approach, his

---

[61] Johnson, *James*, 267-69.

readers can better develop a mental representation of the discourse at all levels. Finally, if his readers heed his exhortations, they will then become "whole" persons in their undivided loyalty to God.

Based on the above top down analysis, I suggest the following outline (i.e., macrostructure) of the letter, based on its hortatory character: Bold points indicate their prominent roles as the thematic and hortatory peaks of the discourse.

Prescript		1:1
1.	Be Joyful in Trials	1:2-15
2.	Do Not Be Deceived about God's Goodness	1:16-18
3.	Become a Good Hearer/Doer of the Word	1:19-27
4.	Do Not Show Favoritism	2:1-13
5.	Show Your Faith by Your Works	2:14-26
6.	Be Consistent in Your Speech	3:1-12
7.	**Follow the Wisdom of God**	3:13-18
8.	**Become a Friend of God**	4:1-10
9.	Do Not Speak Against One Another	4:11, 12
10.	Do Not Plan Presumptuously	4:13-17
11.	You Rich Should Treat the Poor Justly	5:1-6
12.	Wait Patiently for the Lord's Coming	5:7-11
13.	Do Not Swear but Pray	5:12-18
14.	Convert the Erring Brother	5:19, 20

Having completed an analysis of the letter from the top down by discovering its macrostucture, in the commentary that follows we will analyze from the bottom up the successive microstructure levels of clauses, clause complexes, and paragraphs. We will examine in detail the way in which James maps to each individual section of his discourse his over-

---

[62] Two additional studies have helped confirm to me the approach that I take to James. Kenneth Tollefson consistently analyzes the book as a dialectical discourse by paying attention to how an author "uses binary opposition to instruct or persuade the reader/listener in some new element of truth that would otherwise be difficult to obtain." Tollefson also effectively incorporates James' theme of "perfection" into his

all theme of living according to heavenly wisdom rather than earthly wisdom. Our anticipation is that the lowest levels of this discourse will support and illustrate the overall theme conveyed by its highest levels.[62]

ANALYZING THE INDIVIDUAL TEXT UNITS OF JAMES

"A discourse analysis that is not based on grammar is not an analysis at all, but simply a running commentary on a text."[63] This declaration, made not by a Biblical exegete but by a linguist, is at the heart of the following method of analysis of the individual text components in James. Too many commentaries at this point become commentaries on commentaries rather than commentaries on the text itself. Then those comments often sadly become a string of consecutive word studies with little attention to the grammatical structures inherent in the text itself. How shall we go about avoiding those pitfalls and truly engage in a discourse analysis that is rigidly grounded in the grammatical realities of the text of James?

Many expositors and exegetes of Scriptural texts would be surprised to realize how little they trust the text to yield to them the message it communicates. Sadly, handling of a text is too often simply a running commentary on the text marked by intuitive conclusions about the text's structure and semantics that are not based on the grammatical realities of the text itself. One author raised the battle cry to his fellow linguists to "Trust the Text." His words are appropriate also for those of us whose professional calling is to analyze sacred scriptural texts to uncover their meaning.

> I am advocating that we should trust the text. We should be open to what it may tell us. We should not impose our ideas on it, except perhaps just getting started. We should apply only loose and flexible frameworks until we see what the preliminary results are in order to accommodate the new information that will come from the text. We should expect that we will encounter unusual phenomena; . . . and therefore we may find a lot of surprises. We should search for models that are especially appropriate to the study of texts and discourse.[64]

analysis. K. J. Tollefson, "The Epistle of James as Dialectical Discourse," *BTB* 27:2 (1997): 62-69. David Hockman's thesis also reaches the same conclusion about the special role of 3:13-18 as the peak of the discourse. He does this through a discourse analysis model developed by SIL. D. J. Hockman, "A Discourse Analysis of James: An Examination of 3:13-18 as the Doctrinal Peak" (Th.M. thesis, Calvary Baptist Theological Seminary, 2006).

[63] M.A.K. Halliday, *Introduction to Functional Grammar*, xvi.

[64] J.M. Sinclair, "Trust the Text," in M. Coulthard (ed.), *Advances in Written Text Analysis* (London: Routledge, 1994), 25.

This approach is the basis for my application of discourse analysis methodology to the individual text units of James. When we encounter the various issues of interpretation that arise, with all of their attending perplexities, we firmly believe that our author has an overall strategy in mind; that he is competent to convey effectively his message to us; and that the linguistic resources available to him in Hellenistic Greek were adequate to convey his message. Therefore, we believe that his message is grounded in the grammatical realities of his text. In other words, we will steadfastly "trust the text" to convey to us what James would have wanted us to "hear."

We explained how we determine the overall theme of James as it is manifested by the peak of his discourse. That theme of "choosing heavenly wisdom above earthly wisdom" (see 3:13-18) is conveyed through his text by the means of cohesive ties that segment his writing into units introduced by the collocation of a nominative of address (most often ἀδελφοί) with an imperative command. How then will we specifically analyze each of those paragraphs and any sub units within them?

My methodology is an adaptation of one developed over the past two decades by New Testament scholars working within the field of discourse analysis. More specifically, I have been influenced by the model developed by Matthew O'Donnell in his seminal work, *Corpus Linguistics and the Greek of the New Testament*. None of the scholars working from within this perspective should be held responsible for any shortcomings in my own approach, but I acknowledge my indebtedness to them in many ways.[65]

I will approach each section in the following way. I will attempt to:

1. Determine the limits of the paragraph and any sub units within the paragraph by taking note of the linguistic features that justify such a choice. Within the paragraph, we will then isolate the primary and secondary clauses.

2. Assess the role of the participants in the paragraph and relate them to the role of the participants in the entire discourse. James and his readers/hearers are the main participants since no one else is mentioned by name, but groups like the "poor," the "rich," the "widows and orphans," and the "sick" comprise general participants in the discourse.

---

[65] Most of these NT scholars have already been mentioned. Among them are Stanley Porter, Matthew Brook O'Donnell and Jeffrey Reed, whose works have already been cited.

3. Examine the processes and circumstances conveyed by a rigorous attention to the verbal and adverbial word groups contained in the paragraph. Isolating the mainline topic clause followed by supporting comment clauses will be an important step in this regard. This topic/comment analysis forms the heart of the analysis of each paragraph. Fortunately, the way James organizes his own information flow most often by a nominative of address followed by an imperative lends itself well to such an analysis.

4. Trace the semantic patterns and information flow in the paragraph by examining how the features of the text convey its overall "meaning." In this regard, the tracing of what has been called "semantic chains" will take precedence over isolated studies of individual words divorced from their larger context.

5. Finally, we will seek to ascertain how the message conveyed by each paragraph exemplifies and illustrates the overall theme of James which is mapped to each section by the thematic and hortatory peaks of James in chapters 3 and 4. In this way, the overall macro-level topic will be shown to be mapped onto the lower micro level comments and each shown to be consistent with each other.

A further aid to analyzing the textual structure of a passage is a tool like the OpenText.org analysis of the entire NT. Also adapted by electronic Bible programs such as Logos 4.0, its online form is helpful in deciding what are the grammatical elements of a clause/sentence. These elements are included in boxes to show the Subject (S), the Predicator (P), the Complement (C), any Adjunct expressions (A), and the ones addressed (add) in the text. The OpenText analysis of James is included before each pericope is further analyzed.

A newcomer to this approach may feel a bit overwhelmed by what may appear to be a novel analytical methodology expressed in unfamiliar terminology. I encourage the user of this commentary to approach both the text of James and my own text with an eye open to what the canonical text will reveal as we wrestle with its grammar and its meaning. Let us "trust the text" to reveal its own inner workings as we seek to uncover them.

Chapter 1

ANALYSIS OF JAMES ONE

T his discourse analysis of James will proceed paragraph by paragraph. Occasionally, a larger paragraph will be broken down into sub-paragraphs when the linguistic features justify such a breakdown. Each paragraph, or sometimes a sub-paragraph, will be preceded by its Greek text and an English translation. Then will follow an analysis of the primary and secondary clauses with the primary clauses aligned to the left side of the page and the secondary clauses indented. As mentioned previously, the analysis of the online OpenText Syntactically Analyzed NT is utilized. The structure of each clause is indicated by the function of each clause component (S= subject; P= predicator; C= complement; A= adjunct; add= addressee; cj=conjunction). This display at the beginning of each paragraph is very important because it is the information on which the ensuing analysis is based.

1. Paragraph 1 (James 1:1)

Ἰάκωβος θεοῦ καὶ κυρίου Ἰησοῦ Χριστοῦ δοῦλος ταῖς δώδεκα φυλαῖς ταῖς ἐν τῇ διασπορᾷ χαίρειν.	James, a slave of God and of the Lord Jesus Christ, to the twelve tribes which are in the Diaspora. Greetings!

James 1:1 Clause Analysis

S	C
Ἰάκωβος θεοῦ καὶ κυρίου Ἰησοῦ Χριστοῦ δοῦλος	ταῖς δώδεκα φυλαῖς ταῖς ἐν τῇ διασπορᾷ

P

χαίρειν

The opening verse clearly stands as a separate literary unit from that which follows, as would be expected in its role as the salutation of a letter. The most familiar form of an epistolary salutation in a Hellenistic letter is "A to B Greetings," which is exactly the form here. This form also appears in the salutation of another encyclical, also from James, to "the brothers who are of the Gentiles in Antioch and Syria and Cilicia" in Acts 15:23. This exact pattern also appears in the opening of the letter from Claudius Lysias to Felix in Acts 23:26.

The first clause-complex has no expressed predicator, which is consistent with the elliptical form of letter openings during this period. While it is not vital to know what verbal idea is omitted in this ellipsis, one could imagine that the verb γράφει ("writes") is understood. This could also explain the unique function of the independent infinitive χαίρειν ("greetings") in the primary clause concluding verse one. In other words, James not only "writes to the twelve tribes," he also "writes to extend to them greetings." While the above NT references are the only ones to employ this precise verbal form, the infinitive of the verb χαίρω as a greeting can be seen in 2 John 1:10, 11; in its vocative form as a greeting by Judas (Mt. 26:49); by the mockers (Mt. 27:29; Mk. 15:18; Jn. 19:3); by the angel (Lk. 1:28); and in the imperative plural as a greeting by the resurrected Jesus (Mt. 28:9).

Four "participants" who appear in the entire discourse are mentioned in 1:1: James, God, Lord Jesus Christ, and the Twelve Tribes.[95] James, in the role of "actor" throughout the discourse, is self-described here as a "slave" (δοῦλος) of God and of the Lord Jesus Christ. While many commentators mention the use of δοῦλος as an indication of humility, the use of this word to describe the prophets of both Old and New Testaments points more to a noble rather than a humble description.[96] In 3:1 he implies that he also is a "teacher" (διδάσκαλος). The first active agent, God, appears 16 times as "God" (1:1, 5, 13, 20, 27; 2:5, 19, 23; 3:9; 4:4, 6, 7, 8) and 8 times as "Lord" (1:7; 3:9; 4:10, 15; 5:4, 10). The third active agent, the Lord Jesus Christ, is mentioned again by name only in 2:1, "My brothers, show no partiality as you hold the faith in our Lord Jesus Christ, the Lord of glory." However, at least three references to "Lord" (κύριος) in 5:8, 14, 15 also refer to Jesus in his future coming

---

[95] Four named individuals from Israel's history, Abraham, Rahab, Job and Elijah, appear as participants in the role of exemplars to illustrate certain behavior.

[96] 2 Kings 9:7; 17:13; Jer. 7:25; Eze. 38:17; Dan. 9:6, 10; Amos 3:7; Zech. 1:6, et.al. See the discussion in John Painter, *Just James* (Minneapolis: Fortress Press, 1999), 236-37.

and in his role as healer. Further indirect references to the "voice" of Jesus as probable allusions to his teaching will be examined at their appropriate locations in the text. The final participant, functioning in the role of "patient," is the collective group referenced as "the twelve tribes in the Diaspora." This group functions as the "addressee" in the salutation. Other terms applied to this group are "brothers" (ἀδελφοί), used a total of 15 times and "adulteresses" (μοιχαλίδες, 4:4) as well as two negative designations, "sinners" and "double-minded" (ἁμαρτωλοί, δίψυχοί, 4:8). Other designations used for rhetorical effect—"empty person" (2:20) and the two references, "you who say" (4:13) and "you rich" (5:1)—are not literal designations for the addressees. More will be said about each of these terms and their function in the discourse at the appropriate places in the commentary. Two of these participants, however, deserve more attention—James and the twelve tribes.

There has been thus far no treatment of the "introduction" issues that are always found in traditional commentaries, namely the questions about author, recipients, date, genre, language, and structure. That is because these questions can really only be clarified through the analysis of the text itself, the most important source for answering these questions. Therefore, at the appropriate places in the commentary, we will briefly address these issues. The introductory chapter addressed the question of structure and information flow in the discourse. This was part of the discussion of how the "peak" of James identifies its meta-theme, the exhortation to follow Divine rather than human wisdom. A proposed structure/outline of the discourse was also presented at the end of the introduction. In the salutation of 1:1 both the author and the intended recipients of the discourse are clearly mentioned. Who was this "James" and what people are intended by the expression "twelve tribes in the Diaspora?" What are the implications that can be drawn from this information about the date of the book and about the specific form in which it functions as a letter? The question of its literary genre will be discussed in the analysis of the following sub-paragraph (1:2-4).

The issue of the identity of the James in 1:1 as author of the letter attributed to him has developed recently in surprising ways. Rather than moving away from the idea that James, the brother of Jesus, could have been the author, scholarly opinion has moved in the last decades toward greater confidence in the possibility that he was the author. Two of the more articulate scholars in this regard have been Luke

Johnson and Richard Bauckham. These scholars acknowledge that while we cannot know certainly that James was the author, there is no convincing reason for doubting his authorship. He is the best candidate in the field and the reasons for doubting his authorship simply do not stand up to the facts as we know them.[97]

Because this is a commentary that attempts to pay close attention to the language of the text, it is appropriate to respond to the old charge that the literary level of the Greek in this letter indicates that it could not be from the hand of a Galilean peasant as James must have been. Before we cite some evidence to the contrary, I mention the wise observation of a linguist who has offered his own discourse analysis of the text of James. Dell Hymes responded to this familiar charge in the following way. "The excellent Greek has been used as an argument that James of Galilee could not have been the author, but to a linguist *this seems a familiar type of prejudice*, and scholarship has shown the extensive penetration of Greek culture and language in Palestine at the time."[98] Hymes' reference to recent scholarship is evidenced today by the research of such scholars as Sevenster, Hengel, Mussies, Porter, Freyne, and Davids.[99] While none of this can actually prove that James wrote this book, the emerging picture of Galilee in the first century as being at the heart of Hellenization poses serious problems for those confidently questioning the possibility of James being the author on some linguistic basis. On the contrary, the simplicity of the opening greeting in which the author shows no need to argue his own qualifications; the primitive Jewish Christology; the lack of an elaborated creed; the numerous allusions to the oral teaching of Jesus not yet in canonical form; and the author's evident familiarity with Palestinian life and culture all support the idea that the text preserves not only the name of the one called "James the Just," but also the words that come directly from him.

Richard Bauckham has persuasively argued that no James but the brother of Jesus and head of the Jerusalem mother church could expect believers to accept his teaching as authoritative and binding.[100] Just as Second Temple Jewish leaders and also later revered Jerusalem rabbis wrote to the Diaspora communities offering authoritative guidance, so

---

[97] See, e.g., L.T. Johnson, *The Letter of James*, (New York: Doubleday, 1995), 89-121.

[98] Dell Hymes, "The General Epistle of James," *International Journal of the Society of Language*, 62 (1986), 77.

[99] See the Bibliography for these important works.

[100] Richard Bauckham, *James*, (London: Routledge, 1999), 11-18.

James in his role at the center of the Jerusalem church wrote a "diaspora encyclical" to believing Jewish communities. While many would be quick to add that James intended to address Diaspora Jewish communities of believers in Jesus, such a fine distinction at this early time was not appropriate for one who saw the scattered communities of Jewish believers as the beginning of the end time regathering of the scattered tribes. There is no need to argue that the twelve tribes refer to believers of all ethnic backgrounds who were sojourners in some sort of spiritual exile. The reference to "twelve tribes" in ancient Christian literature always referenced the actual tribes of Israel and the context must show whether believing or non-believing Jews were intended.[101] Perhaps James saw no distinction in the address, because he saw himself as the head of a newly constituted twelve tribes. James does not mention the Gentile mission, perhaps because its Pauline manifestation had not yet emerged at this time.

Much of what we have surveyed relates also to the question of the date of the letter. Reliable sources agree on the date of 62 A.D. as the death of James, which obviously provides the *terminus ad quem* for the writing. In this writer's opinion, no one has adequately answered the powerful arguments of John A.T. Robinson for a date of around 48 AD, or possibly a bit earlier. Space does not allow for the marshalling of Robinson's circumstantial evidence for this early date and readers are encouraged to consider his work that is often simply ignored today. Many of his points have been echoed in the treatments of date and authorship by Johnson, Bauckham and Davids. While one still cannot be overly dogmatic, Robinson's conclusion is an accurate description until someone offers a better alternative. "It can take its place, alongside other literature in the process of formation in the second decade of the Christian mission, as the first surviving finished document of the church."[102]

DISCOURSE BOUNDARIES AND COHESION IN 1:2-15

Previously we have argued that the first major division in the body of the letter is 1:2-15. This is based on the nominative plural of address

---

[101] W.C. Van Unnik, "*Diaspora* and *Church* in the First Centuries of Church History," *Sparsa Collecta*, vol. 3 (Leiden: Brill, 1983). James is not referring to the "spiritual dispersion" of all believers living as aliens in this world, which is probably the intention of Peter in his use of the word (1 Peter 1:1). Most commentators have overlooked that James couples the word with the article (τῇ διασπορᾷ), indicating the literal dispersion. Peter omits the article and uses the genitive form of the word (διασπορᾶς) indicating its metaphorical use.

[102] John A.T. Robinson, *Redating the New* Testament (London: SCM Press, 1976), 139.

(ἀδελφοί) collocated with an imperative (ἡγήσασθε) in 1:2 that next appears in 1:16. This is the pattern followed throughout the discourse, with the special exception of the rhetorical questions opening 3:13 and 4:1, which initialize the thematic peak and the hortatory peak of the discourse respectively. Not only do the presence of formal linguistic markers indicate that 1:2-15 is the first main paragraph, but the semantic cohesion throughout this section indicates that it is to be viewed as a unit, while also containing discrete sub-paragraphs.

Commentators from Dibelius onward have noticed the presence of word linkage in this passage. Two of the noted examples are the χαίρειν ending the greeting (1:1) and the χαρὰν as the second word of 1:2 plus λειπόμενοι and λείπεται joining 1:4 and 1:5. In this writer's opinion, however, these word linkages have been greatly overplayed because after this opening paragraph few clear examples like these can be found. A better approach is to stress the semantic cohesion found throughout this paragraph rather than the rhetorical decoration of formal word linkage. This does not imply that James cannot employ a rhetorical flourish, as he does in the alliteration of three consecutive π−words in 1:2 (πειρασμοῖς περιπέσητε ποικίλοις). It is doubtful, however, that these examples are part of a rhetorical strategy to segment his discourse.

The entire paragraph also exhibits semantic cohesion in the following manner. The first sub-paragraph mentions the "trials" (πειρασμοῖς) that serve as the main theme throughout the fourth sub-paragraph in 1:12-15, where the word group πειρα− appears six times. The "testing" (δοκίμιον) of the believer's faith in 1:3 is echoed in the blessed person who has been "tested" (δόκιμος) in 1:12. The endurance (ὑπομονὴ) mentioned twice in 1:3 and 4 is answered by the "endures" (ὑπομένει) of 1:12. Although not the same exact word, the semantic idea of considering our trials to be "all joy" (πᾶσαν χαρὰν) in 1:2 is parallel to the pronouncement of "blessed" (μακάριος) on those who endure such trials (1:12).

In this and in other minor ways not mentioned, the paragraph offers an array of cohesive devices that justify 1:2-15 as the first main paragraph of the discourse. Some recent writers, in an honest attempt to discover some measure of coherence in the letter, have suggested that this section, along with the rest of chapter one, serves as a sort of "table of contents" for the rest of the book.[103] There is some merit to this

---

[103] Bauckham, *James*, 69-73; Johnson, *James*, 14-15.

approach. While it is true that James mentions in 1:2-15 and in the rest of the chapter some themes that he will discuss later, the chapter's proposed role as a table of contents is weakened by the following two facts. First, James discusses in 2:1—5:20 a number of issues that he does not mention in chapter one. Second, the main theme of this opening section, namely "trials" (the πειρα−word group mentioned 7 times) is not mentioned by name in the rest of the book! It is better to see 1:2-15, 1:16-18 and 1:19-27 as three separate paragraphs, each introduced by the formal markers of ἀδελφοί collocated with an imperative. The repetition of themes in chapter one and later in the book should be viewed simply as the prerogative of an author to repeat and expand an idea that he has mentioned earlier in his discourse. More will be said about this special role of chapter one in later comments.

Within the larger paragraph of 1:2-15, there are four sub-paragraphs (1:2-4; 1:5-8; 1:9-11 and 1:12-15). Evidence for the breakdown into these specific sub paragraphs will be presented in the analysis of each individual section.

1. Paragraph 2 (James 1:2-4)

Πᾶσαν χαρὰν ἡγήσασθε, ἀδελφοί μου, ὅταν πειρασμοῖς περιπέσητε ποικίλοις, γινώσκοντες ὅτι τὸ δοκίμιον ὑμῶν τῆς πίστεως κατεργάζεται ὑπομονήν. ἡ δὲ ὑπομονὴ ἔργον τέλειον ἐχέτω, ἵνα ἦτε τέλειοι καὶ ὁλόκληροι ἐν μηδενὶ λειπόμενοι.	Consider it all joy, my brothers, when you encounter trials of various kinds, because you know that the testing of your faith produces endurance. And allow endurance to have its complete effect, so that you may be complete and whole, lacking in nothing.

James 1:2-4 Clause Analysis

C	P	add	A			A
πᾶσαν χαρὰν	ἡγήσασθε	ἀδελφοί μου	**cj** ὅταν	**A** πειρασμοῖς		**P** γινώσκοντες
				P περιπέσητε		
				ποικίλοις		

A (cont.)			
cj	**S**	**P**	**C**
ὅτι	τὸ δοκίμιον ὑμῶν τῆς πίστεως	κατεργάζεται	ὑπομονήν

S	**C**	**P**
ἡ ὑπομονη	ἔργον τέλειον	ἐχέτω
cj δε		

cj	**P**	**C**	**A**	
ἵνα	ἦτε	τέλειοι καὶ ὁλόκληροι	**A**	**P**
			ἐν μηδενι	λειπόμενοι

This section begins immediately after the salutation and is marked by the nominative of address ἀδελφοί collocated with the imperative ἡγήσασθε, and ends with the result participle λειπόμενοι. The topic of the paragraph, therefore, is "joy under trials." The topic shifts in 1:5 with the introduction of a new topic in the word *wisdom* and is concerned with how to find that virtue if it is lacking. Thus while the two paragraphs are closely linked, they are separate topics within the larger paragraph that concerns trials in general.

James 1:2-4 consists of two primary clauses, with each clause featuring an imperative command (ἡγήσασθε and ἐχέτω). The first two of the three secondary clauses support the first primary clause by indicating: 1) *when* the joyful attitude should take place—whenever we encounter various trials; and 2) *why* we should have such an attitude—because we know that trials produce endurance. The second primary clause then continues the exhortation by commanding each individual who is encountering trials to allow this endurance to complete its work in them. Then follows a secondary purpose clause introduced by ἵνα plus the subjunctive ἦτε, which informs the readers that if they have the correct attitude toward their trials it will lead to greater maturity, namely that they would be complete (τέλειοι) and whole (ὁλόκληροι), and thus would not be lacking (λειπόμενοι) in any area of their lives.

Commentators have speculated about the specific type of "trials" to which James refers. Some have seen in this verse evidence that his readers were undergoing a special persecution for their faith, possibly from Jewish authorities. An example of such persecution has been found in a passage like Acts 8:1-3. This conclusion seems unwarranted and unnecessarily limiting in scope. The definer "various" (ποικίλοις), modifying "trials," points away from a focus on persecution. While their problems may have included persecution, their trials were probably those of the types experienced by all believers. Some examples of these trials are mentioned in the immediate and later context, none of which includes what we usually define as "persecution." While the readers were facing bad treatment by others (see 2:1-4 and 5:1-6), there does not seem to be any reference to being persecuted for their faith.

Some commentators have drawn attention to the use in 1:2-4 (as well as in 1:15-18) of the rhetorical device of *gradatio*—the concatenation of terms in which the repetition of one word from the preceding member in a series is in the member that follows (see also Rom. 5:3, 4). In this case, the concatenation would be *trials, endurance, completion* (πειρασμοί, ὑπομονή, τέλειοι). There is some question as to whether the concatenation continues in 1:5-8, although commentators tend to end it at 1:4.[104] The striking aspect is that the final member (τέλειοι) is then paraphrased twice: "complete and whole, lacking in nothing." Dibelius/Greeven have a thorough discussion of *gradatio* with interesting examples from a variety of literature genres.[105] Care should be taken, however, about concluding too quickly that some conscious utilization of this ancient rhetorical device was prominent in James' literary strategy. Many of the features pointed out in rhetorical studies of the NT writers can also be accounted for as present in previous Jewish writings—particularly in the poetic and wisdom literature. A good case could be made that these Jewish writers were drawing more on their own heritage than on some supposed rhetorical training they may, or may not, have received. A more likely inspiration for this figure, even including a form of *gradatio*, is the Jesus *logion* in Mat. 7:7-8: "Ask, and it will be given to you; seek, and you will find; knock, and it will be opened to you. For everyone who asks receives, and the one who seeks finds, and to the one who knocks it will be opened."

---

[104] Brosend suggests extending the *gradatio* through 1:8. William F. Brosend, *James and Jude* (Cambridge: Cambridge University Press, 2004), 34-35.

[105] Martin Dibelius and Heinrich Greeven, *James* (Philadelphia: Fortress Press, 1976), 72.

The clearly hortatory nature of this paragraph is characteristic of James' style throughout the book, as the following chart indicates. James utilizes a total of 55 imperative forms plus 4 imperatival future forms, a higher ratio of imperatives to total words than in any other NT book.

RATIO OF THE NUMBER OF IMPERATIVES TO TOTAL WORDS IN EACH NEW TESTAMENT BOOK

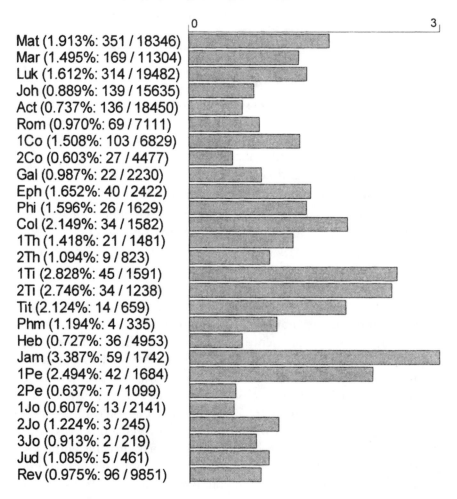

Mat (1.913%: 351 / 18346)
Mar (1.495%: 169 / 11304)
Luk (1.612%: 314 / 19482)
Joh (0.889%: 139 / 15635)
Act (0.737%: 136 / 18450)
Rom (0.970%: 69 / 7111)
1Co (1.508%: 103 / 6829)
2Co (0.603%: 27 / 4477)
Gal (0.987%: 22 / 2230)
Eph (1.652%: 40 / 2422)
Phi (1.596%: 26 / 1629)
Col (2.149%: 34 / 1582)
1Th (1.418%: 21 / 1481)
2Th (1.094%: 9 / 823)
1Ti (2.828%: 45 / 1591)
2Ti (2.746%: 34 / 1238)
Tit (2.124%: 14 / 659)
Phm (1.194%: 4 / 335)
Heb (0.727%: 36 / 4953)
Jam (3.387%: 59 / 1742)
1Pe (2.494%: 42 / 1684)
2Pe (0.637%: 7 / 1099)
1Jo (0.607%: 13 / 2141)
2Jo (1.224%: 3 / 245)
3Jo (0.913%: 2 / 219)
Jud (1.085%: 5 / 461)
Rev (0.975%: 96 / 9851)

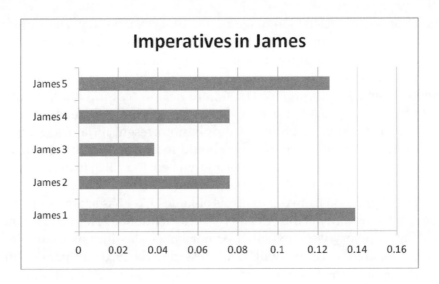

Furthermore, these imperatives are evenly distributed. This can be illustrated by a bar chart that displays how the imperatives are distributed throughout James. The relatively balanced distribution of imperatives in James is unlike some NT books in which the hortatory sections are clearly separate from the indicative sections, e.g., Romans (1-11; 12-16); Ephesians (1-3; 4-6) and Colossians (1-2; 3-4). This distribution illustrates the hortatory character of James and justifies by hard data its genre as a hortatory encyclical.

This type of literature raises the issue of the literary level of the author's Greek, particularly as it relates to the ability of James, the brother of Jesus, to write at such a level. Linguists speak of the *register* of a language, which is *language variety according to use.*[106] Scholars have noted the relatively high number of *hapax legomena* in the letter—62 to be exact. Sometimes this is utilized as evidence of the high literary level of the book. But an understanding of a book's register should create pause before drawing unwarranted conclusions about the literary level of the language. James' hortatory style in which he employs a large amount of vivid imagery including parables and analogies from nature and from cultural activities demands a more specialized vocabulary than another epistle of differing register. A statistical analysis of the vocabulary of the NT, employing the characteristic of "semantic clustering," found that James clustered nearer to the simple Greek of

---

[106] M.A.K. Halliday and R. Hasan, *Language, Context and Text: Aspects of Language in a Social-Semiotic Perspective* (Geelong: Victoria: Deakin University), 126.

the *Didache* than to the language of any other NT book.[107] The similar functions of these two works as practical handbooks to the Christian life argues for a similar register of language variation according to use.

Some characteristics associated with a high literary style, such as in Hebrews and Luke's preface (1:1-4), are not present in James. As one example, the frequent use of an extended periodic sentence, which appears so often in Hebrews, is simply not present in James. From a linguistic viewpoint, therefore, we should recognize that the resources exist in a language for its speakers and writers to utilize in accordance with their purposes in speaking or writing.

This digression from our analysis of James 1:2-4 has again discussed some of the traditional introductory issues mentioned briefly in 1:1. The next introductory issue, whether or not James classifies as traditional Jewish wisdom literature, will be addressed in the next sub-paragraph, which contains the first mention of the word *wisdom*. The last of those issues, James' possible use of Jesus' oral teaching, will be briefly addressed in the discussion of 1:12-15 and more thoroughly analyzed in the analysis of a performance of a Jesus saying in 2:5.

The ideas expressed in James 1:2-4 fit into the overall theme of James as follows. Our approach to this discourse is that 3:13-18 is the discourse peak and conveys the meta-theme that James desires his readers to choose between two polarities—the wisdom from God above or the wisdom from man below. Life as a choice between those two opposite ways of life is a major thrust of his thinking. In other words, his readers can choose either to curse God for the difficult things that come upon them or can view these trials as an opportunity to be joyful. The key is to recognize that such trials produce something in us—the quality of endurance. Another of James' themes—the goal of an undivided and whole life rather than a fragmented one—is brought out clearly in his emphasis that the goal of endurance leads to whole-ness. This is illustrated at the beginning of 1:2 with his reference to "all joy" (πᾶσαν χαρὰν), a rare example in James of fronting the comple-ment of the verb (see 5:11 for the only other occurrence of fronting rather than "default" order of predicate/subject/complement). The rather unique expression conveys the idea of "complete joy" or even "pure joy" (NIV/TNIV). This type of attitude would contrast with a "mixed joy" and would be consistent with the goal of trials as leading one to being "complete and whole, lacking in nothing" (1:4c). This last

---

[107] O'Donnell, *Corpus Linguistics*, 127.

purpose clause in 1:4: (ἵνα ἦτε τέλειοι καὶ ὁλόκληροι ἐν μηδενὶ λειπόμενοι) embodies the desired result of the command to "consider it as all joy" while undergoing trials.[108] It also embodies the overall goal that James has for his readers. To be "complete" (τέλειος) is to be undivided, the opposite of being "double"—a condition that James warns against in many different ways in the letter.

3. Paragraph 3 (James 1:5-8)

Εἰ δέ τις ὑμῶν λείπεται σοφίας, αἰτείτω παρὰ τοῦ διδόντος θεοῦ πᾶσιν ἁπλῶς καὶ μὴ ὀνειδίζοντος καὶ δοθήσεται αὐτῷ. αἰτείτω δὲ ἐν πίστει μηδὲν διακρινόμενος· ὁ γὰρ διακρινόμενος ἔοικεν κλύδωνι θαλάσσης ἀνεμιζομένῳ καὶ ῥιπιζομένῳ. μὴ γὰρ οἰέσθω ὁ ἄνθρω—πος ἐκεῖνος ὅτι λήμψεταί τι παρὰ τοῦ κυρίου, ἀνὴρ δίψυχος ἀκατάστατος ἐν πάσαις ταῖς ὁδοῖς αὐτοῦ.	If any of you lacks wisdom, let him ask God, who gives without hesitation to all and does not reproach and it will be given him. But let him ask in faith, doubting nothing, for the one who doubts is like a wave of the sea that is driven and tossed by the wind. For that person must not suppose that he will receive anything from the Lord. A double-minded man is unstable in all his ways.

James 1:5-8 Clause Analysis
1:5

cj	cj	S	P	C
Εἰ	δέ	τις ὑμῶν	λείπεται	σοφίας

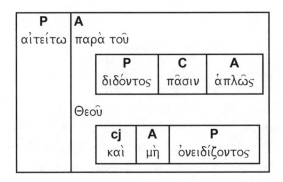

---

[108] James employs the ἵνα plus subjunctive clause elsewhere only in 4:3; 5:9, 12, where each time the purpose is a negative one, unlike the positive purpose envisioned here.

cj	P	C
καὶ	δοθήσεται	αὐτω

1:6

P	cj	A	A	
αἰτείτω	δε	ἐν πίστει	**C** μηδὲν	**P** διακρινόμενος

S		P	A	
cj γὰρ		ἔοικεν	κλύδωνι θαλάσσης	
P ὁ διακρινόμενος			**P** ἀνεμιζομένω	
			cj καὶ	**P** ῥιπιζομένω

1:7

A	cj	P	S			
μὴ	γὰρ	οἰέσθω	ὁ ἄνθρωπος ἐκεῖνος			
C						
	cj ὅτι	**P** λήμψεται	**C** τι	**A** παρὰ τοῦ κυρίου		

1:8

S	C	A
ἀνὴρ δίψυχος	ἀκατάστατος	ἐν πάσαις ταῖς ὁδοῖς αὐτοῦ

This section, 1:5-8, while exhibiting unique characteristics of its own, is connected to the previous section by the word λείπεται, which links it with the closing word of 1:4, λειπόμενοι. The obvious conclusion is that the lacking virtue of wisdom (σοφίας) is what is needed to help complete, perfect and make whole the person encountering trials, the topic of the previous paragraph. The first verb, αἰτείτω ("he should request"), introduces the topic of prayer which dominates the rest of the section with each clause explaining either how one should pray for wisdom or the hindrances to effective praying. While wisdom is an essential aspect in the discussion, it is the effective praying for wisdom that is both the theme and comment throughout. Wisdom is not defined at this point, but in 3:13-18, the thematic peak of the book, heavenly wisdom is contrasted with earthly human wisdom by displaying opposite behaviors. The sub-paragraph ends with a brief description of the "double-souled" person in 1:8, before James returns to exhorting the "lowly brother" in 1:9.

The primary clauses of 1:5-8 deal with the reader's requesting wisdom, God's giving it, the doubter's presumption, and the double-souled person's instability. The protasis of the first class conditional clause, "if anyone lacks wisdom" (Εἰ δέ τις ὑμῶν λείπεται σοφίας) does not function as a hypothetical condition but rhetorically to exhort the readers that the one who lacks wisdom should ask for it. The third person imperative in the apodosis of the conditional sentence does not lessen the urgency of the command but is used only because James has proposed a third person who lacks the wisdom. I suggest the translation "should ask" rather than the traditional "let him ask" to avoid the idea of permission associated with the English word "let." James affirms two attributes of God: that he gives and that he does not reproach the one who asks. The participle διδόντος is in an attributive position modifying θεοῦ. One would expect that the participle would follow the noun describing what God does for those who are the complements or indirect objects (πᾶσιν), as is the case with the following ὀνειδίζοντος. Most commentators ignore this anomaly. Others usually state that the construction does appear occasionally in the NT. The reason for this word order may be that James wished to give prominence to the manner and recipients of God's giving: "without hesitation to all" (πᾶσιν ἁπλῶς).[109]

In the second clause complex of 1:6, the post-positive δέ reminds the reader that the request for wisdom must be with a faith that doubts nothing. He then adds a reason, introduced by γάρ, and his first of many vivid similes: "for the one who doubts is like a wave of the sea that is driven and tossed by the wind."

The third primary clause complex in 1:7, although introduced also

---

[109] The construction is analyzed in *The Ab Urbe Condita Construction in Greek. A Study in the Classification of the Participle.* Language Dissertation No. 28. *Journal of the Linguistic Society of America*, Vol. 15, No. 1 Supplement (1939).

by γάρ, boldly declares that such a wavering "person" (ἄνθρωπος) should never even suppose (μὴ . . . οἰέσθω) that they will receive anything from the Lord. Then follows a clause in 1:8 which translators and commentators have treated differently because of a possible confusion in the punctuation. The most recent critical texts (NA27 and UBS4) put a partial stop before the clause and read it as a statement in apposition to the preceding clause that mentions the wavering person who requests wisdom. The clause is verbless and demands that either a copulative or both a pronoun and copulative be supplied: ἀνὴρ δίψυχος, ἀκατάστατος ἐν πάσαις ταῖς ὁδοῖς αὐτοῦ. The critical texts add a comma following the "double-souled man," thus lending their support to the idea that the clause continues the sentence and further describes the previous person. This is expressed by most of the modern English versions by: "*he is* a double-minded man, unstable in all his ways." However, I suggest that we follow the earlier textual editions and read this as a primary clause, independent in structure from the previous verse. By adding an understood copula and removing the comma following δίψυχος, it would translate: "A double-minded man is unstable in all his ways." This is to be preferred for the following reasons. Verse eight reads like an aphorism and Bauckham has illustrated how James often rounds off his main point in a section by such a stand alone aphorism that illustrates his point.[110] At times the aphorism may seem a bit strained in that it does not always tie in neatly to the previous words. Such is the case here but this would also explain the change to the masculine ἀνήρ from the more generic ἄνθρωπος in the preceding verse. The aphorism contains the ἀνήρ and James faithfully reproduces it, even though his point is that the uncertainty he condemns applies to both male and female. As we have mentioned, earlier versions (Tyndale, Geneva, AV) preferred this approach by seeing a full stop before 1:8 and having no comma in 1:8. Ancient support for reading the verse as an independent clause is in the fourth-century manuscript B (Vaticanus) which indicates a full stop before the words that begin 1:8. Finally, a number of medieval manuscripts and the earlier Harklean Syriac version inserted a γάρ after ἀνήρ, indicating that these scribes understood that 1:8 was to be taken as an independent clause providing the reason why such a person will not receive anything from the Lord. "*For* a doubled-souled man is unstable in all his ways." Its

---

[110] Bauckham, *James*, 35-48. See, e.g., 1:11; 1:25; 2:13; 3:12; 3:18; 4:17.

role as a supporting aphorism is the strongest argument that the verse should stand alone as a concluding statement about the man who requests while doubting.

Words from the two semantic domains of "Possess" (five) and "Believe, Trust" (four) dominate the paragraph's field of ideational content. Among the first field of common words like λείπω, δίδωμι (twice) and λαμβάνω is the adverb ἁπλῶς in 1:5 where it describes the manner in which God gives to all people the wisdom they request.

English versions throughout the last five hundred years have generally translated this adverb as "generously" (NRS, NAU, NIV, ESV) or "liberally" (Geneva, KJV). However, another sense of the word, namely that of "without hesitation," may be more appropriate in the context. BDAG defines this *hapax legomenon* only as "without reservation" and cites classical, Philonic and patristic sources for this meaning.[111] This meaning certainly fits in with James' call for singleness and his aversion to doubleness throughout his discourse. In other words, God's willingness to give "without hesitation" contrasts vividly with the unanswered prayers of the person who prays "with hesitation." With this support from sources outside the NT and also from the context, it is difficult to understand why the versions still cling to the "generously" translation.

Among such common words as πίστις and διακρίνομαι (twice) in the second domain of "Believe, Trust," there is another *hapax legomenon,* namely the rare word δίψυχος in 1:8, where the adjective describes the man who is unstable in all his ways. This word appears in the NT only here and in 4:8. It has been found nowhere else in this form in any previous Greek literature. While the concept of "doubleness" appears in Plato and in Second Temple Jewish literature, this form of the word does not. The word and its cognates appear dozens of times in *Shepherd of Hermas,* in a meaning obviously dependent on its use in James (*Hermas* 12:3; 23:6; 34:1; 39:5, 6; 41:2, et.al.), as well as three times in the Clementine Letters (1Cl. 11:2; 23:3; 2 Cl. 11:2). The *Didache* also uses the verb form along with a number of "double-words" beginning with δι–, in its "two ways" section (*Did.* 2:4; 4:4, 7; 5:1)—one of the many shared semantic concepts in the two books. Most all English versions translate δίψυχος as "double-minded" with Tyndale rendering it as "waveringe mynded." The word is also used in the above Apostolic Fathers as connected to doubting in prayer. In a thorough study of whether this is truly a "Christian word," Porter suggests that James did indeed coin the word and that it is best translated as "double-souled."[112] This translation not only emphasizes the root meaning of this lexeme but also its uniqueness compared to the other "double" words that do appear prior to James.

The stress on requesting wisdom in trials described in the previous passage prepares the reader for the later more detailed description of wisdom in 3:13-18, the passage that in our view serves as the thematic peak of the book and stamps its meta-theme on each individual section. The choosing between two ways or polar opposite behaviors is nowhere else illustrated as clearly as it is in this paragraph. The reader who hesitates at the choice between the two roads before him is strongly condemned here as wavering like the waves of the sea. The δίψυχος description of the man who is unstable in everything he does clearly describes the one who desires it both ways, i.e., to follow both the way of heavenly wisdom in his desire for success in trials AND in his following his own self-sufficient wisdom that results in certain instability in his pursuits. Later in 4:8 the reader is called to convert from this type of "double" thinking.

At this point something should be said about the question of James being part of the Jewish wisdom literature found in both the canonical and the later Jewish writings, some of which were enjoyed by the contemporaries of James. While the literature on this subject is extensive, exact parallels and explanations differ greatly. The German scholar, Ernst Baasland, in an essay translated as "The Letter of James as New Testament Wisdom Literature," has surveyed the different ideas and suggested a creative solution to the tension between James' similarities and differences with traditional Jewish wisdom. Baasland calls James "*the* wisdom writing of the NT which connects the closest to Old Testament wisdom literature." [113] However, James has its own uniqueness in this wisdom tradition because of his evident debt to the wisdom teaching of his brother. In Baasland's words, "The same thing that differentiates James from Jewish wisdom writing is what connects James with the proclamation of Jesus."[114] To James wisdom has received a new center, the starting point of which is belief in the "glorious Messiah, the Lord Jesus" (2:1), and the manifestation of which is that the poor will

---

[111] *BDAG*, 104.

[112] S.E. Porter, "Is dipsychos (James 1,8; 4,8) a 'Christian' Word?" *Biblica* 71 (1990), 469-98.

[113] Ernst Baasland, "Der Jakobusbrief als Neutestamentliche Weisheitsschrift," *Studia Theologica* 36 (1982), 119.

[114] Baasland, 120.

inherit the kingdom (2:5). While there seems to be no dependence on Paul, they are not alien either, with Paul taking wisdom further into more ontological realms. Baasland concludes as follows:

> The lines of wisdom can be traced back to the wisdom literature of the OT. On the other hand, we see a line in the NT, which originates in Jesus and stretches over the parts of the proclamation of Paul (Rom. 2:6, 12; 1 Cor. 1-4, etc.) and which continues over James and other NT letters up to the Apostolic Fathers (the Clements and Origen)."[115]

Some writers have described the approach of James to wisdom literature as "subverting" the traditional wisdom tradition.[116] I am not sure that James would have viewed his approach as subversive. He simply approaches the two ways tradition in Hebraic literature as echoed by Jesus and then applies it to the new kingdom inaugurated by his more famous brother. The poor had a definite role in the social message of the Hebrew prophets. Jesus and James simply focus their role as being more central to the purposes of God and the Messiah in this phase of the Kingdom plan. This may be more accurately described as an extension rather than a subversion of wisdom.

4. Paragraph 4 (James 1:9-11)

Καυχάσθω δὲ ὁ ἀδελφὸς ὁ ταπεινὸς ἐν τῷ ὕψει αὐτοῦ, ὁ δὲ πλούσιος ἐν τῇ ταπεινώσει αὐτοῦ, ὅτι ὡς ἄνθος χόρτου παρελεύσεται. ἀνέτειλεν γὰρ ὁ ἥλιος σὺν τῷ καύσωνι καὶ ἐξήρανεν τὸν χόρτον καὶ τὸ ἄνθος αὐτοῦ ἐξέπεσεν καὶ ἡ εὐπρέπεια τοῦ προσώπου αὐτοῦ ἀπώλετο· οὕτως καὶ ὁ πλούσιος ἐν ταῖς πορείαις αὐτοῦ μαρανθήσεται.	The lowly brother should boast in his exaltation, but the rich in his humiliation, because like a flower of the grass he will pass away. For the sun rises with its scorching heat and withers the grass, and its flower falls, and the beauty of its appearance perishes. So also the rich man will fade away in the midst of his pursuits.

---

[115] Baasland, 139.

[116] P.J. Hartin, " 'Who is wise and understanding among you?' (James 3:13). An analysis of wisdom, eschatology and apocalypticism in the Epistle of James." *SBL 1996 Seminar Papers* (SBL, 1997), 493-501. Todd C. Penner, *The Epistle of James and Eschatology*, JSNT Supplement Series 121 (Sheffield Academic Press, 1996).

James 1:9-11 Clause Analysis
1:9

P	cj	S	A
Καυχάσθω	δε	ὁ ἀδελφὸς ὁ ταπεινὸς	ἐν τῷ ὕψει αὐτου

1:10

S	A
ὁ	ἐν τῇ ταπεινώσει αὐτου
cj δε	
πλούσιος	

cj	A	P
ὅτι	ὡς ἄνθος χόρτου	παρελεύσεται

1:11

P	cj	S	A
ἀνέτειλεν	γὰρ	ὁ ἥλιος	σὺν τῷ καύσωνι

cj	P	C
καὶ	ἐξήρανεν	τὸν χόρτον

cj	S	P
καὶ	τὸ ἄνθος αὐτου	ἐξέπεσεν

cj	S	P
καὶ	ἡ εὐπρέπεια τοῦ προσώπου αὐτου	ἀπώλετο

cj	cj	S	A	P
οὕτως	καὶ	ὁ πλούσιος	ἐν ταῖς πορείαις αὐτου	μαρανθήσεται

James 1:9-11 consists of eight clauses with only one of them functioning as a secondary, causal clause. This straightforward style of affirmations

contrasts clearly with the style of both the preceding and following co-texts, where supporting clauses are as numerous as the mainline claus-es. The ellipsis in the second clause is readily recognized by the reader who knows to provide the missing "should boast" that is clearly stated in the first clause. The single secondary clause in 1:10, introduced by the causal ὅτι ("because like a flower of grass *he* shall pass away") actually serves to introduce a series of five consecutive primary clauses. The tran-sitional conjunction γάρ introduces the first clause that begins the sim-ile of the flower and the burning heat. Parataxis is demonstrated in the repetition of the conjunctive καὶ four times introducing these clauses. In the final clause the fourth καὶ is preceded by the climactic οὕτως ("so" or "thus"), demanding the adjunctive translation of the last καὶ as "also."

The small paragraph demonstrates semantic linkage with the two preceding paragraphs. In 1:2 the "brothers" are exhorted to "consider it all joy" when they encounter trials. Here one example of those broth-ers, a "lowly" one, is to boast (positively) in one type of trial, being lowly. As it is rather odd to exhort someone to be joyful in trials, so it is also odd to exhort someone (third person imperative καυχάσθω) to boast in being lowered. Such is the counter cultural lifestyle of the one who has faith in the "glorious Lord Jesus the Messiah" (2:1). Furthermore, the last clause of this paragraph, "the rich man will fade away in the midst of his pursuits," parallels in structure and thought what is affirmed at the end of the previous paragraph in 1:8: "a dou-ble-minded man is unstable in all his ways." Although the words are different, some translations render the πορείαις αὐτου in the last clause of 1:11 as "his ways," bringing it even closer in semantic paral-lel to the ὁδοῖς αὐτου ending 1:8. In varying language the message is clear: neither the doubting, double-souled person nor the proud, rich person will be successful in the end.

The colorful imagery that James employs here and throughout his book demands a special language register. This is one of the reasons that there is one *hapax legomenon* in this paragraph (εὐπρέπεια); three words that appear only once elsewhere in the NT (ἄνθος, πορεία, μαραίνω); and one other word appearing only once each in Matthew and Luke (καύσων). This passage is typical of the type of language that James uti-lizes to make his vivid points. We need not conclude that this style is evi-dence of a highly literary Greek that would be more appropriate for "classical" writers and supposedly inappropriate for a Galilean like

James. This approach to language register, along with the now abundant evidence of Hellenization in first century Judea, should lay to rest forever the charge that James could not write at this "level" of Greek.

James' careful use of tenses in this paragraph also illustrates the value of an aspectual approach to the study of tense. In a simile from nature he utilizes the future tense when the rich man "will pass away" (παρελεύσεται). In the final verse he declares without a simile in the future tense that the rich man "will fade away" (μαρανθήσεται). Between these two future tenses, he utilizes a series of aorist indicative verbs to describe the symbiotic relationship between the sun and vegetation. "The sun rises (ἀνέτειλεν) with its scorching heat and withers (ἐξήρανεν) the grass, and its flower falls (ἐξέπεσεν), and the beauty of its appearance perishes (ἀπώλετο)." Some traditional grammars, too dependent on the *aktionsart* approach to the aorist as expressing some sort of *punctiliar* action, are forced to refer to this exceptional usage of the aorist as a *gnomic* aorist. It is obvious that these aorists are not referring to action in past time but to actions that take place at many times and are not bound by any past occurrence only. An aspectual approach to tense does not have to explain away this apparent inconsistency with the so-called *normal* use of the aorist, because the aorist does not normally refer to any kind of action, be it in the past or present. The aorist is used to convey *perfective* aspect, viewing the action as a discrete event unrelated to time, unless the context (by deictic indicators) demand that it be in the past. Porter writes:

> Once the time and tense linkage is rightly severed, the gnomic use of the tenses becomes understandable. One of the ways in which language users refer to events is to see them not confined simply to one temporal sphere (past, present, future) but as occurring over time and perhaps as representative of the kind of thing which regularly occurs, especially in nature. In the NT, most of the examples of the gnomic aorist are used with reference to the processes of nature. The English present tense must suffice in translation, so long as one is not misled into thinking the Greek tense form is equivalent to it.[117]

The metatheme of James, evidenced in 3:13-18 by a choice between the polar opposites of human wisdom and divine wisdom, has again mapped itself to the sub-paragraph of 1:9-11. The contrasting attitude

---

[117] S.E. Porter, *Idioms of the Greek New Testament* (Sheffield: Sheffield Academic Press, 1994, 2nd ed.), 38.

and behavior of the lowly person and the rich person is clearly evident. Because the lowly man knows wisdom from above, he can boast about his being exalted. The rich person should boast in his being humbled, because that will eventually take place. Because he has made human wisdom his standard of living, he will eventually fade away like the wilted flower. Such is the inevitable end for those who follow human wisdom.

5. Paragraph 5 (James 1:12-15)

Μακάριος ἀνὴρ ὃς ὑπομένει πειρασμόν, ὅτι δόκιμος γενόμενος λήμψεται τὸν στέφανον τῆς ζωῆς ὃν ἐπηγγείλατο τοῖς ἀγαπῶσιν αὐτόν. Μηδεὶς πειραζόμενος λεγέτω ὅτι ἀπὸ θεοῦ πειράζομαι· ὁ γὰρ θεὸς ἀπείραστός ἐστιν κακῶν, πειράζει δὲ αὐτὸς οὐδένα. ἕκαστος δὲ πειράζεται ὑπὸ τῆς ἰδίας ἐπιθυμίας ἐξελκόμενος καὶ δελεαζόμενος· εἶτα ἡ ἐπιθυμία συλλαβοῦσα τίκτει ἁμαρτίαν, ἡ δὲ ἁμαρτία ἀποτελεσθεῖσα ἀποκύει θάνατον.	Blessed is the man who remains steadfast under a trial, for when he has stood the test he will receive the crown of life, which he has promised to those who love him. Let no one say when he is tempted, "I am being tempted by God," for God cannot be tempted with evil things, and he himself tempts no one. But each person is tempted when he is lured and enticed by his own desire. Then desire when it has conceived gives birth to sin, and sin when it is fully grown gives birth to death.

James 1:12-15 Clause Analysis
1:12

C	S		
Μακάριος	ἀνὴρ		
	S	**P**	**C**
	ὃς	ὑπομένει	πειρασμόν

cj	A		P	C
ὅτι	**C**	**P**	λήμψεται	τὸν στέφανον τῆς ζωῆς
	δόκιμος	γενόμενος		

C	P	C	
ὃν	ἐπηγγείλατο	**P**	**C**
		τοῖς ἀγαπῶσιν	αὐτόν

1:13

S	A	P
Μηδεὶς	**P** πειραζόμενος	λεγέτω

C	A	P
ὅτι	ἀπὸ θεου	πειράζομαι

cj	S	P	C
γὰρ	ὁ θεὸς	ἐστιν	ἀπείραστός κακῶν

P	cj	S	C
πειράζει	δε	αὐτὸς	οὐδένα

1:14

S	cj	P	A		
ἕκαστος	δε	πειράζεται	**A** ὑπὸ τῆς ἰδίας ἐπιθυμίας	**P** ἐξελκόμενος	
			cj και	**P** δελεαζόμενος	

1:15

A	S	A	P	C
εἶτα	ἡ ἐπιθυμία	**P** συλλαβοῦσα	τίκτει	ἁμαρτίαν

S	A	P	C
ἡ ἁμαρτία **cj** δε	**P** ἀποτελεσθεῖσα	ἀποκύει	θάνατον

James 1:12-15 is the fourth sub paragraph in the first main section of the letter: 1:2-15. The passage is introduced by the first of two uses of μακάριος (see also 1:25), and closes with the climactic reference to death at the end of 1:15. Then 1:16 opens with the second of the "address plus imperative" collocations which begins each successive new section. While able to thus stand alone, the passage also has clear affinities with the beginning of the section (1:2-4) with its abundance of references to "testing" (six examples of the πειρα—word group). Other verbal connections with 1:3, 4 are the ὑπομένει and δόκιμος in 1:12. Thus the passage also functions as the end of an *inclusio* that begins in 1:2 and ends in 1:15.

The passage consists of ten clauses, seven of which are primary and three of which are secondary. A large number of embedded clauses (eight) help to complete and also to support the main assertions. Seven of these embedded clauses include circumstantial participles, the most intense concentration of such participles in the letter. These participles convey colorfully the drama of the analogy in 1:13-15 ("lured," "enticed," "conceived," "fully grown").

While the textual tradition of James is stable when compared with other NT books, there are two variant readings in this section that deserve comment. First, Codex Alexandrinus and a few miniscule manuscripts in 1:12 prefer the more generic ἄνθρωπος to the much stronger attested ἀνήρ. Some scribes probably desired to stay away from the more limited masculine sense of ἀνήρ. Second, there is stronger Byzantine attestation for inserting either κύριος or ὁ θεος after the monolectic verb ἐπηγγείλατο because the subject of the verb has not been mentioned thus far in the sentence. One has to go back to 1:5 for the last clearly expressed reference to God, although a reader would not miss the intended subject of the verb here because of the following statement: "to those who love Him." There is, however, very early and strong support for omitting any expressed subject (p43, Aleph, A, B, Coptic). This external evidence combines with the internal principle of *lectio difficilior potior* (the more difficult reading is stronger) to justify the omission of an expressed subject. Recognizing that the alternative readings probably indicate a scribal desire to clarify some perceived obscurities clearly points to the readings in our text as the more original ones. The lack of an expressed subject for the verb may relate to the Jewish tendency to avoid unnecessary deliberate reference to the Deity. This would also be viewed as more of a "problem" by a later scribe removed from the original Jewish context of the language.

Commentators who see a use of the rhetorical device of *gradatio* in 1:2-4 also point to such a rhetorical device in the progression from temptation to desire to conception to birth and finally to death in 1:14, 15. However, the clear analogy of the process of temptation and sin to the process of human birth would be readily recognizable to a reader without any need to resort to such a rhetorical move. This is not meant to imply that writers could not employ such devices, but only to caution against too readily assuming their use when other explanations can be found for the language being used.

Our passage is introduced by a *macarism*, or beatitude, which is pronounced on the one who endures trial, followed by a causal clause with ὅτι, providing the explanation of the blessing: that the one who endures will be blessed by receiving the crown of life. (This is a genitive of apposition: the crown will be "life"). Sometimes it is argued that 1:12 is the proper ending for 1:9-11 and 1:13ff should be viewed separately from 1:12. However, this contradicts the use of the secondary clause following 1:12 explaining the blessing. It also overlooks the verbal linkage between the πειρασμόν in 1:12 and the concentration of four πειρα–words in 1:13, 14. Both man and God (1:12, 13) are joined as participants in this drama of testing by the personification of desire, sin, and death in the vivid birth/death analogy of 1:13-15.

The exact phraseology of the macarism (μακάριος ἀνήρ) is unique in the NT with the only additional use being a quotation from the OT in Rom. 4:8. It is from that rich tradition of the OT, particularly the wisdom literature, that this expression is drawn. The LXX renders "blessed is the man" by μακάριος ἀνήρ in Ps. 1:1; 31:2; 33:9; 39:5; 83:6; 111:1; Prov. 8:34; and 28:14. Post canonical wisdom literature also utilizes this expression in *Sir.* 14:1, 20; 26:1; and *Ps. Sol.* 6:1; 10:1. It appears that James is adapting for his own use the practice of blessing employed by his brother as it was later recorded in the Synoptic Gospels (Mat. 5:3-12). The larger issue about how James creatively adapts Jesus' oral teaching will be addressed later in the commentary on 2:5. What should be noted here is that the OT and Second Temple wisdom literature, Jesus' teaching, and James' language are all part of a continuing flow of traditional wisdom teaching.

A large number of words (ten) from Semantic Domain 88: "Moral/Ethical Qualities and Related Behavior" dominate the paragraph. There are six πειρα—cognates, κακῶν, δελεαζόμενος and ἁμαρτίαν (twice). This creates what has been called a "semantic chain" which begins with the topic statement, "Blessed is the man who remains steadfast under a trial (πειρασμόν)" and continues until the final comment clause, "and sin (ἁμαρτία) when it is fully grown brings forth death."[118] This chain actually reaches back to 1:2. The πειρα—word group does not appear elsewhere in the discourse, a fact that militates against chapter one serving as a table of contents for the remainder of the "volume." The closest verbal parallel to 1:2-15 would be the use of ὑπομένω and ὑπομονή in 5:11. It is more homiletically than exegetically helpful to see the "tests/trials" theme as providing the organizing principle of the discourse as being a series of such "tests."[119]

The key interpretative challenge in this paragraph is how best to translate and understand this word group as describing "tests" (from without) or "temptations" (from within). This is not an easy problem to solve and every commentator wrestles with the issue. Most English translations view the πειρα—word group in 1:2-4 and 1:12 as referring to the general idea of "tests" to prove character, but the references in 1:13-15 as referring to "temptations" to sin. The problem is exacerbated by the statement in 1:13, "he (God) himself tempts no one" and its apparent contradiction with the statements in the OT that He did just that (Gen. 21:1).[119] Space does not permit an adequate discussion of this *crux interpretum* and the reader is referred to the excellent discussion in Johnson for the various views.[121] The lexicons do reveal that the word group involves both concepts and the best view seems to be that James plays on that by moving from one shade of its meaning (testing for a good end) in 1:2-4, 12 to the other shade of meaning (enticement for a bad end) in 1:13-15. God is immediately behind the first idea, which has clearly been implied in 1:2-4. While He is ultimately behind all things as a providential ruler, He is, however, not the immediate seducer to sin. The one who is the tempter, Satan/the Devil, has also been described that way in the Chronicler's handling of David's *faux pas* (cf. I Chron. 21:1 with 2 Sam. 21:1), and he appears later in that role in James 4:7.

---

[118] "A semantic chain (or domain) refers to words grouped according to their shared, distinctive, and supplementary (i.e., contextually relevant) semantic features." Jeffrey T. Reed, *A Discourse Analysis of Philippians* (Sheffield: Sheffield Academic Press, 1997), 297. See pages 296-330.

[119] Many good topical outlines have been produced in this manner. They don't mention if one topic has more prominence than another. See, for example, *"MacArthur Study Bible"* (Nashville: Thomas Nelson, 2006), 1984.

[120] For the suggestion that the expression ἀπείραστός κακῶν should be rendered that God *"ought not to be tested by evil people,"* see Peter Davids, *The Epistle of James* (Grand Rapids: Eerdmans, 1982), 82-83. The subject of the section, however, is not what people do to God but what God does to people.

[121] Johnson, 192-94.

In summary, the passage clearly illustrates the bi-polar choices that James sets before his readers. The person who endures and passes his tests/trials will do so by following heavenly wisdom. The one who succumbs to temptation will do so because he has followed worldly wisdom. An inner force, so often discussed in Jewish literature as the "evil inclination" (*yetser hara*), is the real problem causer—not God! In this discussion, James is in step with the classical Jewish balance, expressed most clearly by the Pharisaic tradition, between both the providential rule of God and the personal responsibility of his creatures.[122]

6. Paragraph 6 (James 1:16-18)

Μὴ πλανᾶσθε, ἀδελφοί μου ἀγαπητοί. πᾶσα δόσις ἀγαθὴ καὶ πᾶν δώρημα τέλειον ἄνωθέν ἐστιν καταβαῖνον ἀπὸ τοῦ πατρὸς τῶν φώτων, παρ᾽ ᾧ οὐκ ἔνι παραλλαγὴ ἢ τροπῆς ἀποσκίασμα. βουληθεὶς ἀπεκύησεν ἡμᾶς λόγῳ ἀληθείας εἰς τὸ εἶναι ἡμᾶς ἀπαρχήν τινα τῶν αὐτοῦ κτισμάτων.	Do not be deceived, my beloved brothers. Every good act of giving and every complete gift is from above, coming down from the Father of the lights with whom there is no variation or shadow due to change. When he desired, he gave birth to us by the word of truth, that we should be a first portion of his created beings.

1:16

A	P	add
μὴ	πλανᾶσθε	ἀδελφοί μου ἀγαπητοί

1:17

---

[122] See the discussion of the rabbinic idea of *yetser hara* in Jacob Neusner, *Dictionary of Judaism in the Biblical Period* (Peabody: Hendrickson, 1996), 312, 668. Caution should be exercised, however, about committing the anachronistic fallacy by confidently using later rabbinic material to illustrate earlier NT ideas.

A	A	P	S
παρ᾽ ᾧ	οὐκ	ἔνι	παραλλαγὴ ἢ τροπῆς ἀποσκίασμα

1:18

A	P	C	A	A		
P βουληθεὶς	ἀπεκύησεν	ἡμᾶς	λόγῳ ἀληθείας	**P**	**S**	**C**
				εἰς τὸ εἶναι	ἡμᾶς	ἀπαρχήν τινα τῶν αὐτοῦ κτισμάτων

This paragraph opens with the collocation of a nominative of direct address, ἀδελφοί μου ἀγαπητοί, with a fronted and negated imperative, πλανᾶσθε. Other such negated collocations appear at 2:1; 3:1; 4:11; 5:9. By this repeated pattern (nominative of address plus imperative) James brings cohesion to his writing and moves the information forward in successive topic shifts. While this device introduces new paragraphs, the semantic connections between the sections should not be over-looked. Some have even viewed this imperative as linked more closely to what was just written than to what follows. Also, some have preferred to view this short paragraph as the closing section of 1:2-18. The nomi-native of address plus imperative also introduces enough of a semantic shift that its use here demands a discrete treatment. James does not want his readers to be led astray from the belief that God gives good gifts.

The paragraph consists of three primary clauses and one secondary clause. Two embedded clauses, anchored by a participle (καταβαῖνον in 1:17) and a purpose infinitive (εἰς τὸ εἶναι in 1:18), serve as adjuncts to the main clause in 1:18. One major difference with the preceding paragraphs is that there are no paragraph level conjunctions joining the clauses. The clauses proceed directly and crisply. There is only one significant variant reading. In 1:17 the rare form ἔνι, a present form of the verb ἔνεστι, is replaced by the more common form εστιν in uncials Aleph and P. This is another clear example of later scribal "correction" to a more acceptable form from that later time. As is usually the case, the canon of *lectio difficilior potior* advises the retention of the *more difficult* reading ἔνι. This shorter form appears elsewhere in the NT only in 1 Cor. 6:5; Gal. 3:28 and Col. 3:11, interestingly only in a negative expression as it does here.

The participants in this paragraph are the brothers and God. Two additional terms are used for the first time in the letter to qualify the participants further. 1) The brothers are *beloved* (ἀγαπητοί), an affectionate term that he also adds to the openings of paragraphs in 1:19 and 2:5. Most commentators do not speculate on why James chooses this adjective to address the brothers at these particular points. I suggest, however, that by using terms for being deceived (πλανᾶσθε in 1:19; παραλογιζόμενοι in 1:22), James is concerned that his readers not be deceived into wrong thinking about God (1:17) and His word (1:22) and what He says about the poor (2:5). The common concern in each of the three paragraphs leads James to revert to the more affectionate expression "beloved brothers." The specific command μὴ πλανᾶσθε appears in other contexts to call attention to a decisive statement about God in epigrammatic form (1 Cor 6:9; Gal. 6:7; Ign. *Eph.* 5:2; *Smyrn.* 6:1). 2) God is called *father* in 1:17, more specifically the *father of the lights* (πατρὸς τῶν φώτων). This reference to God being the creator of the heavenly luminaries that give us light leads perfectly into his point that all gifts, natural and supernatural, come from a loving father. He further describes this loving father by the eloquent expression "with whom there is no variation or shadow due to change" (1:17). The abrupt introduction of a divine attribute at this point should be understood in light of James' desire to guide his readers toward being whole and complete (1:4). The God who has gifted "us" to become his spiritual creation by the word of truth is also undivided and complete. It is not necessary to see in this statement an abstract theological description. As elsewhere the concern of James is more ethical than metaphysical. Furthermore, there is no need to discern in the clause παρ' ᾧ οὐκ ἔνι παραλλαγὴ ἢ τροπῆς ἀποσκίασμα some allusion to Stoic philosophy. The expression is entirely consistent with both Biblical and Hellenistic Jewish thinking expressed in Philo.[123]

There are two often overlooked linguistic issues in this paragraph. One has to do with the sometimes challenging problem of synonyms (δόσις and δώρημα in 1:17) and the unique use of a passive participle (βουληθεὶς in 1:18). Did James intend to make a distinction between the two terms δόσις and δώρημα? Both terms can simply mean "gift." There have been some wise cautions issued about making too fine of a distinction between synonyms, with Trench's work often being the focus of concern.[124] I believe that here, however, we are justified in seeing

---

[123] *Wisdom* 7:17 ff.; *Deus imm.* 22; *Leg. All.* 2:33.

[124] D.A. Carson, *Exegetical Fallacies*, 2nd ed. (Grand Rapids: Baker Books, 1996), 47-53.

a careful difference in nuance between these words. Both of these words are rare in the NT, with δόσις only appearing elsewhere in Romans 5:16. It is used in the LXX only in *Sirach* 34:18, and only twice in the Apostolic Fathers (*Hermas*). The corresponding δώρημα only appears in Phil. 4:15. It is used in the LXX 21 times, in Philo 4 times, and again in *Hermas* once. The more common word δῶρον appears 19 times in the NT and 170 times in the LXX. It is the word that is most often used for human gifts to God. The two words in James 1:17 are describing divine gifts. A general observation is that nouns ending in –σις express the action of the verbal root while nouns ending in –μα stress the result of the verbal root. With this observation, I believe that it is justified to conclude that James wants us to know that every act of God's giving is "good" (ἀγαθὴ) and every result of his giving is "complete" (τέλειον).[125] An author's use of the resources in the lexico-grammar of a language implies a choice. While we need to be careful about imagining distinctions based on a too facile approach to the lexis, we should not ignore such choices when the evidence demands that we do so. The appropriateness of these nuanced definitions in the context should not be missed. Just as the good and complete God gives us only good and complete gifts, so He desires his new creations to be good and complete persons!

The rare use of the aorist *passive* participle βουληθείς initiating 1:18 merits reflection. The participle form of βούλομαι appears 13 times in the NT, but everywhere else it is in the present form βουλόμενος. *LSJM* mentions it as used only twice in secular Greek literature.[126] This specific form is not in the LXX, but Philo uses it 20 times of the Divine will, most often in a temporal sense. Typical of the uses in Philo is *On the Virtues*, 188: "For when God determined (βουληθείς) to establish this in us out of his own exceeding mercy and love for the human race, he did not find any temple on earth more beautiful or more suited for its abode than reason." Therefore, the "instrumental" use of the participle here by most English versions should be questioned. Typical is the KJV and ESV's "Of his own will … ," or the CSB's "By his own choice . . ." In light of the only other use of βουληθείς in Judaeo-Christian literature, a temporal rather than instrumental force should be preferred

---

[125] J.H. Thayer, *A Greek-English Lexicon of the New Testament* (New York: Harper and Brothers, 1898), 157, 161, 618.
[126] *LSJM*, 325.

while the instrumental dative conveys that his word was the means by which he gave birth to us: "*When he decided, he gave birth to us by the word of truth* (λόγῳ ἀληθείας)."

This semantically rich paragraph serves as an appropriate bridge between 1:2-15 which describes God's gracious giving of wisdom for the trials of those who ask him for it and 1:19-27 which stresses the further role of the word of God in the believer's experience. The reader is again challenged to choose between the polar opposites of a God who is either good and gracious or evil and indifferent to His creatures. The way of wisdom is to acknowledge God's goodness.

7. Paragraphs 7, 8, 9 (James 1:19-27)

Ἴστε, ἀδελφοί μου ἀγαπητοί/ἐστω δὲ πᾶς ἄνθρωπος ταχὺς εἰς τὸ ἀκοῦσαι, βραδὺς εἰς τὸ λαλῆσαι, βραδὺς εἰς ὀργήν· ὀργὴ γὰρ ἀνδρὸς δικαιοσύνην θεοῦ οὐκ ἐργάζεται. διὸ ἀποθέμενοι πᾶσαν ῥυπαρίαν καὶ περισσείαν κακίας ἐν πραΰτητι, δέξασθε τὸν ἔμφυτον λόγον τὸν δυνάμενον σῶσαι τὰς ψυχὰς ὑμῶν. Γίνεσθε δὲ ποιηταὶ λόγου καὶ μὴ μόνον ἀκροαταὶ παραλογιζόμενοι ἑαυτούς. ὅτι εἴ τις ἀκροατὴς λόγου ἐστὶν καὶ οὐ ποιητής, οὗτος ἔοικεν ἀνδρὶ κατανοοῦντι τὸ πρόσωπον τῆς γενέσεως αὐτοῦ ἐν ἐσόπτρῳ· κατενόησεν γὰρ ἑαυτὸν καὶ ἀπελήλυθεν καὶ εὐθέως ἐπελάθετο ὁποῖος ἦν. ὁ δὲ παρακύψας εἰς νόμον τέλειον τὸν τῆς ἐλευθερίας καὶ παραμείνας, οὐκ ἀκροατὴς ἐπιλησμονῆς γενόμενος ἀλλὰ ποιητὴς ἔργου, οὗτος μακάριος ἐν τῇ ποιήσει αὐτοῦ ἔσται. Εἴ τις δοκεῖ θρησκὸς εἶναι μὴ χαλι— ναγωγῶν γλῶσσαν αὐτοῦ ἀλλὰ ἀπατῶν καρδίαν αὐτοῦ, τούτου μάταιος ἡ θρησκεία. θρησκεία καθαρὰ καὶ ἀμίαντος παρὰ τῷ θεῷ καὶ πατρὶ αὕτη ἐστίν, ἐπισκέπτεσθαι ὀρφανοὺς καὶ χήρας ἐν τῇ θλίψει αὐτῶν, ἄσπι— λον ἑαυτὸν τηρεῖν ἀπὸ τοῦ κόσμου.	Know this, my beloved brothers: every person must be quick to hear, slow to speak, slow to anger; for the anger of man does not produce the righteousness God requires. Therefore put away all filthiness and rampant wickedness and receive with meekness the implanted word, which is able to save your souls. But become doers of the word, and not hearers only, deceiving yourselves. For if anyone is a hearer of the word and not a doer, he is like a man who looks intently at his natural face in a mirror. For he looks at himself and goes away and at once forgets what he was like. But the one who looks carefully into the perfect law of liberty, and perseveres in it, being not a forgetful hearer but one who does the work, this one will be blessed in his doing. If anyone thinks he is religious while not bridling his tongue but deceiving his heart, this person's religion is worthless. A religion pure and undefiled before God the Father is this: to visit orphans and widows in their affliction, to keep oneself unstained from the world.

1:19

P	add
Ἴστε	ἀδελφοί μου ἀγαπητοί·

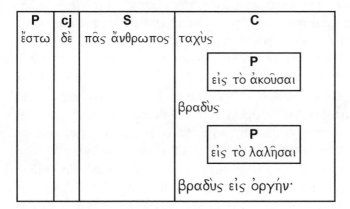

P	cj	S	C
ἔστω	δὲ	πᾶς ἄνθρωπος	ταχὺς

with nested:

			C
ἔστω	δὲ	πᾶς ἄνθρωπος	ταχὺς
			P: εἰς τὸ ἀκοῦσαι
			βραδὺς
			P: εἰς τὸ λαλῆσαι
			βραδὺς εἰς ὀργήν·

1:20

S	C	A	P
ὀργὴ ἀνδρὸς [γὰρ]	δικαιοσύνην θεου	οὐκ	ἐργάζεται.

1:21

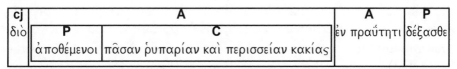

cj	A		A	P
διὸ	**P**: ἀποθέμενοι	**C**: πᾶσαν ῥυπαρίαν καὶ περισσείαν κακίας	ἐν πραΰτητι	δέξασθε

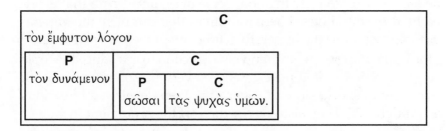

C		
τὸν ἔμφυτον λόγον		
P: τὸν δυνάμενον	**C**	
	P: σῶσαι	**C**: τὰς ψυχὰς ὑμῶν.

James 1:19-27 is introduced, as is the custom throughout, by the collocation of the nominative plural of address (ἀδελφοὶ) with an imperative

(ἴστε). Following the suggestion of UBS4, we further discern three sub paragraphs (1:19-21; 22-25; 26-27). The διὸ clause in 1:21 concludes the first section. The reiterated macarism pronouncement (οὗτος μακάριος . . .) concludes the second section. The third section (1:26, 27) consists of three illustrations of what it means to be a "doer of the word" in 1:22-25.

The first sub-paragraph consists of five clauses, four primary and two secondary participial clauses along with three embedded infinitive clauses. There is one significant textual variant and one punctuation problem. The textual issue involves a number of variants centering on whether 1:19 begins with ἴστε or ὥστε. The critical text reading (ἴστε) not only has the firm external support of the Alexandrian family but the perfect imperative form is consistent with the collocation of imperative and address nominatives at the beginning of the other paragraphs. The consequential ὥστε variant reading, supported by the Byzantine manuscripts, looks very much like a later scribal attempt to avoid the rare ἴστε. This variant, however, necessitates the dropping of the δὲ in the second clause to smooth out the syntax, which the later Byzantine manuscripts also do.

In its form ἴστε can be either Perfect Imperative or Indicative. Since James uses the imperative more than any other NT writer (see above) and his appeals to his readers' knowledge are usually in the form of a rhetorical question (4:4), the use of the imperative is favored. Since this is the only time that a perfect imperative opens a new paragraph, and since choice implies meaning, we should ask if there may be a reason for its use. The discourse role of the perfect conveys greater prominence than the other tense forms.[127] It is important to notice, however, that the function of the imperative ἴστε is not the same as the imperatives that introduce the other paragraphs. The word functions here as a "meta-comment" to call attention to the imperative ἔστω that is followed by three infinitives. These infinitives that complete the imperative actually comprise the imperatival function of the paragraph rather than the initial imperative ἴστε, and also function to introduce the topic of the paragraph. These three elements, "every person must be quick to hear, slow to speak, slow to anger," are then developed in various ways through 1:27. They also convey three of the prominent themes of

---

[127] Porter uses the term *frontground to* describe the discourse role of the perfect tense form compared to the *foreground* role of the present/imperfect and the *background* role of the aorist. *Idioms*, 302-03.

the entire discourse: 1) Being swift to hear and do; 2) Being slow to speak; and 3) Being slow to anger. Some commentators see 1:21 as embodying a three point outline of chapters 2-4. While there is some merit to this approach, especially in light of the perfect imperative, we should not fail to see that these three themes are also expounded right in this paragraph. The topic "quick to hear" is commented on in 1:22-25. The topic "slow to speak" is commented on in 1:27. The topic "slow to anger" is commented on in 1:20, 21.

The punctuation problem in 1:21 is whether to place a comma before or after the ἐν πραΰτητι. The critical text places it after, thus making the phrase modify the participle ἀποθέμενοι by showing the manner in which we are to put off anger. No English version that I have been able to find, however, translates ἐν πραΰτητι with the previous clause. Even the footnote in UBS4 acknowledges that among other texts and versions only a marginal reading in the Revised English Bible places the comma after the phrase. Perhaps the editors were uncomfortable with the fronting of a prepositional phrase before the imperative δέξασθε. James does this again, however, in 2:1 (ἐν προσωπολημψίαις ἔχετε). Discourse considerations recognize that the fronting of the phrase also lends prominence to the attitude in which the brothers are to receive the word—with humility, not with anger.

Semantically, it is important to note that the implanted λόγον in 1:21 is the second link in a semantic chain (domain 67) that extends from the λόγῳ ἀληθείας in 1:18 to the third link, ποιηταὶ λόγου, in 1:22 and then to the final νόμον τέλειον in 1:25. Receiving, responding to, and obeying the word is the semantic theme that controls the entire paragraph. The imperative commands in the passage highlight the focus on hearing and receiving the word.

Anger, filthiness and wickedness impede the right reception of the word and are the attitudes that must be "put off." The attendant circumstance participle ἀποθέμενοι embedded in the fourth clause assumes the mood of the following imperative δέξασθε and parallels the Pauline dynamic of "putting off" and "putting on" in Ephesians 4:17 ff. When rightly received, the word that has been implanted by the gracious God in the soul of the believer is able to save the soul. This expression does not refer to the initial act of salvation, as is often assumed, but to the ongoing and continuous (imperfective aspect of δυνάμενον) work of restoring and rescuing the inner life of believers. This is obvious when one recognizes that James is addressing "brothers" (1:19) who have already been "birthed" through the supernatural word (1:18).

The relationship of the ideational "message" in this section to the overall meta-theme of James is obvious. Those who receive the word with a gentle attitude are those who follow the wisdom from above (see 3:13, 17). Those whose wrath impedes God's word in their "souls" follow the wisdom from below (see 3:14-16). James knows no middle way.

1:22

P	cj	C
γίνεσθε	δὲ	ποιηταὶ λόγου

cj	A	A	C	A		
καὶ	μὴ	μόνον	ἀκροαταὶ		P	C
					παραλογιζόμενοι	ἑαυτούς

1:23

cj	cj	S	C	P
ὅτι	εἴ	τις	ἀκροατὴς λόγου	ἐστὶν

cj	A	C
καὶ	οὐ	ποιητής

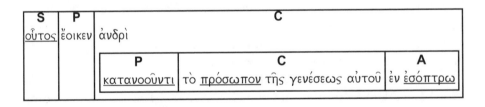

S	P	C		
οὗτος	ἔοικεν	ἀνδρὶ		
		P	C	A
		κατανοοῦντι	τὸ πρόσωπον τῆς γενέσεως αὐτοῦ	ἐν ἐσόπτρῳ

1:24

P	cj	C
κατενόησεν	γὰρ	ἑαυτὸν

cj	P
καὶ	ἀπελήλυθεν

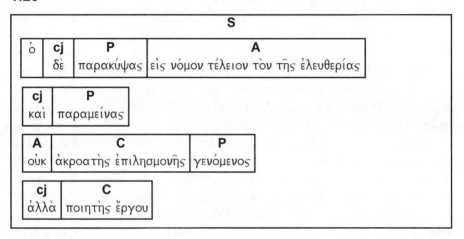

cj	A	P	C	
καὶ	εὐθέως	ἐπελάθετο	**C**	**P**
			ὁποῖος	ἦν

1:25

S			
ὁ	**cj** / δὲ	**P** / παρακύψας	**A** / εἰς νόμον τέλειον τὸν τῆς ἐλευθερίας

cj	P
καὶ	παραμείνας

A	C	P
οὐκ	ἀκροατὴς ἐπιλησμονῆς	γενόμενος

cj	C
ἀλλὰ	ποιητὴς ἔργου

S	C	A	P
οὗτος	μακάριος	ἐν τῇ ποιήσει αὐτοῦ	ἔσται

The post-positive δέ links with the preceding verses by developing the idea that the one who truly receives the word which saves him (1:20, 21) is the one who "becomes" a doer of the word, not just a "hearer" of the word. The primary clauses (1:22, 25) serve as an inclusio with the secondary clauses embodying a parable from life about a person who forgets what he looks like in the mirror (1:23, 24). The parable illustrates the meaning of "deceiving yourselves" (1:22b) and contrasts with the hearer/doer who will be ultimately blessed because of his obedience (1:25).

The comparison between the two different types of hearers is brought into sharp relief by the effective use of the demonstrative pronoun οὗτος in 1:23 and 1:25. In 1:23 the conditional clause proposes a forgetful hearer and adds: "this one" is like a person who forgets what he looks like in the mirror. On the contrary, the δέ of 1:25 describes a hearer who obeys and adds: "this one" will be blessed in his doing. The secondary conditional clause contrasts with the primary clause which affirms the beneficial result of obeying what he commanded in 1:22: become a doer and not just a hearer.

Furthermore, attention to the aspectual functions of the verbs vividly highlights the forgetful actions of the hypothetical mirror-gazer in 1:24. He looks (κατενόησεν) at himself, he departs (ἀπελήλυθεν), and he at once forgets (ἐπελάθετο) what he looked like. Many commentators simply ignore the change in tense from the aorist to the perfect and back to the aorist. Moo refers to the "gnomic aorist" and posits some sort of similar function for the perfect, while Davids suggests the idea of different forms for stylistic variety.[128] *BDF* and Porter prefer the category "Omnitemporal" for these aorists which grammaticalize perfective aspect. The perfective aspect of the aorist deals with observed processes (see 1:11) and conceives the situation as complete.[129] Porter does not clarify the specific role of the perfect tense in this verse. He does define the aspectual function of the perfect tense as "stative."[130] In a later work he further describes the stative aspect of the perfect tense form as describing a "state of affairs."[131] This is the best approach to James' use of the perfect tense here, particularly when one sees the issue through a discourse model which views the perfect as "frontgrounding" the action in the discourse.[132] In other words, what James wants the reader to focus on is the forgetful looker's state of having departed from looking in the mirror. It is interesting that a nineteenth century commentator, Henry Alford, called attention to this stative function of the perfect tense in the following way.

> We might have had all aorists, but seeing that the *departing* begins a permanent **state of absence** from the mirror, that is chosen to be designated by a perfect. The forgetting is also a permanent state, but the Apostle rather chooses in this case to bring out the act itself, as one *immediately* (εὐθέως) and suddenly taking place.[133]

James' fondness for using the perfect tense in this stative aspectual role while juxtaposed with an aorist can also be seen in 2:10, "For whoever keeps (aorist τηρήσῃ) the whole law, yet stumbles (aorist πταίσῃ) in one point, he has become (perfect γέγονεν) guilty of all."

---

[128] Douglas Moo, *The Letter of James* (Grand Rapids: Eerdmans, 2000), 125. Davids, 98.

[129] Porter, *Verbal Aspect in the Greek of the New Testament* (New York: Peter Lang, 1982), 318-19.

[130] Porter, *Verbal Aspect*, 245-290.

[131] Porter, *Idioms*, 40.

[132] See Porter's treatment of the perfect in 1:21 and footnote 31.

[133] Henry Alford, *The Greek New Testament*, vol. 4 (Chicago: Moody Press, 1958), 288.

The semantic chain introduced in 1:21 with the word λόγος (Domain 33) continues to permeate this paragraph with the lexemes λόγος (1:22) and νόμος (1:25). Both here and throughout the discourse (see e.g., 2:8: the "royal law" and the "scripture"), these individual words are not intended to convey distinct functions of the Divine "word/law/scripture." Their semantic identity involves the same revelation from the one God, whether that word was stated through the writings of the law and the prophets or through the wisdom teaching of the Messiah who faithfully communicated the Divine will (1:1; 2:1). To bifurcate the "word" into various discrete components would be foreign to James. He saw them all as part of one piece: the will of the one God expressed through His messengers. We will give further attention to how the teaching of Jesus forms part of that wisdom continuum of word/law in our treatment of 2:5, 6.

It is important to clearly see what James is contrasting in his parable and application. He is not contrasting two types of "looking," namely a casual glance in the mirror with a studied peering into the word. Fine distinctions between the meanings of the two verbs, with the κατανοέω of 1:23, 24 supposedly being the more casual glance and the participle form of παρακύπτω being the more intent gaze, miss the point of the comparison. Uses elsewhere of the first verb do not indicate a less serious "glance" (Acts 11:16; 27:39; Rom. 4:19; and esp. Heb. 3:1; 10:24). The contrast is not between how the two look at their respective object, but between the one forgetting what he saw and the second persevering (παραμείνας) in his look and not forgetting what he saw. When one gives careful attention to what the word teaches by not forgetting what it teaches, this person will be blessed. It is the blessed one who will obey the word and not forget what he has heard by not allowing the word to affect his "doing."

James' call to follow wisdom from above and reject wisdom from below is again clearly stamped on this section of his discourse. His call to wholeness implies a rejection of hearing only and a choice to follow through on obedience to the word.

1:26

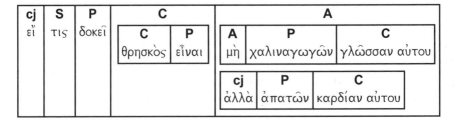

1:27

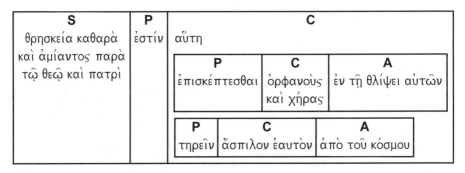

In keeping with the topic/comment linguistic analysis of discourse mentioned earlier, this sub-paragraph (1:26, 27) is the concluding *comment* about the *topic* introduced at the beginning of this second main paragraph in James 1:19a: "every person must be quick to hear, slow to speak, slow to anger." James comments on being "slow to anger" in 1:19-21; he comments on being "quick to hear" in 1:22-25; and he comments (among other matters) on being "slow to speak" in 1:26, 27. The short passage also serves to introduce themes which are further elaborated in the next three chapters. In chapter 2, James further develops how we must be "quick to hear" what God says about the poor in 2:1-5 and to put what we have heard to work in 2:12-26. In chapter 3:1-12, James vividly illustrates that we should be "slow to speak" by the many analogies of the dangers of the tongue. In 3:13-4:10, James warns that the failure to be "slow to wrath" exemplifies devilish wisdom and is the cause of conflicts among his readers. In this strategic manner, therefore, 1:26, 27 functions anaphorically as it recalls 1:19 and then cataphorically as it anticipates chapters 2-4.

There are two primary clauses in 1:26, 27. The first ("this person's religion is worthless") functions as the apodosis of a first class conditional clause initiating 1:26 ("If anyone thinks he is religious. . ."). The second primary clause in 1:27 functions to define what is the "religion that is pure and undefiled." This is done by two embedded epexegetical infinitive clauses forming the two-fold complement of the clause: "to visit (ἐπισκέπτεσθαι) orphans and widows in their affliction; to keep (τηρεῖν) oneself unstained from the world." The OpenText analysis above visually displays this development of the text.

There are three special linguistic features in these two verses. The first is the continued use of the demonstrative pronoun, which appears twice in 1:23 and 25, the first time functioning anaphorically and the second time functioning cataphorically. If the supposed religious person does not bridle his tongue and thus deceives his own heart, "the religion of this (τούτου) person is worthless" (vs. 26). On the contrary, the religion that is pure and undefiled is characterized by "this (αὕτη): to visit orphans and widows in their affliction; to keep oneself unstained from the world" (vs. 27). The second feature is the notable asyndetic character of these clauses. Most translations recognize this and insert the conjunction "and" before the complement in the first clause and between the parallel infinitive clauses in the second clause. The third feature, on the other hand, is the use of the conjunction καὶ in the second clause in vs. 27: "A religion pure *and* undefiled before God *and* the Father is this. . . ." It is pointless to see a distinction in meaning between the first two adjectives. Furthermore, the article preceding God and father indicates the identity of the one described by these two substantives. Thus it appears that James employs hendiadys in both expressions. The sense would be as follows. "A completely pure religion before our Divine Father is as follows."

Most commentators do not take notice of these peculiar modes of expression, probably because it is difficult to discern any clear reason for them. I suggest that an explanation lies in the special transitional character of 1:26, 27. For example, note the ideas repeated from the previous paragraph. The ἀπατῶν καρδίαν αὐτου echoes the παραλογιζόμενοι ἑαυτούς of 1:22, and these verses provide prime examples of what 1:22 exhorted as being "doers" and not just "hearers" of the word. These verses also look ahead with the first mention in Greek literature of the word χαλιναγωγῶν which is repeated later in 3:2. The warning about the world also anticipates its mention again in 4:4. These summary transitional themes combine with the special linguistic features to indicate 1:26, 27 as the peak of chapter one which stands out from the rest of the chapter by these unique characteristics.

The language of 1:26, 27 also features a high degree of cultic words. For example, θρησκὸς and θρησκεία most probably exemplify "religion" in its outward features. Furthermore, καθαρὰ, ἀμίαντος, τηρεῖν and ἄσπιλον echo Jewish cultic purity laws.[134] But consistent elsewhere with his wisdom approach to the Torah, James subverts these cultic associations by applying the terms not to ceremonial religious observances but to ethical praxis. The terms are exemplified in caring for the societal marginalized and in avoiding the world's standards. James echoes not only the approach of the Hebrew prophets to these issues, he also reflects his brother's vital concerns, with the poor (here represented by "orphans and widows") being the ones in 2:5 who are rich in faith and heirs of the kingdom.

Since this passage expresses the peak concerns of James, we should not be surprised that his overall message of following heavenly, not earthly wisdom is quite clear. Wisdom governs the tongue (James 3:1-17), so it also does here. The wisdom of the "world" (James 3:13; 4:4) is to be rejected because this will keep one from being spoiled by its values. James' emphasis on wholeness can also be seen in his description of the right type of religion. It is a religion that is pure, not mixed with any foreign elements.

---

[134] The entries in *BDAG* for these lexemes cite numerous examples of their cultic associations in both the LXX and in non-Christian Greek literature.

Chapter 2

ANALYSIS OF JAMES TWO

M ost commentators acknowledge that James 2:1-13 forms a separate section with self-contained cohesive ties and coherence of thought. The inconsistent practice of "partiality" in 2:1 is the topic and the rest of the section is the comment on that topic. This is evidenced not only by the repetition of the word in 2:9, but also by the vivid parable in 2:2-4 and the adaptation of a Jesus-saying in 2:5,6 buttressed by the application of a "royal law" in 2:8-13. James here elaborates his earlier points about the "lowly" brother in 1:9 and the orphans and widows in 1:27. Three sub-paragraphs consist of 2:1-4, 2:5-7, and 2:8-13. Each of these is developed around a statement first from the law (2:1); then from Jesus (2:5); and then from both the law and Jesus (2:8). The translation and analysis of 2:1-13 will proceed around these three sections.

10. Paragraph 10 (James 2:1-4)

Ἀδελφοί μου, μὴ ἐν προσωπολημψίαις ἔχετε τὴν πίστιν τοῦ κυρίου ἡμῶν Ἰησοῦ Χριστοῦ τῆς δόξης. ἐὰν γὰρ εἰσέλθῃ εἰς συναγωγὴν ὑμῶν ἀνὴρ χρυσοδακτύλιος ἐν ἐσθῆτι λαμπρᾷ, εἰσέλθῃ δὲ καὶ πτωχὸς ἐν ῥυπαρᾷ ἐσθῆτι, ἐπιβλέψητε δὲ ἐπὶ τὸν φοροῦντα τὴν ἐσθῆτα τὴν λαμπρὰν καὶ εἴπητε· σὺ κάθου ὧδε καλῶς, καὶ τῷ πτωχῷ εἴπητε· σὺ στῆθι ἐκεῖ ἢ κάθου ὑπὸ τὸ ὑποπόδιόν μου, οὐ διεκρίθητε ἐν ἑαυτοῖς καὶ ἐγένεσθε κριταὶ διαλογισμῶν πονηρῶν;	My brothers do not hold to the faith of our Lord Jesus Christ, the Lord of glory, while committing acts of partiality. For if a man wearing a gold ring and fine clothing comes into your assembly, and a poor man in shabby clothing also comes in, and if you pay attention to the one who wears the fine clothing and say, "You sit here in a good place," and you say to the poor man, "You stand over there," or, "Sit down at my feet," have you not made distinctions among yourselves and become judges with evil thoughts?

Clause Analysis of 2:1-4

2:1

add	A	A	P	C
Ἀδελφοί μου	μὴ	ἐν προσωπολημψίαις	ἔχετε	τὴν πίστιν τοῦ κυρίου ἡμῶν Ἰησοῦ Χριστοῦ τῆς δόξης

2:2

cj	cj	P	A	S
ἐὰν	γὰρ	εἰσέλθῃ	εἰς συναγωγὴν ὑμῶν	ἀνὴρ χρυσοδακτύλιος ἐν ἐσθῆτι λαμπρᾷ

P	cj	cj	S
εἰσέλθῃ	δὲ	και	πτωχὸς ἐν ῥυπαρᾷ ἐσθῆτι

2:3

P	cj	A	
ἐπιβλέψητε	δὲ	**P**	**C**
		ἐπὶ τὸν φοροῦντα	τὴν ἐσθῆτα τὴν λαμπρὰν

cj	P
και	εἴπητε

S	P	A	A
σὺ	κάθου	ὧδε	καλῶς

cj	C	P
καὶ	τῷ πτωχῷ	εἴπητε

S	P	A
συ	στῆθι	ἐκεῖ

cj	P	A
ἢ	κάθου	ὑπὸ τὸ ὑποπόδιόν μου

2:4

A	P	A
οὐ	διεκρίθητε	ἐν ἑαυτοῖς

cj	P	C
καὶ	ἐγένεσθε	κριταὶ διαλογισμῶν πονηρῶν;

This paragraph opens and closes with primary clauses (2:1, 4). The first clause begins with the nominative of address, "my brothers," followed by the negated imperative "do not hold." This is one of the cohesive devices used by James to introduce a new paragraph. When this device introduces a new topic, as is the case here, it serves as one of the twelve (12) main divisions of the letter (1:2 e.g.).[135] The second primary clause serves as the apodosis of a long conditional clause (2:2-4) that contains five secondary clauses, each containing a subjunctive verb (see the underlined above) introduced by the one ἐὰν beginning 2:2. This approach is typical of James, who often opens a paragraph with a primary clause of mainline material (usually a command) and then sets forth a number of clauses that serve as supporting material for the initial command (1:19) or a rhetorical question which further amplifies his topic (3:13; 4:1). We have written previously of the topic/comment sequence at the paragraph level and this paragraph is a clear example of that approach.

The substantive "partiality" in 2:1 (προσωπολημψίαις) appears in this specific form for the first time in Greek literature (like δίψυχος in 1:8).[136] This semantic theme, however, is often mentioned in the OT (see Lev. 19:15 and Deut. 1:15). James also quotes Lev. 19:18 in 2:8 and that chapter plays a key role throughout the book.[137] The preposition ἐν

---

[135] This verse along with 5:19 are the only occasions where ἀδελφοί μου is prominently located by fronting the clause in which it is found. This is a fact generally overlooked by commentators. These two instances together form an *inclusio* initiating the first and last paragraphs of the main body of the letter.

[136] Paul uses the noun in Rom. 2:11; Eph. 6:9; and Col. 3:25, where it refers to Divine impartiality. It is here assumed that the letter of James was written prior to these Pauline writings.

[137] L.T. Johnson, "The Use of Leviticus 19 in the Letter of James," in *Brother of Jesus Friend of God* (Grand Rapids: Eerdmans, 2004), 123-35.

probably has a temporal force here. It is often overlooked that the word is plural in form; thus it probably refers to "acts of partiality." Hence a permissible translation is: "while committing acts of partiality." James' readers are commanded not to hold to faith in Jesus while at the same time practicing acts of favoritism or social discrimination. This verse contains the second reference to Jesus by name, the first being in the salutation (1:1). The genitival "glory" (τῆς δόξης) has been taken adjectivally by a number of versions and commentators—"our glorious Lord Jesus Christ."[138] If the latter words in the genitive chain all modify Lord, however, we have a translation as follows: "our Lord Jesus Christ, the Lord of glory."[139]

In regards to the expression πίστις Χριστου, the question is whether the genitive functions as an object in relation to the head noun ("faith in Christ") or as a subject ("Christ's faithfulness").[140] Many commentators simply assume an objective genitive here and do not even comment on the issue. Later in the chapter James uses the noun to refer to an individual's faith, although the specific object of that faith is not mentioned in those verses (2:14, 17, 18, 20, 22, 24, 26). The presence of the article before the substantive (τὴν πίστιν) has led James Dunn, normally a defender of the "objective" view, to argue that the presence of the article is evidence of the subjective genitive.[141] Thus, the translation of the arthrous noun with the predicator ἔχετε would be: "My brothers do not *hold to the faith of our Lord Jesus Christ, the Lord of glory,* while showing acts of partiality." It is *the* faith of Jesus that is later manifested in the Jesus *logion* in 2:5 and in the "royal law" of 2:8. It is *the faith that comes from Jesus* that would never show partiality. Thus the following context also argues for a subjective genitive in 2:1. It is not necessary to resort to the translation, "faithfulness," a rare meaning

---

[138] NASB, NIV, NLT, NET, NRSV. Dibelius, 128; Davids, 106, e.g.

[139] ESV, KJV, RSV. See also Moo, 101. The attempt to make τῆς δόξης a synonym for Jesus ("our glory") suffers from unduly rearranging the word order and from the fact that δόξα is never used as a title for Deity in the OT, only as a modifier. In the NT "glory" is often used as a shorthand for Jesus' resurrection (Lk. 24:26; Acts 22:11; Heb. 2:7; 1 Peter 1:11). This should be carefully noted when considering James' apparent lack of references to the saving acts of Jesus.

[140] The bibliography of works related to this discussion is quite large. For an updated bibliography and an excellent presentation of arguments for both translations see Appendix One and Two by James D.G. Dunn and Richard B. Hays in Richard B. Hays, *The Faith of Jesus Christ*, 2nd ed. (Grand Rapids: Eerdmans, 2002), 249-97.

[141] Dunn, 252-53. See also the presence of the article in Rev. 2:13 and 14:12, as well as Rom. 3:3.

of that word in any case. Johnson well points the way forward. "The use of Jesus' sayings throughout the composition suggests a meaning like 'the faith of Jesus in God as reflected in his teaching,' or perhaps 'the faith that is from Jesus Christ,' in the sense 'declared by Jesus'."[142]

As was mentioned, 2:2, 3 is an elaborate protasis of a conditional clause, of which 2:4 is the apodosis. The complexity of the five subjunctives (see the underlined verbals in the clause analysis above) is increased by two embedded clause-quotations in 1:3 expressing the commands delivered to the rich person and to the poor person about their seating arrangements. It is best to read all the secondary clauses as part of one protasis rather than to break them up into separate sentences. Grammarians refer to this type of protasis as a Third Class Conditional Clause. Porter states: "A third class conditional with ἐὰν and the subjunctive, in distinction to a first class conditional, is more tentative and simply projects some action or event for hypothetical consideration."[143] While this point cannot be the determining factor, it does support the view that James is raising a hypothetical situation and that he is not necessarily describing a scene that has taken place in their assemblies. It is interesting in this regard to notice how in the immediately preceding paragraph (1:26, 27), he used a first class conditional clause protasis (εἴ τις δοκεῖ θρησκὸς εἶναι . . .). This condition assumes the reality of the protasis for the sake of the argument, which fits the rhetorical force of James' admonition that follows. Elsewhere James often makes an assertion or a command and follows it up with a parable or hypothetical situation (1:22-25). This also supports the idea that the scene described in the synagogue may have taken place, but it is not necessarily a scene that actually has taken place.

The apodosis of the conditional clause (2:4) is actually a question which (with conjunction οὐ) expects a positive answer. Question asked: "Have you not made distinctions among yourselves . . .?" Answer expected: "Yes, we have." They have become "judges with evil motives," in the sense of judges characterized by evil motives. This is best identified as a genitive of description, the most essential use of the genitive case.[144]

The name of the meeting place in this example is "your synagogue" (συναγωγὴν ὑμῶν), the only place in the NT where this specific term is

---

[142] Johnson, 220.
[143] Porter, *Idioms*, 262.
[144] Wallace, 88.

used for gatherings of Jesus-followers (see the related ἐπισυναγωγὴ in Heb. 10:25). This again points to the Jewish-Christian nature of the letter and to the continuity between the "torah-based" communities and the "Jesus-based" communities in these early days of the movement. James refers in 5:14 to the elders of the "assembly" (πρεσβυτέρους τῆς ἐκκλησίας). As it is elsewhere in the NT, ἐκκλησία is the gathering of believers, but συναγωγη is used for their gathering *place*—a usage that even continued into the second century (Justin *Dial.* 134.3; Ign. Pol. 4:2; Ign. *Trall.* 3:1).

While this passage has been usually applied to discrimination in public worship, the context may point to another explanation. In an influential article, R.B. Ward argued that the scene in this passage is not a worship service but a "court" session to render judgment on a case brought before it.[145] James condemns the partiality of those who are "judges" (κριταὶ) who "made discriminatory distinctions" (διεκρίθητε). The paronomasia is evident in the original (διακρίνω and κριταὶ). The reference in 2:6 to the poor being drawn into "courts" (κριτήρια) continues the semantic chain of κρι-lexemes and further supports this view in the context. Furthermore, the OT warning about showing partiality was addressed to Israel's judges (Deut. 1:17; Lev. 19:15). Ward also cited striking linguistic and social parallels, although from later Rabbinic materials. While a legitimate application of the partiality principle can certainly be applied to the favoring of the rich in their seating assignments in the assembly's "pews," it appears that the passage makes much more sense if we imagine the assembly leaders gathered to decide cases (see Matt. 18:15-17 ; 1 Cor. 6:1-6). Perhaps the unjust way in which the rich landowners withheld pay to their day laborers, so strongly condemned in 5:1-6, was the kind of legal issue that was being handled in this scene. As is so true today, it is in legal proceedings that the poor often suffer discrimination because they do not have an adequate recourse available to them. While that may happen in secular contexts, James insists that it must not happen among those who believe in the Lord of Glory who became poor for our sake. Jesus' specific contribution to this issue and James' application of it follows in the next sub-paragraph.

---

[145] R.B. Ward, "Partiality in the Assembly," HTR 62 (1969), 87-97.

11. Paragraph 11 (James 2:5-7)

Ἀκούσατε, ἀδελφοί μου ἀγαπητοί· οὐχ ὁ θεὸς ἐξελέξατο τοὺς πτωχοὺς τῷ κόσμῳ πλουσίους ἐν πίστει καὶ κληρονόμους τῆς βασιλείας ἧς ἐπηγγείλατο τοῖς ἀγαπῶσιν αὐτόν; ὑμεῖς δὲ ἠτιμάσατε τὸν πτωχόν. οὐχ οἱ πλούσιοι καταδυναστεύουσιν ὑμῶν καὶ αὐτοὶ ἕλκουσιν ὑμᾶς εἰς κριτήρια; οὐκ αὐτοὶ βλασφημοῦσιν τὸ καλὸν ὄνομα τὸ ἐπικληθὲν ἐφ᾽ ὑμᾶς;	Listen, my beloved brothers, has not God chosen those who are considered poor by the world to be rich in faith and heirs of the kingdom which he promised to those who love him? But you have dishonored the poor person. Do not the rich oppress you, and do they not drag you into courts? Do they not blaspheme that honorable name which has been pronounced over you?

Clause Analysis of 2:5-7

2:5

P	add
Ἀκούσατε	ἀδελφοί μου ἀγαπητοι

A	S	P	C	A				
οὐχ	ὁ θεὸς	ἐξελέξατο	τοὺς πτωχοὺς τῷ κόσμῳ	πλουσίους ἐν πίστει καὶ κληρονόμους τῆς βασιλείας				
					C	P	C	
					ἧς	ἐπηγγείλατο	P	C
							τοῖς ἀγαπῶσιν	αὐτόν;

2:6

S	cj	P	C
ὑμεῖς	δε	ἠτιμάσατε	τὸν πτωχόν

A	S	P	C
οὐχ	οἱ πλούσιοι	καταδυναστεύουσιν	ὑμῶν

cj	S	P	C	A
καὶ	αὐτοὶ	ἕλκουσιν	ὑμᾶς	εἰς κριτήρια

2:7

A	S	P	C		
οὐκ	αὐτοὶ	βλασφημοῦσιν	τὸ καλὸν ὄνομα		
				P	**A**
				τὸ ἐπικληθὲν	ἐφ᾽ ὑμᾶς

This section opens with the familiar nominative of address, ἀδελφοί μου, fronted by an imperative, Ἀκούσατε. This collocation, however, does not justify the conclusion that an entirely new section of James is being introduced. Three linguistic features must be present for that to be the case: (1) a nominative of address; (2) an imperative command or rhetorical question, plus (3) a new semantic theme. A new semantic component justifies the introduction of a new major paragraph. This was evidenced before at 1:2; 1:16; 1:19; and 2:1. It will be seen later at 2:14; 3:1; 3:13; 4:1; 4:11; 4:13; 5:1; 5:7; 5:12 and 5:19. Uses of ἀδελφοί and an imperative alone at other locations like this one serve to span the topic introduced in 2:1 throughout the section by making a particular application of the new semantic theme within the section. This can also be seen at 3:10, 12; 5:9, 10. Here the imperative Ἀκούσατε functions as a "meta-comment" calling attention to the following question. Therefore, 2:5 is the beginning of a new sub-paragraph (2:5-7) of the larger unit, 2:1-13.

The five primary clauses in 2:5-7 convey three rhetorical questions, which also provide a link with the rhetorical question asked in 2:4. The hypothetical scene in 2:2, 3 is now over and James drives home his point by means of these questions, each of which is expressed with the negative particle οὐχ/οὐκ and thus expects a positive answer. The rhetorical force of these questions effectively makes three emphatic statements which James expects his readers to affirm. (1) God has chosen the poor by the world's standards to be the rich heirs in His kingdom. (2) The rich dishonor the poor and oppress them. (3) In doing so, the rich dishonor the name which is held in honor by the poor. The themes of honor and shame, so prominent in the social system of the ancient world, are quite evident in these rhetorical questions.[146] Therefore, the readers should honor those whom God honors. Conversely, they should not show partiality by honoring those who dishonor those whom God honors.

---

[146] Bruce J. Malina, *The New Testament World*, 3rd ed. (Louisville: WJK Press, 2001), 27-57.

The words in 2:5 clearly echo a passage like Matthew 5:3, "Blessed are the poor in spirit, for theirs is the kingdom of heaven." It is at this point that we should pay closer attention to two larger issues that are raised in James 2:5-7. They are 1) the presence of the *logia* of Jesus in James, and 2) the specific identity of the "poor" and the "rich" in the letter. This divergence is in keeping with our conviction that most introductory issues can only be solved by the exegesis of the book itself. Hence they are treated here rather than in a separate introductory chapter.

Vernon Robbins has suggested that texts are marked by layers of meaning that make up their "texture."[147] More specifically, he suggests that Scriptural texts contain an Inner texture, an Intertexture, a Sociocultural texture, and an Ideological texture. To explore Inner Texture means to examine features in the language of the text itself. This type of analysis is exemplified in our treatment of the clausal structure of 2:5-7. To examine the Intertexture means to examine how texts outside the text inform our understanding of the text itself. The field of "intertextuality" is concerned, for example, about how an author may utilize other authors by quotation or allusion. To examine the Sociocultural texture is to attempt to understand the world that produced the text and employs the insights of social scientific criticism and cultural anthropology. To explore the Ideological texture means to examine the implied author's beliefs, or his ideology. These textures have striking affinities with the textual, interpersonal and ideational components of a text mentioned earlier as part of a Hallidayan approach to language use.

In approaching the intertextuality of a passage like 2:5-7, the question of James' employing "Jesus material" arises. This issue is also relevant in the next sub-paragraph (2:8-13) where quotations from the OT are utilized and one is called the "royal law" and the "law of freedom." Furthermore, intertextuality is a vital area of study throughout the letter. Does James consciously utilize sayings from Jesus and, if so, how does he use them?

Every writer on James addresses the issue of the *logia* of Jesus in the book. To date the most thorough treatment of the issue is the published dissertation by David Deppe.[148] Deppe analyzes in detail the twenty five most common sayings in James that writers have referred

---

[147] Vernon K. Robbins, *Exploring the Texture of Texts* (Valley Forge: Trinity Press, 1996).
[148] D. B. Deppe, *The Sayings of Jesus in the Epistle of James* (Chelsea, MI: Bookcrafters, 1989).

back to Jesus. He applies a very conservative set of standards and concludes that there are only eight firm allusions to Jesus' teaching as we know them in the Synoptic Gospels. Those allusions are set out by means of the following chart.[149]

Eight Firm Allusions		
James Reference	Synoptic Reference	Subject
Jas. 1:5	Mt. 7:7; Lk. 11:9	ask and you will receive
Jas. 2:5	Lk. 6:20b; Mt. 5:3	kingdom belongs to poor
Jas. 4:2c,3	Mt. 7:7; Lk. 11:9	ask and you will receive
Jas. 4:9	Lk. 6:21, 25b	those who laugh will mourn
Jas. 4:10	Mt. 23:12; Lk. 14:11; 18:14b	humble will be exalted
Jas. 5:1	Lk. 6:24	woe to the rich
Jas. 5:2,3a	Mt. 6:19, 20: Lk. 12:33b	do not treasure up wealth
Jas. 5:12	Mt. 5:33-37	oaths

An allusion is defined as the presence of substantial verbal similarities as well as a common context and emphasis of content. It may be, however, that Deppe's standards are too strict and probably err on the conservative side. For example, there are a number of probable allusions based on more than casual verbal similarities. Consider the following parallels, each one of which has been suggested by more than one writer on the subject.

---

[149] The following charts were constructed from the data in Deppe and from the author's own analysis.

Other Probable Allusions		
James Reference	**Synoptic Reference**	**Subject**
Jas. 1:22-25; 2:14-17	Mt. 7:24-27; Lk. 6:46-49	doers of the word
Jas. 4:11, 12	Mt. 7:1, 2; Lk. 6:37	against judging others
Jas. 1:19, 20	Mt. 5:22	against anger
Jas. 3:12	Mt. 7:16; ; Lk. 6:44	fruit from the tree
Jas. 1:12; 5:10, 11	Mt. 5:11, 12; Lk. 6:22, 23	blessing on those who endure
Jas. 3:18	Mt. 5:9;	being peacemakers
Jas. 2:13	Mt. 5:7	results of mercy

Furthermore, when we do not look for exact verbal parallels, we can also discern the following common themes shared by James and Jesus.

Common Themes		
James	**Jesus**	**Theme**
Jas 1:2; 5:10,11	Mat. 5:11, 12	joy in tribulation
Jas. 1:6	Mt. 21:21	faith and doubting
Jas. 1:22-25; 2:14	Mt. 7:21,24-26	hearing and doing
Jas. 2:8	Mt. 22:39	the love commandment
Jas. 2:13	Mt. 5:13; 9:13	mercy
Jas. 4:4	Mt. 6:24; Lk. 16:13	serving God vs. loving the world
Jas. 4:11, 12; 5:9	Mt. 7:1; Lk. 6:37	refraining from judging
Jas. 1:12; 5:10, 11	Mt. 5:11, 12; 10:22	persevere in trials/receive blessing

Despite the large number of shared expressions and themes, not one of them qualifies as a direct verbal quotation of the *logia* of Jesus as we have them in the Synoptic Gospels. The closest example is James' warning about oaths in 5:12 with its striking verbal similarities to Matt. 5:33-37. But even there James is not quoting exactly the words of Jesus as we have them in Matthew. Perhaps we have not approached this issue in the best way when we try to find undoubted allusions based on the standards of exact quotations. Richard Bauckham has provided the best solution to this problem.[150] He compares James' use of Jesus material to Sirach's use of the canonical *Proverbs*. In no place does *Sirach* quote that canonical book, but any reader recognizes the large amount of shared themes and expressions in the two books. Bauckham suggests that *Sirach* adapts and reshapes hundreds of individual verses from *Proverbs* without ever actually quoting any of them. He argues that James approaches the sayings of Jesus in the same way. Without ever clearly quoting a saying of Jesus, James adapts for his purpose dozens of those sayings and reshapes them for his own specific purpose. Bauckham's suggestion, therefore, frees us from the need for a painstaking verbal comparison between James' statements and the *logia* of Jesus. Another aspect of the question is that we need not even suppose that James had a written Gospel in front of him. James may have simply recalled the oral traditions of Jesus' sayings before they were ever written down by Matthew, Mark, or Luke. The voice of Jesus, therefore, is heard distinctly in the book of James, but not in the form of literal citations. By using Latin expressions from synoptic criticism, we may safely conclude that in James we may not have the *ipsissima verba* of Jesus, but we do hear loudly the *ipsissima vox* of Jesus.

Some authors have criticized James as being one of the least "Christian" books of the NT.[151] Some have even argued that the book was originally a Jewish treatise to which someone added the Christianizing references in 1:1 and 2:1.[152] When we realize, however, the thorough way in which Jesus' teachings permeate the writing, we could conclude that, after the Gospels, James is the most "Jesus-centered"

---

[150] Bauckham, *James*, 74-108.

[151] A. Julicher, *An Introduction to the NT*, tr. J.P. Ward (New York: Putnam, 1904), 225. Dunn writes: "The letter of James is the most Jewish, the most undistinctively Christian document in the NT." J.D.G. Dunn, *Unity and Diversity in the New Testament*, 3rd ed. (London: SCM Press, 2006), 271.

[152] L. Massibeau, "L'Epitre de Jacques est—elle l'oeuvre d'un Chretien?" RHR 32 (1895): 249-83.

book in the NT canon. While Paul theologizes about Jesus, he displays a measured interest in the teachings of Jesus (see Acts 20:30). However, almost every point that James makes is grounded or illustrated by an adapted saying or aphorism that echoes in some way a *logion* of his brother. Finally, when James' use of the orally transmitted sayings of Jesus is acknowledged, it becomes probably the strongest argument for the early dating of the book.

The second of the two side issues that must be mentioned at this point is the identity of the "poor" and the "rich" in James. Earlier we cited Halliday's approach that language is a "social semiotic."[153] Thus we use language to interact with other people, to establish and maintain relations with them, to influence their behavior, to express our viewpoint to others and to elicit or change theirs. It is necessary, therefore, at certain points in this analysis, to discuss the interpersonal components of language register. In James' use of language, who are the "poor" and the "rich" who figure so prominently here in 2:1-7 and at other key locations in his book?

Bruce Malina has thoroughly analyzed the social conditions of the first century Mediterranean world. He describes it as a "limited goods" society in which people did not move up and down in their status but sought to maintain the status into which they were born. By also analyzing the way in which the word "poor" is associated in the NT with other types of suffering people, he offers these insightful conclusions.

> Being classified as poor was the result of some unfortunate turn of events or some untoward circumstances. Poor persons seem to be those who cannot maintain their inherited status due to the circumstances that befell them and their families, such as debt, being in a foreign land, sickness, death of a spouse, or some personal physical accident. Consequently, the poor would not be a permanent social standing but some sort of revolving category of people who unfortunately cannot maintain their inherited status. Thus day laborers, landless peasants, and beggars born into their situation were not poor persons in first century society. And "poor" would most certainly not be an economic designation. Furthermore, the opposite of rich would not necessarily be poor. To repeat, in the perception of people in a limited-goods society, the majority of people are neither rich nor poor, just equal in that each has a status to maintain in some honorable way. Personal assessment is not economic but a matter of lineage. Thus, in this context, rich and

---

[153] Halliday, *Social Semiotic.*

poor really refer to *the greedy* and *the socially ill-fated*. The terms do not characterize two poles of society as much as two minority categories, the one based on the shameless drive to expand one's wealth, the other based on the inability to maintain one's inherited status of any rank.[154]

As mentioned previously, Malina calls *honor* and *shame* two of the most "pivotal values of the Mediterranean world."[155] The importance of these values also has great application to James' discussion of the rich and poor in the court scene of chapter two. The poor man would be shamed and the rich man would be honored by this type of behavior. But the Divine standard, as exemplified both in the Jesus *logion* of 2:5 and later in the "royal law" mentioned in 2:8, subverts the accepted societal norms and indicates the counter-cultural nature of James' ethical standard for the community of believers. The point that he makes in 2:7 should not be missed when seen in this context. To slightly paraphrase it: "Do not they speak *shamefully* (βλασφημοῦσιν) of that *honorable* name (τὸ καλὸν ὄνομα) which has been pronounced over you (τὸ ἐπικληθὲν ἐφ ὑμᾶς)?" That name may have been "Christian" since it had recently been used of the believers in Antioch (Acts 11:40), probably communicating the idea of "Messianist." Whatever was its original context, it soon came to be a name that was worn with honor (1 *Peter* 4:16; *Didache* 12:4). James probably refers to the naming of poor believers at their baptism, indicating their new owner. James himself quotes the prophecy in Amos 9:15 where the LXX uses the same language to describe the naming of Gentiles by Yahweh, their new owner, when they are brought into the eschatological kingdom (*Acts* 15:17—ἐφ οὓς ἐπικέκληται τὸ ὄνομά μου).

---

[154] Malina, 100.
[155] Malina, 27.

12. Paragraph 12 (James 2:8-13)

Εἰ μέντοι νόμον τελεῖτε βασιλικὸν κατὰ τὴν γραφήν· ἀγαπήσεις τὸν πλησίον σου ὡς σεαυτόν, καλῶς ποιεῖτε· εἰ δὲ προσωπολημπτεῖτε, ἁμαρτίαν ἐργάζεσθε ἐλεγχόμενοι ὑπὸ τοῦ νόμου ὡς παραβάται. ὅστις γὰρ ὅλον τὸν νόμον τηρήσῃ πταίσῃ δὲ ἐν ἑνί, γέγονεν πάντων ἔνοχος. ὁ γὰρ εἰπών· μὴ μοιχεύσῃς, εἶπεν καί· μὴ φονεύσῃς· εἰ δὲ οὐ μοιχεύεις φονεύεις δέ, γέγονας παραβάτης νόμου. Οὕτως λαλεῖτε καὶ οὕτως ποιεῖτε ὡς διὰ νόμου ἐλευθερίας μέλλοντες κρίνεσθαι. ἡ γὰρ κρίσις ἀνέλεος τῷ μὴ ποιήσαντι ἔλεος· κατακαυχᾶται ἔλεος κρίσεως.	If you really are fulfilling the kingly law according to the Scripture, "You shall love your neighbor as yourself," you are doing well. But if you are showing partiality, you are committing sin and thus are convicted by the law as transgressors. For whoever observes the whole law but stumbles in one point has become accountable for all of it. For he who said, "Do not commit adultery," also said, "Do not murder." And if you do not commit adultery but you murder, you have become a transgressor of the law. So speak and so act as those who are to be judged under the law of liberty. Because judgment is without mercy to one who has shown no mercy. Mercy triumphs over judgment.

Clause Analysis of 2:8-13

2:8

cj	cj	C		A
εἰ	μέντοι	νόμον	βασιλικὸν	κατὰ τὴν γραφήν·
		P τελεῖτε		

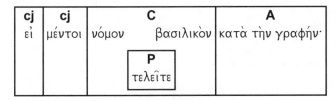

P	C	cj	C
ἀγαπήσεις	τὸν πλησίον σου	ὡς	σεαυτόν,

A	P
καλῶς	ποιεῖτε·

2:9

cj	cj	P
εἰ	δὲ	προσωπολημπτεῖτε

■ *The Book of James—A New Perspective*

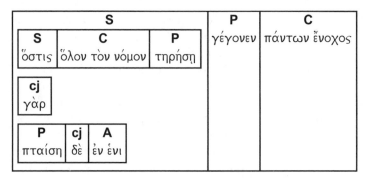

C	P	A		
ἁμαρτίαν	ἐργάζεσθε	**P** ἐλεγχόμενοι	**A** ὑπὸ τοῦ νόμου	**A** ὡς παραβάται

2:10

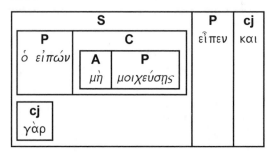

S			P	C
S ὅστις	**C** ὅλον τὸν νόμον	**P** τηρήσῃ	γέγονεν	πάντων ἔνοχος
cj γὰρ				
P πταίσῃ	**cj** δὲ	**A** ἐν ἑνὶ		

2:11

S		P	cj
P ὁ εἰπών	**C** [**A** μὴ | **P** μοιχεύσῃς]	εἶπεν	καὶ
cj γὰρ			

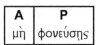

A	P
μὴ	φονεύσῃς

cj	cj	A	P
εἰ	δὲ	οὐ	μοιχεύεις

P	cj
φονεύεις	δε

P	C
γέγονας	παραβάτης νόμου

2:12

A	P
οὕτως	λαλεῖτε

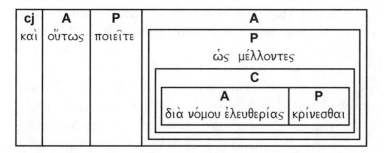

cj	A	P	A
καὶ	οὕτως	ποιεῖτε	P — ὡς μέλλοντες
			C
			A: διὰ νόμου ἐλευθερίας | P: κρίνεσθαι

2:13

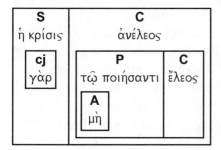

S	C
ἡ κρίσις	ἀνέλεος
cj — γὰρ	P: τῷ ποιήσαντι (A: μὴ) | C: ἔλεος

P	S	C
κατακαυχᾶται	ἔλεος	κρίσεως

This section (2:8-13) forms the third and final sub-paragraph of the larger discourse unit beginning at 2:1. The topic introduced there was a strong warning against discrimination and partiality in the community. Throughout the larger section this is especially applied to how this unacceptable favoritism is practiced against the poor to the advantage of the rich. The connection between the sections is evidenced by the use of the verb προσωπολημπτεῖτε in 2:9, recalling the noun προσωπολημψίαις in 2:1. In the first sub-paragraph (2:1-4), partiality is shown to be inconsistent with a Torah-saying (Leviticus 19:15) alluded to in 2:1. In the second sub-paragraph (2:5-7), partiality is shown to be inconsistent with a Jesus-saying alluded to in 2:5 (the believing poor as heirs of the kingdom as expressed in Matt. 5:3 and Luke 6:20). In this last sub-paragraph (2:8-13), partiality is shown to be inconsistent with a Torah-saying (Lev. 19:18 regarding loving one's neighbor) that is also a Jesus-saying (Matt. 22:39) which James calls a royal law (2:8). As was mentioned, in 2:1-13 James begins a skillful midrashic treatment of Leviticus 19:12-18 which he continues at later points in his discourse (4:11; 5:4, 9, 12, 20). Intertextuality, involving both the OT and the sayings of Jesus, will continue to be a major factor in James from this point onward.

The section begins with two first class conditional clauses in 2:8 and 9, strongly contrasted by his using a variation of the μέν . . . δέ construction. On the one hand, if his readers "really" (μέντοι) are fulfilling the royal law of loving one's neighbor, then they "are doing well" (καλῶς ποιεῖτε). On the other hand (δέ), if they show partiality, they are "committing sin" (ἁμαρτίαν ἐργάζεσθε). James uses the μέν . . . δέ contrast elsewhere only in the strikingly contrasting statements about wisdom from above and below (3:17, 18). This strong contrast heightens the severity of the inconsistent behavior in those who are guilty of partiality—the theme introduced in 2:1. He then adds a result participle after the second conditional clause in 2:9 showing how those who show such partiality are guilty of law breaking: "and thus are convicted (ἐλεγχόμενοι) by the law as transgressors." This result clause emphasizes the severity of this behavior as being, not just a poor choice, but a breaking of a Torah commandment.

That specific Torah commandment is Lev. 19:18, which he quotes in verse 8. This is the first time James actually quotes the OT, although he had alluded to Lev. 19: 15 when he mentioned partiality in 2:1. He will continue to utilize and adapt Lev. 19:12-18 throughout his letter. He calls this commandment a "royal law"—the way in which it is rendered by every English translation. This translation may have obscured for English readers what James intends to communicate. The Greek word for "royal" (βασιλικὸν) recalls the cognate word "kingdom" (βασιλείας) in 2:5. This is the kingdom to which the believing poor are heirs, an allusion to the beatitude of Matt. 5:3 and Luke 6:20. This further recalls the "faith of the Lord Jesus Christ" in 2:1, whose name is called over those believing poor in 2:7. Thus, by the Messianic king citing Lev. 19:18 as part of his program of counter cultural values, it became the royal or "kingly" law. James would not make a distinction between the Torah and Jesus' teaching. James bases his argument on the Torah as it was understood and applied by the new King over the reconstituted twelve tribes, the glorious Lord Jesus Christ. Thus, although sounding a bit awkward, it may be of value to translate the expression as the "kingly law" to make clearer his allusion to the beatitude about the kingdom in 2:5.

Describing those who break the "kingly law" as transgressors (2:9b) leads into the next part of this section (2:10-11) that elaborates what is meant by transgressing the law. The post-positive γὰρ in 2:10 explains that if one obeys all but one law, he has still become guilty of all of them (γέγονεν πάντων ἔνοχος). In 2:11 he illustrates this by the sixth and seventh words of the Decalogue, the prohibitions against adultery and murder. This is the second example of James' citation of the OT (Exo. 20:13, 14). If a person does not commit one but commits the other he still is "a transgressor of the law" (γέγονας παραβάτης νόμου). The use of the perfect tense of γίνομαι in both verses front-grounds the state of affairs in which the law-breaker is found—he is a guilty transgressor.

Being guilty of breaking all of the law if someone is guilty of breaking one law must be understood in light of 2:11: "For he who said, 'Do not commit adultery,' also said, 'Do not murder'." There is only one lawgiver, a point he will later declare firmly in 4:12. So there is one whole law, not just many individual laws. The clear implication is that readers cannot simply choose to obey some laws—the big ones?—and neglect the other ones like the royal law of love to a neighbor. Just as God is one so the law is one, another emphasis on being single rather than double that characterizes the entire work. Perhaps the rendering "has become accountable for all of it" better conveys the sense of the expression (NRSV, ESV).

James applies his comment on partiality in this subsection (2:8-13) with two imperatives in 2:12, each introduced by οὕτως plus, two indicative aphorisms in 2:13, introduced by a causal γὰρ. "So (οὕτως) speak and so (οὕτως) act as those who are to be judged under the law of liberty. Because (γάρ) judgment is without mercy to one who has shown no mercy. Mercy triumphs over judgment." If we do not recognize James' emphasis on the unitary nature of the law as taught by Jesus, we may seek to discover some different referent for the "law of liberty" under which we are judged. However, the "perfect law" (1:25); the "law of liberty" (1:25; 2:12); the "royal law" (2:8); the "law" (2:9, 11); and the "whole law" (2:10) are all in continuity with the law as expounded by Jesus. When we recognize this, we can see the wholeness of the entire law as James wishes us to understand it. It is the one law in its multi-faceted aspects, given by the one Lawgiver in Heaven and interpreted by His messianic law interpreter on earth.

James ends his exhortation on partiality with two parallel clauses in 2:13. The first is introduced again by the post-positive γάρ, and is negative in tone, concluding the exhortation against discrimination: "Because judgment is without mercy to one who has shown no mercy." The second, while parallel in structure as a primary clause, is more positive in tone: "Mercy triumphs over judgment." The asyndeton of the second clause is characteristic both of James' style and of the stand-alone nature of an aphorism specifically applied to partiality. The pair of aphorisms both round off this section (2:1-13) and anticipate the next section (2:14-26). "Mercy" is the virtue that partiality denies to the poor (2:4) while it shows practical provision for the needs of the poor (2:15, 16).

James' effort throughout his book to portray the binary opposition of behaviors in the two ways ethical tradition finds clear illustration in this passage. Favoring the rich at the expense of the poor is an example of the wisdom from below that contrasts with the wisdom from above. Divine wisdom honors those whom God honors—the heirs of His kingdom—and manifests behavior that is "full of mercy and good fruits and impartiality" (3:17). Partiality in favor of the rich is evidence of the "selfishness" that is from below (3:14, 16). One cannot dishonor those whom God has honored.

James 2:14-26

The second main paragraph of James 2 displays clearly the discourse markers that set it off as a separate section of the letter, the most distinct being the opening nominative of direct address ἀδελφοί μου (see 1:2; 1:16; 1:19; 2:1). Combined with this direct address marker is the introduction of a new topic, the inseparability of faith and actions. And yet the paragraph is not totally isolated from the previous context, since it brings together three themes previously introduced: Hearing/Doing (1:22-25); Discrimination (2:1) and the Poor (2:5). While 1:22-25 did stress the importance of not only hearing but doing the word, it is in this passage that the faith/actions theme finds its fullest treatment in the book. Of the sixteen occurrences of πίστις in James, eleven are in 2:14-26. Of the fifteen occurrences of ἔργον, twelve appear here, all in the plural form. Nine of the occurrences of ἔργον occur closely with πίστις—a collocation that occurs nowhere else, although the theme of behavior matching profession permeates the book. See, e.g., 3:13: "Who is wise and understanding among you? By his good conduct let him show his actions in the meekness of wisdom."

However, the unique collocation of faith and actions in this section should not obscure the fact that this passage has many anaphoric links with what precedes.

Consider the striking verbal and semantic patterns repeated from 2:1-13:

1. Brothers are warned about how they should "have faith" (2:1 and 2:14).

2. A vivid and compelling example is then offered (2:2-4 and 2:15-17).

3. The non-compassionate treatment of the ill-clad poor (2:2 and 2:15).

4. Proofs from both logic and scripture are offered (2:5-12 and 2:20-26).

5. An aphoristic saying rounds off and concludes each paragraph (2:13 and 2:26).

6. The comment "you do well" is used each time in an ironic sense (2:8 and 2:19).

7. His readers are "called" by a name (2:7) and Abraham was "called" by a name (2:23).

Earlier we noted the semantic linkage of this passage also with 1:22-25. Other connections with chapter one are as follows: the order of "faith—work—perfect" in 1:3, 4 and 2:22; the expression "able to save" in 1:22 and 2:14; the use of τέλ– semantic domain words in 1:4, 15, 17, 25 and ἐτελειώθη in 2:22 (as well as 2:8. 3:2; 5:11); the similar explanation of δικαιοσύνη in 1:20 and 2:22, 23; and the similar use of the adjective μόνον in 1:22 and 2:24.

Because of their many similarities, a good case can be made that both 2:1-13 and 2:14-26 are two parts of one unit devoted to the same topic. However, the use of ἀδελφοί coupled with the collocation of the faith/works vocabulary in the second section does justify its separate treatment. The NA/UBS texts further divide 2:14-26 into three sub-paragraphs (2:14-17; 2:18, 19; and 2:20-26). This seems justified since each of these sub-paragraphs has certain shared linguistic characteristics. The rhetorical question Τί τὸ ὄφελος (What good is it?) opens the argument in 2:14 and closes it in 2:17, followed by an aphorism in 2:18 about the uselessness of a faith that is not accompanied by actions. Between these bookends is the parable about the neglect of the poor person's need. The adversative conjunction ἀλλ' in 2:18 then introduces the imagined interlocutor's objection which is answered in 2:19. The strong words issued to the vain person in 2:20 challenge his knowledge which is then supplied by the exemplars, Abraham and Rahab, in 2:21-25. James concludes with another aphorism summarizing the point of the entire paragraph. Faith that is not accompanied by appropriate actions, like a body without a spirit, is dead. He then develops the inner texture of these three sub-sections as follows.

13. Paragraph 13 (James 2:14-17)

Τί τὸ ὄφελος, ἀδελφοί μου, ἐὰν πίστιν λέγῃ τις ἔχειν ἔργα δὲ μὴ ἔχῃ; μὴ δύναται ἡ πίστις σῶσαι αὐτόν; ἐὰν ἀδελφὸς ἢ ἀδελφὴ γυμνοὶ ὑπάρχωσιν καὶ λειπόμενοι τῆς ἐφημέρου τροφῆς εἴπῃ δέ τις αὐτοῖς ἐξ ὑμῶν· ὑπάγετε ἐν εἰρήνῃ, θερμαίνεσθε καὶ χορτάζεσθε, μὴ δῶτε δὲ αὐτοῖς τὰ ἐπιτήδεια τοῦ σώματος, τί τὸ ὄφελος; οὕτως καὶ ἡ πίστις, ἐὰν μὴ ἔχῃ ἔργα, νεκρά ἐστιν καθ ἑαυτήν.	What good is it, my brothers, if someone says that they have faith but they do not have the accompanying actions? Can that kind of faith save him? If a brother or sister is poorly clothed and lacking in daily food, and one from among you says to them, "Go in peace, be warmed and filled," without giving them the things needed for the body, what good is that? So also that kind of faith, if it is not accompanied by actions, is dead being by itself.

Clause Analysis of 2:14-17

2:14

C	S	add
Τί	τὸ ὄφελος	ἀδελφοί μου

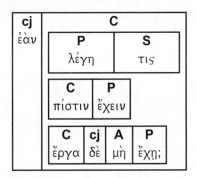

cj	C		
ἐὰν	**P** λέγῃ	**S** τις	

	C πίστιν	**P** ἔχειν	

| | **C** ἔργα | **cj** δὲ | **A** μὴ | **P** ἔχῃ; |

A	P	S	C	
μὴ	δύναται	ἡ πίστις	**P** σῶσαι	**C** αὐτόν;

2:15

cj	S	C	P
ἐὰν	ἀδελφὸς ἢ ἀδελφὴ	γυμνοὶ	ὑπάρχωσιν

cj	C	
καὶ	**P** λειπόμενοι	**C** τῆς ἐφημέρου τροφῆς

2:16

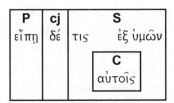

P	cj	S	
εἴπῃ	δέ	τις	ἐξ ὑμῶν
			C αὐτοῖς

P	A
ὑπάγετε	ἐν εἰρήνῃ

P	A	P
θερμαίνεσθε	καὶ	χορτάζεσθε

A	P	cj	A	C
μὴ	δῶτε	δὲ	αὐτοῖς	τὰ ἐπιτήδεια τοῦ σώματος

C	S
τί	τὸ ὄφελος;

2:17

A	cj	S	cj	A	P	C	C	P	A
οὕτως	καὶ	ἡ πίστις	ἐὰν	μὴ	ἔχῃ	ἔργα	νεκρά	ἐστιν	καθ' ἑαυτήν

The Open Text analysis indicates that there are four primary clauses in this section. The first is a rhetorical question in 2:14a that serves also as the apodosis of a third class conditional clause. The entire verse conveys the topic of the overall paragraph, the remainder of which (2:13-26) is the comment on that topic (a real faith is demonstrated by appropriate actions). The indirect discourse expressed by the infinitive (ἔχειν) gives voice to the imagined person who later engages with the author as a rhetorical interlocutor. That imagined person is later directly quoted in the parable in 2:18, 19 and finally addressed in the second person in 2:20 as "O vain person." This interpersonal dynamic is vividly portrayed through the diatribe format, progressively increasing in intensity throughout the section.

The second rhetorical question concluding 2:14 brings into doubt the nature of a faith professed but not accompanied by appropriate actions. The accompanying negative adjunct μὴ indicates an expected negative reply. Furthermore, the use of the article before πίστις serves an anaphoric function, referring back to the type of deficient faith that was described in the earlier conditional sentence. In other words, the sense conveyed is: "No. That kind of faith cannot save the person who says that they have it."

James' fondness for parables, already seen in 1:22-25 and in 2:2-4, is illustrated again by introducing a person who, like the poor person in 2:2, is inadequately dressed. A person was considered "naked" (γυμνοὶ) if they did not have adequate clothing for public appearance.[156] The word was used of a working fisherman in John 21:7. James did not need a modern translator to unpack a generic masculine word because he

---

[156] BDAG, 208.

clearly refers to a "brother or sister" who is lacking not only clothing but also the food necessary for that day. The pointed description of the indifferent response to these needy people in 2:16 clearly portrays the guilty person as being part of the community of people James is addressing. This person, although only theoretically described, is "from among you" (ἐξ ὑμῶν). The serious callousness of this heartless response is that it is spoken by someone else in the believing community. This second conditional sentence in 2:16 inverts the apodosis from the earlier conditional sentence by ending with the repeated rhetorically powerful question, "what good is it?" This inversion heightens the rhetorical punch of James' response.

The concluding verse of the section is an effective aphorism that adds to the already declared doubt about the nature of such faith ("what good is it?) by openly declaring that such a faith (ἡ πίστις) is actually "dead." The type of faith that lacks the necessary accompaniment of loving acts is a faith that has no life at all. Some equate this faith with a weaker form of faith that simply needs awakening from slumber.[157] This explanation, however, blunts the severity of James' attack, which he repeats verbatim in the final aphorism of the paragraph (2:26). I have chosen not to translate ἔργα in this section by its traditional rendering "works." This is because of the baggage the English word carries in some circles that associate it with achieving merit for salvation. The word in James simply refers to actions that demonstrate Christian love and give evidence of a genuine faith. It is also easy to see an allusion to the dominical words of Matt. 25:35-46 ("I was naked and you did not clothe me"). This is another illustration of how James utilizes and adapts a Jesus saying without directly quoting it.

Paragraph 14 (James 2:18, 19)

Ἀλλ᾽ ἐρεῖ τις· σὺ πίστιν ἔχεις, κἀγὼ ἔργα ἔχω· δεῖξόν μοι τὴν πίστιν σου χωρὶς τῶν ἔργων, κἀγώ σοι δείξω ἐκ τῶν ἔργων μου τὴν πίστιν. σὺ πιστεύεις ὅτι εἷς ἐστιν ὁ θεός, καλῶς ποιεῖς· καὶ τὰ δαιμόνια πιστεύουσιν καὶ φρίσσουσιν.	But someone will say, "You have faith and I have actions."* Show me your faith apart from your actions, and I will show you my faith by my actions. You believe that God is one; you do well. Even the demons believe-and shudder! *or "Do you have faith?" "I also have actions…"

---

[157] See Z.C. Hodges, *The Epistle of James* (Irving, TX: Grace Evangelical Society, 1994), 62-63, for a similar interpretation of "dead."

2:18

cj	P	S
Ἀλλ	ἐρεῖ	τις

S	C	P
σὺ	πίστιν	ἔχεις

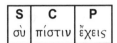

S	C	P
κἀγὼ	ἔργα	ἔχω

P	C	C	A
δεῖξόν	μοι	τὴν πίστιν σου	χωρὶς τῶν ἔργων

S	C	P	A	C
κἀγώ	σοι	δείξω	ἐκ τῶν ἔργων μου	τὴν πίστιν

2:19

S	P
σὺ	πιστεύεις

cj	C	P	S
ὅτι	εἷς	ἐστιν	ὁ θεός

A	P
καλῶς	ποιεῖς

cj	S	P
καὶ	τὰ δαιμόνια	πιστεύουσιν

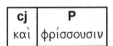

cj	P
καὶ	φρίσσουσιν

The voice of the hypothetical interlocutor was briefly heard in the previous section through his indifferent response to a real need: "Be warmed and filled." Now James gives that person a voice of debate and challenge in 2:18, 19. The passage is quite challenging despite its rapid fire presentation of nine primary clauses. It is the shorthand way in which the debate is presented, combined with the lack of quotation marks in the original, that actually contribute to its difficulty to sort out. The commentaries explain the various possibilities about where to end the quotation that begins with "You have faith" (σὺ πίστιν ἔχεις). The problem is compounded by the fact that the opponent's statement seems to be opposite of what we would expect him to say. The suggestion most often made is that the statement should be taken as "One has faith and another has actions" with the stinging response by James that the two can't be divided, but must remain together. While any interpreter must avoid dogmatism, the suggestion by David Edgar should be seriously considered.[158] He argues that σὺ πίστιν ἔχεις is a question by itself, expressing doubts about the author's own faith, just as the author had done in referring to his deedless faith as "dead." James then responds, "I also have actions. Show me your faith without actions and I will show you my faith by my actions." This actually fits the context well, and is more satisfying than other forced interpretations. The doubled κἀγὼ initiating the third and fifth clauses thus adds a rhetorical intensity to James' reply. That κἀγὼ can begin a sentence is evidenced a number of times elsewhere in Greek literature.[159]

When James cites an adaptation of the Shema of Deut. 6 he is on very Jewish ground. The article before "God" (ὁ θεός) conforms to the prevailing form of Jewish orthodoxy. The biting sarcasm of his response to the confession, καλῶς ποιεῖς, echoes an earlier statement in 2:8. Each of these is a response to the readers' incomplete obedience to the two statements that comprise Jesus' summation of the law, i.e., love to others and to God (see Matt. 22:37-39). By not favoring those favored by God (2:5), they fail to demonstrate the whole-hearted devotion to God demanded by the very Shema they claim to affirm (Deut. 6:6-8). "The intention of the allusion is not so much to point out its inadequacy by itself, as to draw attention to its full consequences."[160] So much attention has been given to the shuddering of the demons (see

---

[158] D.H. Edgar, *Has God Not Chosen the Poor?* (Sheffield: Sheffield Academic Press, 2001), 170-71. Edgar cites an article by H. Nietzel, "Eine alte crux interpretum im Jakobusbrief 2.18," ZNW 73 (1982): 286-93.

[159] Nietzel, 290-91.

[160] Edgar, 171-72.

Mark 1:24) that it has drawn proper attention away from the powerful sarcasm of this passage. Furthermore, the links with the Jesus tradition again should not be missed. While intertextual links to Lev. 19 also permeate this passage, it is Jesus' use of that material that provides the meaning and application that James employs.

Paragraph 15 (James 2:20-26)

Θέλεις δὲ γνῶναι, ὦ ἄνθρωπε κενέ, ὅτι ἡ πίστις χωρὶς τῶν ἔργων ἀργή ἐστιν; Ἀβραὰμ ὁ πατὴρ ἡμῶν οὐκ ἐξ ἔργων ἐδικαιώθη ἀνενέγκας Ἰσαὰκ τὸν υἱὸν αὐτοῦ ἐπὶ τὸ θυσιαστήριον; βλέπεις ὅτι ἡ πίστις συνήργει τοῖς ἔργοις αὐτοῦ καὶ ἐκ τῶν ἔργων ἡ πίστις ἐτελειώθη, καὶ ἐπληρώθη ἡ γραφὴ ἡ λέγουσα· ἐπίστευσεν δὲ Ἀβραὰμ τῷ θεῷ, καὶ ἐλογίσθη αὐτῷ εἰς δικαιοσύνην καὶ φίλος θεοῦ ἐκλήθη. ὁρᾶτε ὅτι ἐξ ἔργων δικαιοῦται ἄνθρωπος καὶ οὐκ ἐκ πίστεως μόνον. ὁμοίως δὲ καὶ Ῥαὰβ ἡ πόρνη οὐκ ἐξ ἔργων ἐδικαιώθη ὑποδεξαμένη τοὺς ἀγγέλους καὶ ἑτέρᾳ ὁδῷ ἐκβαλοῦσα; ὥσπερ γὰρ τὸ σῶμα χωρὶς πνεύματος νεκρόν ἐστιν, οὕτως καὶ ἡ πίστις χωρὶς ἔργων νεκρά ἐστιν.	Do you want to be shown, O foolish person, that the faith that is not accompanied by actions is barren? Was not Abraham our father justified by actions when he offered up his son Isaac on the altar? You see that faith was active along with his actions, and faith was completed by his actions. In this way the Scripture was fulfilled that says, "Abraham believed God, and it was counted to him as righteousness"—and he was called "friend of God." You see that a person is justified by actions and not by faith alone. And in the same way was not also Rahab the prostitute justified by actions when she received the scouts and sent them out by another way? For just as the body apart from the spirit is dead, so also the faith not accompanied by actions is dead.

The harsh address to the author's debate opponent (ὦ ἄνθρωπε κενέ) connects this passage to the previous one. The way that the question is posed, however, actually serves as an introduction to his final argument—two examples from Israel's past that illustrate that a person is justified not by faith that is alone but by faith that is accompanied by actions (2:24). Thus the passive translation ("wish to be shown") of the active infinitive γνῶναι is justified on rhetorical grounds. The following examples are persuasive to a person willing (Θέλεις) to accept them.

2:20

P	cj	C	add
Θέλεις	δὲ	γνῶναι	ὦ ἄνθρωπε κενέ

cj	S	C	P
ὅτι	ἡ πίστις χωρὶς τῶν ἔργων	ἀργή	ἐστιν

2:21

S	A	P
Ἀβραὰμ ὁ πατὴρ ἡμῶν	οὐκ ἐξ ἔργων	ἐδικαιώθη

A		
P	C	A
ἀνενέγκας	Ἰσαὰκ τὸν υἱὸν αὐτοῦ	ἐπὶ τὸ θυσιαστήριον

2:22

P
βλέπεις

cj	S	P	A
ὅτι	ἡ πίστις	συνήργει	τοῖς ἔργοις αὐτου

cj	A	S	P
καὶ	ἐκ τῶν ἔργων	ἡ πίστις	ἐτελειώθη

2:23

cj	P	S
καὶ	ἐπληρώθη	ἡ γραφὴ ἡ λέγουσα

P	cj	S	C
ἐπίστευσεν	δὲ	Ἀβραὰμ	τῷ θεῷ

cj	P	C	A
καὶ	ἐλογίσθη	αὐτῷ	εἰς δικαιοσύνην

cj	C	P
καὶ	φίλος θεοῦ	ἐκλήθη

2:24

P
ὁρᾶτε

cj	A	P	S
ὅτι	ἐξ ἔργων	δικαιοῦται	ἄνθρωπος

cj	A	A	A
καὶ	οὐκ	ἐκ πίστεως	μόνον

2:25

A	cj	cj	S	A	P
ὁμοίως	δὲ	καὶ	Ραὰβ ἡ πόρνη	οὐκ ἐξ ἔργων	ἐδικαιώθη

A		
P	**C**	
ὑποδεξαμένη	τοὺς ἀγγέλους	
cj	**A**	**P**
καὶ	ἑτέρα ὁδῷ	ἐκβαλοῦσα

2:26

cj	cj	S	C	P
ὥσπερ	γὰρ	τὸ σῶμα χωρὶς πνεύματος	νεκρόν	ἐστιν

A	cj	S	C	P
οὕτως	καὶ	ἡ πίστις χωρὶς ἔργων	νεκρά	ἐστιν

James repeats his topic statement for the second of what will be three times (17, 20, 26). In this second occurrence, however, the adjective describing the deficient faith is ἀργή , not νεκρά. It is not surprising, therefore, that some later scribes attempted to bring this into agreement with 2:17 and 2:26. The entire Byzantine family does so with the reading νεκρά, but it is also joined by Sinaiticus and Alexandrinus. Metzger defends the UBS/NA ἀργη reading, which "not only is strongly supported by B C 322 323 945 1739 it vg cop arm, but may involve a subtle play on words (ἔργων ἀργή [α + εργη])."[161] I suggest another reason for the change to ἀργή at exactly this point. It has to do with the semantic meaning conveyed by the word in the author's overall rhetorical strategy. The word is most often translated by "indolent," "unemployed," "useless." "It is also used in the sense of 'incapable of action or of live operation'."[162] In 2 Pet. 1:8 it is parallel to ἄκαρπος ("unfruitful"). With this in mind, it is striking to see that the next person mentioned in the argument is Abraham (2:21-24). Who better could serve as an example of a person who, although once "unfruitful" and "barren," produced an unexpected heir who then becomes part of the text illustrating that faith accompanied by actions is not "barren"?[163]

To "show" (2:20) his opponent evidence for a faith accompanied by actions, James offers two exemplars from Israelite history. The parallel way in which he structures the action of each exemplar can be seen in the OpenText analysis of 2:21 and 2:25 above. In each sentence a rhetorical question expecting a positive answer with the subject's name (Abraham, Rahab) is followed by a one word description (father, prostitute), with the adjunct "by works" concluding each initial primary clause. Each secondary clause then opens with a temporal participle (ἀνενέγκας, ὑποδεξαμένη), followed by their complements/direct objects ("Isaac" and "the scouts") and the appropriate adjuncts ("on the altar" and "another way"). This parallel construction is more than an attractive ornament. It focuses the reader's attention on the specific action that demonstrates the exemplar's faith. This is important because it is attractive to focus on Abraham's hospitality (so celebrated in Rabbinic tradition) as a parallel to Rahab's hospitality. It would have been easy for James to do just that but he chose to focus on the

---

[161] Metzger, 610.

[162] *TDNT*, ed. Gerhard Kittel, vol. 1 "ἀργός" (Grand Rapids: Eerdmans, 1964), 452.

[163] In keeping with the insights of speech-act theory, this is an illustration of what an author intends to do with his words (the illocution) rather than just the surface meaning of the word (the locution).

supreme action by which Abraham evidenced his faith—the Akedah of Isaac.[164] While it is possible that the plural ἔργων may include his earlier hospitality (as it does with Rahab), it more likely refers to all of Abraham's actions that culminated in the dramatic scene on one of the hills of Moriah (see Gen. 21:1; 1 Mac. 2:52; Sirach 44:19-21; Heb. 11:17-19).

Why does James choose these two as his exemplars of faith in action? Perhaps it was because each came from a "Gentile" background and each became ideal prototypes of converts. Perhaps it was because each was celebrated in Jewish tradition for their hospitality. Perhaps it was because each was from an opposite end of the moral spectrum, thus illustrating the need for faith and actions for both types of readers. Perhaps James himself provides the answer by alerting us earlier in the passage to the importance of including a male and female when he departs from his use of the generic "brothers" to condemn the one who neglects either "a brother or a sister" who is in need (2:15).

Verses 22 and 23 further describe the undivided character of Abraham's faith and actions. Three semantically related verbs convey the inseparable nature of the two. In 2:22 the active verb συνήργει declares that Abraham's faith and actions "were working together." The imperfect aspect describes that process as taking place throughout Abraham's experience from the time he believed God in Genesis 15 (2:23) until the Akedah in chapter 22. The passive verb, ἐτελειώθη ("was completed"), describes his faith as completed by the appropriate action(s).[165] In other words faith is incomplete if it is not accompanied by actions, another example of James' stress on wholeness. In 2:23 Abraham's believing God (Gen. 15:6) was "fulfilled" (ἐπληρώθη) in the Akedah. The English word "fulfill" often conveys the idea of prophecy and fulfillment, yet Gen. 15:6 is a past tense indicative statement, not a future prophetic announcement. But the verb πληρόω here means "give true or full meaning," as it also does in Matt. 5:17 and Gal. 5:14.[166] As was mentioned, this description of "complete" faith in 2:22, 23 is also quite compatible with James' emphasis throughout his letter on a "whole" or "undivided" life. That faith can exist without the appropriate accompanying actions is so inconceivable to James that he calls his opponent something akin to our modern

---

[164] *Akedah* is the Hebrew term for "binding," referred to in Gen. 22:9. In Jewish tradition, it has become the title by which to refer to the entire incident.

[165] Note also the chiastic rhetorical flourish in 2:22: faith-works-works-faith.

[166] Louw and Nida, 405.

[167] Louw and Nida give the meaning of κενέ ηερε as "foolish" or "stupid," 388.

"blockhead" (ἄνθρωπε κενέ) for suggesting that they can be separate.[167]

James concludes his discussion of Abraham by adding the climactic, "he was called 'friend of God' " (φίλος θεοῦ ἐκλήθη). The verb suggests that someone called Abraham by this title. In the two times that Abraham was referred to by a similar name in canonical literature, however, the substantive in the Hebrew and its LXX translation has the idea of "loved one," and the Greek word is not φίλος (Isa. 41:8; 2 Chron. 20:7) and τηςγαπημενῳ in 2 Chron. 20:7). It seems that James is not directly referring to either the Isaiah or Chronicles reference, but to the Jewish literary tradition. In Second Temple Jewish literature there are a number of places where Abraham is called God's friend by the word φίλος.[168]

Before introducing his second exemplar, James anticipates his conclusion by appealing to his interlocutor, "You see (ὁρᾶτε) that a person (ἄνθρωπος) is considered righteous (note the present δικαιοῦται) not by faith alone" (2:24). From what he has already written, James must be referring to the type of "faith" that consists only in verbal affirmation of God's unity (see 2:19), but is not accompanied by actions appropriate to the correct kind of faith. In other words we know that Abraham's having faith in God in Gen. 15:6 was fruitful and alive because he demonstrated it to be so by the things that he did later.

With the second δὲ in this paragraph (see 2:20), James introduces another exemplar of faith and actions—Rahab, the prostitute (2:25). James resists the attempts by later Jewish writers to blunt the nature of Rahab's profession (Josephus referred to her as an "innkeeper," Ant. 5, 8). This prostitute received "the scouts" and sent them out another way. This translation of τοὺς ἀγγέλους has been chosen because it is hard to see how they were "messengers." James does not employ the LXX verb in Joshua (κατασκοπέω) nor the noun in Hebrews 11:31 (κατασκοπός). I suggest that he consciously chose this word in reflection on Abraham's hospitality to the ἄγγελοι (see Gen. 19:1). As Abraham showed acts of kindness to those ἄγγελοι that came to him, so Rahab showed the same actions to the ἄγγελοι who came to her. Although no mention is made of Rahab's faith, readers would know about her faith from her confession in Josh. 2: 9-13. James emphasizes that no matter what she said, she acted out her faith by sending out the

---

[168] See the extensive excursus on Abraham in Dibelius, 168-74.

scouts "by another way" (ἑτέρᾳ ὁδῷ).

The paragraph ends in the familiar way our author rounds off his argument—with an aphorism expressed in a simile. "For just as (ὥσπερ) the body without a spirit is dead, so (οὕτως) also the faith that is not accompanied by actions is dead." Here James returns to his main point stated in 2:17 with his wording altered slightly from ἀργή in 2:20 to νεκρά here.

Readers may notice that no mention has been made in this entire discussion about the controversy about James's and Paul's differing emphases on justification. That absence has been deliberate. I wanted to make an effort to demonstrate that the argument of James makes perfect sense by itself without any reference to Paul. Too often James has been read only as a foil to Pauline theology. I argue that while James is not anti-Pauline, he should be viewed as ante-Pauline. This is not only because I see him writing prior to Galatians and Romans, but because I believe that James and Paul are using the same words in different senses. The commentaries treat this controversial issue in depth and I refer readers especially to the excellent treatments by Johnson and Bauckham. In addition to the above, however, I would offer the view that Paul's focus is on the "works of the law" while James' focus is on works of love and kindness. Paul also emphasizes a believing person's entrance into justification by faith while James emphasizes what a valid faith looks like. Any definition of the great Reformation distinctive "sola fide" should always be nuanced in light of James 2:24. According to Paul, New Testament faith is never absolutely alone since it is always accompanied by hope and love (1 Cor. 13:13). In one of the two books where Paul teaches justification by faith "alone," he offers the following balanced statement, "For in Christ Jesus neither circumcision nor uncircumcision counts for anything, but only faith (πίστις) working (ἐνεργουμένη) through love" (Gal. 5:6). To that statement I am sure that James would have uttered a hearty "Amen."

Chapter 3

ANALYSIS OF JAMES THREE

16. Paragraph 16 (James 3:1-12)

Μὴ πολλοὶ διδάσκαλοι γίνεσθε, ἀδελφοί μου, εἰδότες ὅτι μεῖζον κρίμα λημψόμεθα. πολλὰ γὰρ πταίομεν ἅπαντες. εἴ τις ἐν λόγῳ οὐ πταίει, οὗτος τέλειος ἀνὴρ δυνατὸς χαλιναγ— ωγῆσαι καὶ ὅλον τὸ σῶμα. Ἴδε τῶν ἵππων τοὺς χαλινοὺς εἰς τὰ στόματα βάλλομεν εἰς τὸ πείθεσθαι αὐτοὺς ἡμῖν, καὶ ὅλον τὸ σῶμα αὐτῶν μετάγομεν. ἰδοὺ καὶ τὰ πλοῖα τηλικαῦτα ὄντα καὶ ὑπὸ ἀνέμων σκληρῶν ἐλαυνόμενα, μετάγεται ὑπὸ ἐλαχίστου πηδαλίου ὅπου ἡ ὁρμὴ τοῦ εὐθύνοντος βούλεται. οὕτως καὶ ἡ γλῶσσα μικρὸν μέλος ἐστὶν καὶ μεγάλα αὐχεῖ. ἰδοὺ ἡλίκον πῦρ ἡλίκην ὕλην ἀνάπτει· καὶ ἡ γλῶσσα πῦρ· ὁ κόσμος τῆς ἀδικίας ἡ γλῶσσα καθίσταται ἐν τοῖς μέλεσιν ἡμῶν, ἡ σπιλοῦσα ὅλον τὸ σῶμα καὶ φλογίζουσα τὸν τροχὸν τῆς γενέσεως καὶ φλογι— ζομένη ὑπὸ τῆς γεέννης. πᾶσα γὰρ φύσις θηρίων τε καὶ πετεινῶν, ἑρπετῶν τε καὶ ἐναλίων δαμάζεται καὶ δεδάμασ— ται τῇ φύσει τῇ ἀνθρωπίνῃ, τὴν δὲ γλῶσσαν οὐδεὶς δαμάσαι δύναται ἀνθρώπων, ἀκατάστατον κακόν, μεστὴ ἰοῦ θανατηφόρου. ἐν αὐτῇ εὐλογοῦμεν τὸν κύριον καὶ πατέρα καὶ ἐν αὐτῇ

3 [1]Not many of you should become teachers, my brothers, for you know that we who teach will receive a stricter judgment. [2]For we all stumble in many ways. If anyone does not stumble in what he says, he is a perfect man, able also to bridle his whole body. [3]Look! We put bridles into the mouths of horses so that they obey us and we guide their whole bodies. [4]Look! The ships also, though they are so large and are driven by strong winds, are guided by a very small rudder wherever the will of the pilot directs. [5a]So also the tongue is a small member, and yet it boasts of great things. [5b]Look! Such a small fire sets ablaze such a great forest! [6]And the tongue is a fire. The tongue is set as the unrighteous world among our members, staining the whole body, setting on fire the entire course of life, and is itself set on fire by hell. [7]For every kind of beast and bird, of reptile and sea creature, can be tamed and has been tamed by mankind, [8]but no human being can tame the tongue. It is a restless evil, full of deadly poison. [9]With it we bless our Lord and Father, and with it we curse people who are made in the likeness of God.

καταρώμεθα τοὺς ἀνθρώπους τοὺς καθ ὁμοίωσιν θεοῦ γεγονότας, ἐκ τοῦ αὐτοῦ στόματος ἐξέρχεται εὐλογία καὶ κατάρα. οὐ χρή, ἀδελφοί μου, ταῦτα οὕτως γίνεσθαι. μήτι ἡ πηγὴ ἐκ τῆς αὐτῆς ὀπῆς βρύει τὸ γλυκὺ καὶ τὸ πικρόν; μὴ δύναται, ἀδελφοί μου, συκῆ ἐλαίας ποιῆσαι ἢ ἄμπελος σῦκα; οὔτε ἁλυκὸν γλυκὺ ποιῆσαι ὕδωρ.	[10]From the same mouth come blessing and cursing. My brothers, these things ought not to be so. [11]Does a spring pour forth from the same opening both fresh and salt water? [12]Can a fig tree, my brothers, bear olives, or a grapevine produce figs? Neither can a salt pond yield fresh water.

Martin Dibelius' view that James lacks any unified structure is cited by every commentator on the book. It is sometimes overlooked that Dibelius did recognize that there were three consecutive sections of James that were "treatises" on three different subjects—2:1-13 on the evils of favoritism; 2:14-26 on the inseparability of faith and works; and 3:1-12 on the effects of the tongue. While Dibelius did view 3:1-12 as only an assemblage of "school materials" whose clauses often crash into each other and have no connection with their context, it does comprise a discrete section with its own integrity.[169] Most agree that the passage is a paragraph on its own, being introduced by the familiar ἀδελφοί μου plus the imperative Μὴ . . . γίνεσθε and then concluding by a series of agricultural analogies (3:11, 12).

The verbal links of our passage with earlier and later ideas should not be overlooked. The most obvious is the verbal connection with 1:27, where reference is made to "not bridling" (μὴ χαλιναγωγῶν) one's tongue, while 3:2 states that the person who controls his tongue "is able also to bridle (χαλιναγωγῆσαι) the entire body." James's discussion of "speech ethics" in 3:1-12 has other deep roots in chapter one. Some commentators have seen the three asyndetic imperatives of 1:19: "everyone should be swift to hear, slow to speak, slow to wrath" as a table of contents for the rest of the book with "slow to speak" being elaborated in 3:1-18.[170] James further

---

[169] Dibelius, 182.

[170] The "swift to hear" of 1:19 is then elaborated in 2:1-13 and the "slow to wrath" is expanded in 4:1-5:6. There is something to commend this approach, but this writer believes that this view does not account for other subjects discussed in chapters 2-5 and does not explain the role of 5:7-20. It is better to see the three commands of 1:19 as the topics that are commented on in their following co-text, (1:20-27). Then 1:26, 27 serves as a bridge to the following chapters where the three issues of speech ethics (ch. 3), care for the poor (ch. 2) and the dangers of world-friendship (ch. 4) are expanded. See the earlier comments on 1:19-27.

continues his emphasis on speech ethics with his later warnings not to speak against a brother (4:11); not to speak presumptively about the future (4:13); and not to swear (5:12).

Another helpful approach to these three "treatises" is found in a socially informed understanding of the ancient Mediterranean context of James. Bruce Malina points out that in the first century the nature of a person was viewed as comprising three zones, each related to parts of the body. First was the "zone of emotion-fused thought" (the activities of the eyes and heart). Second was the "zone of self-expressive speech" (the activities of the mouth and ears). Third was the "zone of purposeful action" (the activities of the hands and feet). "The idea is that all human activities, states, and behaviors can be and are chunked in terms of these three zones. When all three zones are explicitly mentioned, then the speaker or writer is alluding to a total and complete human experience."[171] While Malina does not apply this specifically to James, this paradigm is quite useful in explaining how James seeks to regulate all areas of his readers' lives. In 2:1-13 he describes their emotion-fused thought (with a discriminatory attitude). In 3:1-12 he describes their self-expressive speech (with a destructive tongue). In 2:14-26 he describes their lack of purposeful interaction (by not extending a helping hand). In keeping with his emphasis on wholeness as opposed to doubleness (related clearly in the following passage, 3:13-18—the peak of the book), James thus describes a complete person as one who is singly focused and whole in all the zones of their personality.

The sub-sectional analysis of 3:1-12 is as follows. In 3:1, 2 a new topic is introduced—the great responsibility of teachers in the assemblies of Jesus-believers in the Diaspora. This is due to a teacher's obvious use of the tongue to teach. This topic is then developed by first illustrating the powerful and positive effect of such a small member of the human body (3:3-5a). Then the negative power of the tongue—large in relation to its small size—is illustrated in 3:5b-12. In each of these two sections, colorful rhetorical figures are employed from both the animate and inanimate natural worlds. In addition to drawing many colorful analogies from common life, James also employs a rich intertexture, drawing from both the Jewish wisdom literature and also from the sayings of Jesus, adapted for his own purposes. The following analysis will illustrate how he powerfully argues his point that not many should become teachers.

---

[171] Malina, 70. See 68-75 for his discussion and application of these "three zones of human behavior."

Clause Analysis of 3:1, 2

3:1

A	S	C	P	add	A			
Μὴ	πολλοὶ	διδάσκαλοι	γίνεσθε	ἀδελφοί μου	**P** εἰδότες			
					cj ὅτι	**C** μεῖζον κρίμα	**P** λημψόμεθα	

3:2

A	cj	P	S
πολλὰ	γὰρ	πταίομεν	ἅπαντες.

cj	S	A	A	P
εἰ	τις	ἐν λόγῳ	οὐ	πταίει,

S	C		
οὗτος	τέλειος ἀνὴρ δυνατὸς		
	P χαλιναγωγῆσαι	**cj** καὶ	**C** ὅλον τὸ σῶμα.

The opening sentence in 3:1 is a complex clause employing another of his many imperatives (γίνεσθε) collocated with the familiar nominative of direct address (ἀδελφοί μου). The imperative with μὴ appears in only seven of the nearly sixty imperatives in the book. The actions warned against in this way are being deceived (1:16), showing partiality (2:1), are boasting and lying (3:14), slandering (4:11), complaining (5:9), and swearing an oath (5:12). James' choice of the present imperative of γίνομαι stresses the dynamic action of "becoming" teachers, rather than the stative force that would be stressed by the verb εἰμί. The use of πολλοὶ recognizes that there must be teachers in the assemblies, but that this should not be a role that many should aspire to because of the great responsibility attached to it. Teachers were prominent in the Jewish-Christian assemblies (Heb. 5:12; Acts 13:1) and were ranked just below apostles and prophets by Paul (1 Cor. 12:28; Eph. 4:11). They were associated with the prophets but higher than the ἐπίσκοποι and διάκονοι in the *Didache* (13:2; 15:1, 2). A scene to which James refers is preserved in Acts 13:1 where five prophets and teachers are mentioned. It is possible that the "Christians" at Antioch was among the first to hear James' warning read out to them in the presence of these teachers!

A secondary clause introduced by εἰδότες provides the reason why few should pursue the role of teacher, namely that teachers will be examined more strictly due to the seriousness of their role. James elsewhere uses a causal participle only in 1:3 where he also appeals to his readers' knowledge: "because you know (γινώσκοντες) that the testing of your faith produces endurance."[172] Our author switches, for the first time, to a first person plural verb (λημψόμεθα). This usage is characteristic of this paragraph, being repeated in vss. 2, 3 (twice), and 9 (twice). James uses this first person plural verb elsewhere only in 5:11 and 17. This is more than just a lapse into an "editorial we," and indicates a self-designation. James considers himself as a "teacher."

In the following paragraph, characteristics of a "sage" (σοφὸς) are described. In ancient Israel a teacher (*rabbi*) and a sage (*chokham*) were terms for the same person. Thus this chapter, while maintaining an application in a general sense to all believers, has a particular application to teachers and sages—one of whom was James himself. If we are correct in viewing his self-designation of δοῦλος (1:1) as describing the noble and honored role of one of Israel's prophets (see the comments there), then his identity as a prophet/teacher/sage seems confirmed. But this is only implied because his readers are the ones in focus here. Few of them should become teachers because "we who teach will receive a stricter judgment" (κρίμα). The sense of the expression is not that the teachers' punishment will be more severe but that they will be more strictly examined due to the effect, both for good and bad, which their speech can produce. The eschatological motivation for this type of paranesis was sounded also in 1:12 where the faithful one will receive (note also the verb λήμψεται) the crown of life and in 5:7, 8 where the patient believer like the patient farmer receives (note also the verb λάβῃ) the fruit of his labor. Adapting another Jesus *logion* at this point appears almost to be certain. This can be in a general sense from the saying about the inconsistency between saying and doing in a judgment

---

[172] A fine distinction in "knowing" between the verbs γινώσκω and οἶδα, maintained by some older commentators, does not seem justified. See Mayor, 34.

context (Matt. 7:15 ff.). But more specifically, this echoes Jesus' warning about the teaching of the scribes (Israel's teachers!) in Mark 12:38-40 and Luke 20:45-47. Note particularly the verbal similarity: οὗτοι λήμψονται περισσότερον κρίμα (Mark 12:40 and Luke 20:47).[173]

This subsection (vss. 1, 2) introducing the larger paragraph (vss. 1-12), then adds two clauses. The first is a primary clause introduced by the post-positive γάρ that serves as a reason for his warning in the opening clause. Our author often uses the same pattern of argumentation. First, he issues a command, then he offers an example of the transgression of the command, then he supports his point by further argument, and he finally concludes with an aphorism to round off his point. This can be seen in the previous chapter (2:1-13) where he issues the command (2:1), introduces an example (2:2-4, introduced by γάρ), then offers further support for his point (2:5-12), and closes with an aphorism (2:13). In this paragraph, he issues a command (3:1), provides a reason (3:2), offers extended support by analogies (3:3-11), and concludes with an aphorism (3:12).

The neuter plural πολλά is an adverbial accusative, signified by its classification in the OpenText analysis as an "Adjunct," not as a "Complement," to the main verb. However, "we all stumble *in many ways*" is not a simple restatement of the theological observation in Rom. 3:23. The use of the first person plural here signifies a realistic personal anthropology on our author's part. This does not disqualify him from being a teacher, but it alerts the readers to how great is the challenge for those who aspire to be teachers. Many commentators seek to root this statement in the Hellenistic moral treatises where the verb πταίω certainly does appear. However, we do not need to go outside the traditional Jewish wisdom literature to find statements which James could echo in his use of the verb twice in this verse. In those wisdom writings there are metaphorical uses of the verb in relation to speech in *Test Job* 38:1 and similar uses in *Deut.* 7:25 and *Sirach* 2:8. However, even in addition to similar ideas found in the many Jesus *logia* about speech (e.g., Matt. 12:37), James may have another nearer reason for using this word. He already has the verb close at hand by using it in 2:10: "For whoever observes the whole law but stumbles (πταίσῃ) at one point has become accountable for all of it." Furthermore, since our author soon illustrates his point about the tongue with an analogy of a horse (to keep it from

---

[173] The same expression in Matt. 23:14 apparently indicates a later Byzantine effort to bring Matthew into closer agreement with Mark and Luke.

stumbling), his use of this verb has reasons based in the context rather than in its use in non-Jewish material.

This section concludes with a first class conditional clause that functions both anaphorically in its use of the verb χαλιναγωγῆσαι (see 1:26) and cataphorically to point to the literal use of the noun χαλινοὺς in the next verse. The statement also recalls the important word τέλειος (see 1:4) as embodying the goal of every believer. The primary clause functioning as the apodosis of the conditional clause exhibits a couple of unique Jamesian linguistic features. The apodosis beginning with the unusual demonstrative pronoun οὗτος is characteristic of our author's style, as he uses the word in the same way in 1:23 and uses it following a participle in 1:25. This "unnecessary" use of the demonstrative is the author's way of emphasizing the prominence of the role that this "perfect man" fulfills. Another stylistic characteristic is the asyndeton in the description of the perfect man, "able also to bridle the entire body" (δυνατὸς χαλιναγωγῆσαι καὶ ὅλον τὸ σῶμα). No conjunction or relative pronoun, which might be expected, is present. One final example of his style is the expression "perfect man," using the word ἀνήρ. This word usually refers to a "male" rather than the more generic ἄνθρωπος. He uses ἀνήρ six times and ἄνθρωπος seven times. Is this another example of stylistic variation, or is there a pattern that emerges? Mayor addresses this question with an important observation.

> St. James commonly uses ἀνήρ with some characteristic word, as μακάριος i.12, κατανοῶν i.23, χρυσοδακτύλιος ii.2, τέλειος iii.2, keeping ἄνθρωπος for more general expressions, ἐκεῖνος, πᾶς, οὐδείς, etc. This agrees fairly with the use in the LXX and Gospels: in the other epistles ἀνήρ is almost exclusively used in opposition to γυνή.[174]

This observation keeps one from making unwarranted conclusions about the maleness of these expressions and also points up the necessity of considering an author's individual style to avoid making universal statements about the semantics of New Testament Greek.

The author's comment about the mature man's being able to "bridle the whole body" prepares the reader for his colorful analogies in the following verses. This expression is repeated in 3:3 and 3:6. The verb "to bridle" leads to an analogy with a horse and its "bridle."

---

[174] Mayor, 42.

Clause Analysis of 3:3-5

3:3

P
ἴδε

A	P	A		
τῶν ἵππων	βάλλομεν	**P**	**A**	**C**
C		εἰς τὸ πείθεσθαι	αὐτοὺς	ἡμῖν
τοὺς χαλινοὺς				
εἰς τὰ στόματα				

cj	C	P
καὶ	ὅλον τὸ σῶμα αὐτῶν	μετάγομεν.

3:4

P
ἰδοὺ

cj	S	A		P	A
καὶ	τὰ πλοῖα	**C**	**P**	μετάγεται	ὑπὸ ἐλαχίστου πηδαλίου
		τηλικαῦτα	ὄντα		
		cj	**A**	**P**	
		καὶ	ὑπὸ ἀνέμων σκληρῶν	ἐλαυνόμενα	

cj	S	P
ὅπου	ἡ ὁρμὴ τοῦ εὐθύνοντος	βούλεται

3:5

A	cj	S	C	P
οὕτως	καὶ	ἡ γλῶσσα	μικρὸν μέλος	ἐστὶν

cj	C	P
καὶ	μεγάλα	αὐχεῖ.

P
ἰδοὺ

S	C	P
ἡλίκον πῦρ	ἡλίκην ὕλην	ἀνάπτει·

The clause display adapted from OpenText.org illustrates how this sub-paragraph consists of nine crisp primary clauses with three embedded infinitive (1) and participle (2) clauses in 3:3,4. A secondary relative clause concludes verse 4.

I have altered the way in which OpenText displays verse 3, because I have chosen not to follow the critical NA27/UBS text at this point. I prefer the reading ἴδε instead of εἰ δὲ, which changes the verse from a conditional clause to two primary clauses, the first of which is the imperative command, "look," or as it has traditionally been translated "behold." Thus the protasis and apodosis in the conditional sentence becomes "Look! We put bridles into the mouths of horses so that they obey us and we guide their whole bodies." This is the sense of the AV, although the Textus Receptus follows a few late Byzantine manuscripts which have the clearly assimilating ἰδοὺ, instead of the ἴδε found in C, P, the Byzantine family and a few early versions. The εἰ δὲ reading has support among manuscript representatives of the Alexandrian and Western families, although this matter is complicated by the unique ΕΙΔΕ ΓΑΡ in Sinaiticus. The entire issue is further complicated by the recognized danger of itacism among the scribes. It is well known that εἰ and ι were pronounced identically in ancient times, even as they are today in Modern Greek (ee). This means that scribes could change either an εἰ to an ι or vice versa! Because of the diversity of manuscript evidence and the possibility of itacism, the UBS committee gave a {C} rating to εἰ δὲ in their text. This was because some of the committee felt εἰ δὲ was the more difficult reading—a fact that we will discuss later. Metzger wisely comments, "The editor must choose the reading that, in his judgment, is most appropriate in the context."[175]

---

[175] Metzger, 611.

Although I am reticent to dissent from the critical text, I have chosen the ἴδε because of the following internal reasons. 1) In every other case in which the conditional εἰ δὲ appears in James, the δὲ is clearly adversative to what had just been stated (1:5; 2:9, 11; 3:14; 4:11). That is not the case if there is a conditional sentence beginning 3:3. 2) If 3:3 is a conditional sentence, the καὶ beginning the proposed apodosis seems out of place. While translators recognize this by rendering it "also," it is not the normal role of an apodosis to add information to the protasis but to show the result of fulfilling the hypothetical protasis. 3) Since our author uses the Aorist Middle Imperative of ὁράω (ἰδού) to call attention to the ship/rudder in 3:4 and the fire/forest in 3:5a, the parallelism with using the Aorist Active Imperative of ὁράω (ἴδε) in 3:3 is evident. I have tried to display that parallelism by bolding the parallel imperatives in my clausal display above. 4) The post-positive καὶ in 3:4 seems to point back to the preceding illustration in a way that supports the idea that James is calling attention to a previous command to "look" at something in natural life. 5) While Metzger writes that a majority of the UBS committee preferred εἰ δὲ as the more difficult reading,[176] couldn't the same thing be said about ἴδε, since it breaks the exact parallelism with the ἰδού in verse 4 and 5? If someone objects that it would be odd for James to mix ἴδε and ἰδου in such a close context, I call attention to the following places where the two imperatives are utilized in close context: Eccl. 2:1 (LXX); Mark 3:32, 34; Matt. 25:6, 20, 22, 25; John 16:29, 32; Gal. 1:20; 5:2.

Mayor effectively defends the ἴδε reading. He calls attention to how James also interchanges αἰτεῖτε and αἰτεῖσθε in 4:3, the same type of shift between active and middle voices in the same verse. He even offers a suggestion about the difference between the voices in 3:3,4, i.e., that the middle voice calls for the subject to become even more involved in the action. "Look at the details of the ship and its rudder."[177] Whether or not Mayor's analysis of the reasons for the variation in voice is valid, the arguments for the priority of the ἴδε seem compelling to adopt it with more than the expected degree of caution in a disputed reading.

While textual issues deal mainly with the external evidence of manuscript age and quality, the added internal evidence of context and even discourse considerations, such as this example, ought to be given due consideration. In my opinion, the function of the discourse

---

[176] Metzger, 611.
[177] Mayor, 418-420.

markers ἴδε and ἰδου to call attention to the three examples from natural life—the horse/bridle, the ship/rudder and the fire/forest—powerfully combine to make an effective rhetorical argument for the power of the tongue, both for good and for evil. Therefore, he wants to ask us to "look" at them with special attention!

Two more issues call for a brief mention. First, I have chosen the translation "bridles" rather than "bits" for the accusative noun χαλινοὺς in 3:4. This translation brings out more clearly the verbal connection with the verb χαλιναγωγῆσαι in 3:2 (also in 1:27), which was our author's reason for choosing the bridle example in the first place. The bit actually does not control the horse, since the bit is part of the bridle controlled by the rider. The usage of the verb and noun support the translation "bridle."[178] Secondly, we should be careful not to think that it is the bridle and the rudder that control the horse and the ship. It is actually the rider (alluded to in the purpose clause of 3:3: εἰς τὸ πείθεσθαι αὐτοὺς ἡμῖν) and the pilot of the ship (clearly mentioned in the relative clause of 3:4: ὅπου ἡ ὁρμὴ τοῦ εὐθύνοντος βούλεται). This is consistent with James's recognition that the driving forces behind one's actions are the inward hearts and motives (1:14, 15; 2:2:18; 3:13-17; 4:1, 2). Our actions are simply the outward manifestations that emerge from within. The tongue is controlled by the heart.

Because of the more detailed attention given to structural issues, only a brief treatment will be made of some discourse and linguistic features in the remainder of this paragraph, 3:6-12. The clausal display will, however, help to provide a response to the famous remark of Dibelius on this passage describing the power of the tongue. He clearly summarizes the "treatise" as follows.

> The small member has a great effect (images of the horse and the ship), the small tongue does great damage (images of the fire and the beasts). To this is added the metaphors of the spring and the beasts in vv 9-12, with the moral, "The tongue ought not to have such effects."

But since the great commentator and form critic seemed to always find something to annoy him in our author's style, he quickly adds,

> But the neat arrangement which is indicated here does not quite obtain in the treatise. Instead we observe how the ideas bump against

---

[178] BDAG, 1076.

or even clash with one another—evidence that the author is transmitting school material.[179]

Due respect should always be directed to the two German "Martins" (the other was Martin Luther) whose views dominated the study of James for over four centuries. However, recognizing James' style—e.g., his fondness for asyndeton and his avoidance of secondary clauses and inferential particles—will keep us from criticizing his language. This is something that a linguist finds odd in any case. Our task is not to pronounce judgments on the rightness or wrongness of an author's language, but to analyze how that author utilizes the resources of the language to convey his message. When we do that with James, we can appreciate afresh his vivid and direct appeal to his hearers to choose an undivided life. Furthermore, by recovering his original text, we can sometimes soften the supposed bumps and clashes which Dibelius noticed.

Clausal Analysis of 3:6-8

3:6

cj	S	C
καὶ	ἡ γλῶσσα	πῦρ·

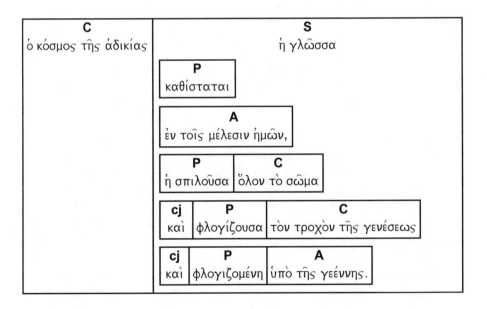

---

[179] Dibelius, 182.

3:7

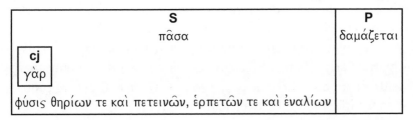

	S πᾶσα	P δαμάζεται
cj γὰρ		
φύσις θηρίων τε καὶ πετεινῶν, ἑρπετῶν τε καὶ ἐναλίων		

cj	P	A
καὶ	δεδάμασται	τῇ φύσει τῇ ἀνθρωπίνῃ,

3:8

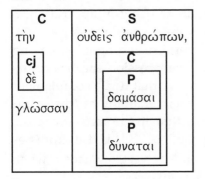

C τὴν	S οὐδεὶς ἀνθρώπων,
cj δὲ	**C**
γλῶσσαν	**P** δαμάσαι
	P δύναται

C
ἀκατάστατον κακόν, μεστὴ ἰοῦ θανατηφόρου.

The final clause of 3:5: ἰδοὺ ἡλίκον πῦρ ἡλίκην ὕλην ἀνάπτει· (Look! Such a small fire sets ablaze such a great forest!), while completing the triad of attention-getters (ἴδε in 3:3; ἰδου in 3:4), should begin 3:6 because it introduces the figure "fire" that is the subject of the verse. Thus, the clause has both an anaphoric and a cataphoric function in the paragraph. The double use of the adjective ἡλίκου/ἡλίκην to describe a small fire than can consume a large forest has befuddled beginning Greek students and has led commentators to find a word play of opposite meanings that can be found in other Greek literature.[180] However, I suggest that a better approach is to recognize that the word simply expresses alarm at the size

---

[180] See Dibelius for references to Antiphanes, Lucian, and Epictetus, 191.

of something ("such a, what a, how!") with the context supplying whether the size of the noun described is large or small, or, as in this case, both small and large! Its use in all of Greek literature seems to bear this out.[181] The word play would then be in the close combination of ἡλίκην and ὕλην, particularly when one recognizes that the words not only share rough breathers but also share the same sound. The η and υ were probably pronounced the same way in ancient times (i.e, "ee").

Only a few comments on linguistic features of the five consecutive primary clauses in 3:6-8 can be allowed. After affirming that the tongue is that fire to which he referred to metaphorically, James describes the awful power of that metaphor in the rest of the verse. Both the OpenText clausal analysis and the *Lexham Discourse Greek NT* view the noun-genitive expression ὁ κόσμος τῆς ἀδικίας as the complement of the following verb καθίσταται, rather than as being in apposition to the previous statement.[182] The *NET Bible* expresses well the sense of the expression: "The tongue represents the world of wrongdoing among the parts of our bodies." The fronting of the expression emphasizes its prominence in the clause—a further argument that it is a complement to the verb rather than simply an appositional renaming of "the world is a fire." It is in the nominative case, rather than in the accusative case, because it serves as a "Nominative of Apellation."[183] This use expresses a title or a name given to the controlling verb's subject, ἡ γλῶσσα, when we would expect a complement in the accusative case.

The repetition of the three vivid participles describing the power of the tongue as fire (σπιλοῦσα, φλογίζουσα, φλογιζομένη), has caused many commentators to attempt detailed explanations of their meaning. Sometimes explanations of the unique expression τὸν τροχὸν τῆς γενέσεως reach into the areas of Stoic philosophy or other Greek naturalists. Such efforts seem doomed, since the language is so metaphorical that we are meant to feel the rhetorical impact of the fiery figures rather than to find some clear analogy in nature. The expressions here and in the entire paragraph are rooted in Second Temple Jewish literature.[184]

---

[181] LSJM, 768; BDAG, 436.

[182] Older English versions such as Tyndale, Geneva and the AV, as well as the modern NASB and ESV, translate the expression as in apposition to the preceding statement. The ASV, RSV, NIV/TNIV, NRSV, NLT, CSB, and NET view it as being a complement to the following verb.

[183] Wallace, 61.

[184] Ps. 32:9; *Sirach* 14:1, 20:1-8; Prov. 10:19; Ecc. 5:1; *1 Enoch* 48:7. See also Luke 16:9, 11; 18:6.

With all of this concern about the details of meaning, we should not miss the point that James is the only writer outside the Gospels to use the noun γέεννα. This could be further intertextual evidence of the use of Jesus *logia* (see, e.g., Matt. 5:29, 30; 18:9; 23:33). Riesner also points out that the figure was drawn from the valley (*Ge Hinnom*) to the west and south of Jerusalem, which was quite near the home of James and the early Jesus followers.[185]

The deep anthropological skepticism expressed in 3:7,8—wild beasts can be tamed, but not the tongue—continues a theme that is almost contradictory, namely, we are supposed to control the tongue, but we cannot do so! However, James' use of paradox is not meant to be pessimistic. It is meant to graphically challenge us to the difficult task of managing this small member. Furthermore, perfection in James and elsewhere in the NT, does not convey sinlessness but wholeness— a moral integrity that avoids doubleness. This, of course, leads to the final subsection where the dangers of inconsistency and the importance of wholeness are stressed.

Clausal Analysis of 3:9-12

3:9

A	P	C
ἐν αὐτῇ	εὐλογοῦμεν	τὸν κύριον καὶ πατέρα

cj	A	P	C
καὶ	ἐν αὐτῇ	καταρώμεθα	τοὺς ἀνθρώπους

	P
τοὺς	γεγονότας,

A
καθ ὁμοίωσιν θεοῦ

3:10

A	P	S
ἐκ τοῦ αὐτοῦ στόματος	ἐξέρχεται	εὐλογία καὶ κατάρα.

---

[185] R. Riesner, *James*, in *Oxford Bible Commentary*, eds. J. Barton and J. Muddiman (Oxford: Oxford University Press, 2001), 1260.

A	P	add	S		
οὐ	χρή,	ἀδελφοί μου,	**S**	**A**	**P**
			ταῦτα	οὕτως	γίνεσθαι.

3:11

A	S	A	P	C
μήτι	ἡ πηγὴ	ἐκ τῆς αὐτῆς ὀπῆς	βρύει	τὸ γλυκὺ καὶ τὸ πικρόν;

3:12

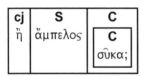

A	P	add	S	C	
μὴ	δύναται,	ἀδελφοί μου,	συκῆ	**C**	**P**
				ἐλαίας	ποιῆσαι

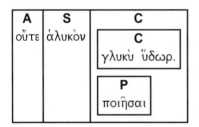

cj	S	C
ἢ	ἄμπελος	**C**
		σῦκα;

A	S	C
οὔτε	ἁλυκὸν	**C**
		γλυκὺ ὕδωρ.
		P
		ποιῆσαι

James continues his asyndeton style with a series of primary clauses, eight of them in 3:9-12 with only two of the clauses connected by a conjunction (καὶ in 3:9). One participle (γεγονότας) introduces an embedded clause, also in 3:9b. The admonition against doubleness in the use of the tongue (3:9, 10) is followed by three rhetorical questions, drawn from the figures of springs and vineyards (3:11, 12a). He concludes the paragraph with an aphorism in 3:12b: "A salt pond cannot yield fresh water." The evident use of ellipsis in these last verses indicates that he is drawing his argument to a rhetorically effective close. He understands that his readers will recognize the missing words and that they will know the obvious answer to the questions that are expressed with the negative particles μήτι and μή. That answer is: "No, these things can't be true!" In the same way, this tongue cannot be used for two incompatible purposes, to bless God and others and at the same time to curse God and others. The use of the expression ἀδελφοί μου in both 3:10 and 12 does not introduce new material, but intensifies the appeal to apply what is being said and helps to span the entire paragraph (see also 2:5 and 5:19).

We should recognize again the echoes of various Jesus *logia* in these word pictures (see esp. Matt. 7:16 and Lk. 6:44). Riesner again reminds us of the possible reflections of Palestinian nature scenes. The image of salt and sweet springs side by side would be obvious to one who lived on the edges of the Jordan rift valley and the Dead Sea.[186]

Soon James will develop his point that the teacher/sage must display heavenly wisdom rather than earthly attitudes (3:13-18). This opposition of actions, described in the following passage which we have called the prominent thematic peak of the letter, has left its stamp on every paragraph. We are urged to display heavenly wisdom by the use of the tongue to bless and edify. We display earthly wisdom by using the tongue to curse and destroy. Many of us, however, desire to use our tongues to display both of these inconsistent actions. James again calls us to be mature and whole (τέλειος) and to avoid the doubleness (δίψυχος) which leads to instability (1:8; 3:16).

17. Paragraph 17 (James 3:13-18)

3:13 Τίς σοφὸς καὶ ἐπιστήμων ἐν ὑμῖν; δειξάτω ἐκ τῆς καλῆς ἀναστροφῆς τὰ ἔργα αὐτοῦ ἐν πραΰτητι σοφίας. ¹⁴εἰ δὲ ζῆλον πικρὸν ἔχετε καὶ ἐριθείαν ἐν τῇ καρδίᾳ ὑμῶν, μὴ κατακαυχᾶσθε καὶ ψεύδεσθε κατὰ τῆς ἀληθείας. ¹⁵οὐκ ἔστιν αὕτη ἡ σοφία ἄνωθεν κατερχομένη ἀλλὰ ἐπίγειος, ψυχική, δαιμονιώδης. ¹⁶ ὅπου γὰρ ζῆλος καὶ ἐριθεία, ἐκεῖ ἀκαταστασία καὶ πᾶν φαῦλον πρᾶγμα.	Jas 3 ¹³Who is wise and understanding among you? He should demonstrate by his good conduct his actions done with the gentleness that wisdom brings. ¹⁴But if you have bitter jealousy and selfish ambition in your hearts, stop boasting and being false to the truth. ¹⁵This is not the wisdom that comes down from above, but is earthly, unspiritual, demonic. ¹⁶ For where jealousy and selfish ambition exist, it is there that will be disorder and every vile practice.

---

[186] Riesner, 1260. For an insightful analysis of the way in which James utilizes his Palestinian background to effectively communicate his metaphors and similes, see the largely overlooked volume by Palestinian resident, Eric Bishop. *Apostles of Palestine: The Local Background to the New Testament Church* (London: Lutterworth Press, 1958), 177-94.

¹⁷ἡ δὲ ἄνωθεν σοφία πρῶτον μὲν ἀγνή ἐστιν, ἔπειτα εἰρηνική, ἐπιεικής, εὐπειθής, μεστὴ ἐλέους καὶ καρπῶν ἀγαθῶν, ἀδιάκριτος, ἀνυπόκριτος. ¹⁸καρπὸς δὲ δικαιοσύνης ἐν εἰρήνῃ σπείρεται τοῖς ποιοῦσιν εἰρήνην.	¹⁷But the wisdom that comes from above is first pure, then peaceable, gentle, open to reason, full of mercy and good fruits, impartial and sincere. ¹⁸And a harvest of righteousness is sown in peace by those who work for peace.

The Prominent Role of 3:13-18 in the Discourse

Previously we have argued that this paragraph has the most promi-nent role in the overall structure of the Letter from James. This is due to its special linguistic features that set it apart from other paragraphs along with its semantic function of conveying the essential message of the entire discourse. The paragraph has verbal links with both previ-ous and subsequent material, thus serving as a transitional section, but also functions as a summation of the entire discourse. Therefore, here we will expand on the crucial role of this paragraph which we have called the thematic "peak" of James.

Dibelius thought that 3:13-17 had internal cohesion but had no real connections with what precedes or follows in the letter. He also thought that 3:18 was an isolated saying, belonging neither with the previous group and separate from 4:1ff.[187] It can be shown, however, that Dibelius was simply wrong in this estimation. It is my opinion that he allowed his view that James is composed of loosely arranged paranetic material to sometimes negatively influence his critical judgment. A number of writers both before and after Dibelius have affirmed the unity of this paragraph and its vital verbal and semantic connection both to its immediate co-text and also to the distant sections of the discourse.

At the beginning of the twentieth century, two other German schol-ars argued for the central role of 3:13-18. C.F.G. Heinrici, in a volume on the literary character of the NT writings, acknowledged that James, like the proverbial writings of the OT, consisted of a large number of discrete sections of familiar wisdom material. There was, however, something that held all the variant sayings together.

> Der zusammenhaltende Gedanke ist die Einsharfung der rechten Weisheit, die von oben kommt (3, 13-18). Alle einzelnen Warheiten

---

[187] Dibelius, 207-08.

sind ihre Fruchte.[188] [The connecting thought is the emphasis on the true wisdom, which comes from above (3:13-18). All of the other individual truths are its fruits.]

In an earlier article, Herman Cladder also set forth a strong argument for literary coherence in the book, with 3:13-18 also functioning as both its linguistic and semantic center.[189]

Dibelius greatly influenced a succeeding generation of writers, but in the last decades a number not only have found a coherent structure in James, but also have argued for the over-arching structural and semantic role of 3:13-18. James Reese views 3:13-18 as "the heart of the letter" where its "core message" (the teacher's awesome responsibility) is located and developed.[190] In a number of books and articles, Patrick Hartin has "argued that this (3:13-18) is the central pericope in the epistle, the other pericopes forming an embrace around it."[191] Luke Cheung has stressed the central function of 3:13-18 as a link passage in the book which many of the previous and subsequent paragraphs echo both linguistically and thematically.[192] In a published dissertation utilizing a form of discourse analysis, Mark Taylor affirms that this passage summarizes the burden of the letter thus far and prepares the way for the strong rebuke that follows. These anaphoric and cataphoric roles of the passage lead him a similar conclusion as these aforementioned writers.

> Functionally, 3:13-18 gathers key concepts raised in 1:2-3:12 and anticipates the next major movement in the discourse. Contextually, the passage reveals grounding in Jewish concepts of wisdom, emphasizing the practical obedience of a life marked by the possession of wisdom as a gift of God.[193]

In the introduction I referred to the unpublished thesis of David Hockman which views our passage as the discourse "peak" of the book

---

[188] C. F. G. Henrici, *Der literarische Charakter der neutestamentliche Schriften* (Leipzig: Durr, 1908), 75.

[189] H. Cladder, "Die Anlage des Jakobusbriefes," *ZKT* 28: 37-57.

[190] J.M. Reese, "The Exegete as Sage: Hearing the Message of James," *BTB* 12: 83.

[191] P.J. Hartin, "Who is wise and understanding among you?" *SBLSP* (1996): 483. See also *James and the 'Q' Sayings of Jesus*, JSNTSup 47 (Sheffield: Sheffield Academic Press, 1991), 29-32; and *A Spirituality of Perfection* (Collegeville: Liturgical Press, 1999), 72-75.

[192] L. L. Cheung, *The Genre, Composition and Hermeneutics of the Epistle of James* (Milton Keynes: Paternoster Press, 2003), 75-85, 138-147.

[193] M.E. Taylor, *A Text-Linguistic Investigation into the Discourse Structure of James* (London: T&T Clark, 2006), 116.

and also Tollefson's article stressing the key role of the paragraph in the dialectical discourse of James. Suffice it to conclude that a number of recent scholars have also concluded that 3:13-18 is the key to pulling the seemingly disparate sections of James together into some coherent structure.

Such a conclusion, however, cannot be based simply on the linguistic features in the structural "peak" of the book, although those indicators must be present as well. The semantic content of the paragraph must also convey the main themes of the book for the paragraph to function clearly in a prominent role as the thematic peak of James. I believe that these semantic indicators are also present in this passage. James conveys here his burden that his readers adopt a lifestyle that is based on the wisdom that comes from God above and that they must reject any anti-wisdom that comes from human viewpoint alone. It is my contention that each individual paragraph of the discourse displays the stamp of that theme. The intensely imperative paragraph that follows (4:1-10), for example, reaches a hortatory peak in calling the reader to accept the friendship of God and reject the friendship of the world. In the words of the previous thematic peak, that means that we must reject the anti-wisdom of this "below" world and to accept the true wisdom of the "above" world. For the person who may want it both ways, James reserves the stinging message of not being "double-minded," but choosing rather the wholeness of a single and pure life marked by a moral integrity rooted in Divine wisdom.

Clausal Analysis of 3:13-18

3:13

C	S
Τίς	σοφὸς καὶ ἐπιστήμων ἐν ὑμῖν;

P	A	C	A
δειξάτω	ἐκ τῆς καλῆς ἀναστροφῆς	τὰ ἔργα αὐτοῦ	ἐν πραΰτητι σοφίας.

3:14

cj	cj	C	A
εἰ	δὲ	ζῆλον πικρὸν	ἐν τῇ καρδίᾳ ὑμῶν,
		P ἔχετε	
		καὶ ἐριθείαν	

A	P
μὴ	κατακαυχᾶσθε

cj	P	A
καὶ	ψεύδεσθε	κατὰ τῆς ἀληθείας.

3:15

A	P	S	C	
οὐκ	ἔστιν	αὕτη	ἡ σοφία	
			A ἄνωθεν	**P** κατερχομένη

cj	C
ἀλλὰ	ἐπίγειος, ψυχική, δαιμονιώδης.

3:16

cj	cj	S
ὅπου	γὰρ	ζῆλος καὶ ἐριθεία,

A	S
ἐκεῖ	ἀκαταστασία καὶ πᾶν φαῦλον πρᾶγμα.

3:17

S	A	cj	C	P
ἡ **cj** δὲ ἄνωθεν σοφία	πρῶτον	μὲν	ἀγνή	ἐστιν,

A	C
ἔπειτα	εἰρηνική, ἐπιεικής, εὐπειθής, μεστὴ ἐλέους καὶ καρπῶν ἀγαθῶν, ἀδιάκριτος, ἀνυπόκριτος.

3:18

S	A	P	C		
καρπὸς δικαιοσύνης	ἐν εἰρήνῃ	σπείρεται			
δὲ				P	C
				τοῖς ποιοῦσιν	εἰρήνην.

This paragraph opens with a rhetorical question addressed to those "among you" (ἐν ὑμῖν)—the first of six occurrences of this expression, all in the latter half of the book. The next paragraph opens with another challenging rhetorical question asked of those "among you" (ἐν ὑμῖν; 4:1). The remaining four times that this expression occurs are in the closing paragraph (5:13, 14, 19, 20). This indicates that James at this point begins to close in on the fallacies and foibles of congregational lives in the Diaspora. The question in 3:13a is answered immediately by an imperative (δειξάτω) clause that echoes an earlier use of this specific imperative (twice in 2:18) and also echoes the same semantic point, namely that his readers must demonstrate by their right behavior their faith (2:18) and also their wisdom (3:13b). More specifically, it is that gentleness that has its origin in wisdom (σοφίας as a genitive of source). Although this is only the second use of this specific noun (see 1:5), it appears twice in 3:15 and 17, and introduces the topic which will be commented on in the rest of the paragraph.

The use of σοφὸς in the opening question also strengthens the point that wisdom is the topic which will be explained. Coupled with σοφὸς is the added characteristic, "and understanding" (καὶ ἐπιστήμων). This word does not convey the semantic overtones of a "sympathetic understanding," but is more in the semantic field of its partner, σοφὸς. Louw and Nida define this field, including also συνετός (32.27), as "pertaining to being able to understand and evaluate—'intelligent, insightful, understanding'."[194] Although this specific combination of words does not appear elsewhere in the NT, the collocation would be familiar to those who honored the wisdom traditions of Israel and the wise men of that tradition. When Moses wondered how he could bear the burden of leading the people, he decided by issuing the following command. "Assign for yourselves men, wise and

---

[194] Louw and Nida, 384.

discerning (σοφοὺς καὶ ἐπιστήμονας) and prudent (συνετοὺς) for your tribes, and I will appoint them as your leaders" (Dt. 1:13). The response of the people was to do just that and such wise and understanding men were so appointed (1:15). In Dt. 4:6 Israel was told that if they kept the statutes, they would be a wise and understanding (σοφὸς καὶ ἐπιστήμων) people"—the exact pair of wisdom words found in Jas. 3:13. Daniel was referred to by the same two coupled adjectives (Dan. 1:4; 5:11) and Sirach also collocates the two words (21:15). Therefore, attending to the intertexture of James suggests that this he is asking for one who desires to be a "sage" in ancient Israel. This connects the paragraph to the opening of the previous one where a warning was issued against too many desiring to be teachers (3:1). The teacher was a "rabbi." The "sage" was one who taught wisdom. The requirement for the rabbi was to be perfect in the use of his tongue (3:2-12). The requirement for the sage is that he demonstrates by his behavior the gentleness that comes from heavenly wisdom (3:13, 17).

The next three verses (3:14-16) introduce a negative tone, because James loves portraying the oppositions of actions in his ethical paranesis. The Jewish "two ways" tradition could also be invoked here, as he describes the characteristics of anti-wisdom by means of a vice list. Many commentators have pointed out that he never calls this behavior a type of wisdom, but he does state that "this is not the wisdom that comes down from above, but is earthly, unspiritual, demonic" (3:15). He begins his portrayal of anti-wisdom by a first class conditional sentence in 3:14: "εἰ δὲ ζῆλον πικρὸν ἔχετε καὶ ἐριθείαν ἐν τῇ καρδίᾳ ὑμῶν, μὴ κατακαυχᾶσθε καὶ ψεύδεσθε κατὰ τῆς ἀληθείας." Too often those trained in traditional grammar settle for a description of the syntax of a first class conditional clause (εἰ plus the indicative in the protasis . . .) with little recognition for what an author is doing with the conditional clause. Richard Young has framed a rhetorical approach to conditional clauses in light of speech-act theory that focuses on what an author is attempting to do with the clause.[195] Here, for example, James is not making a statement, but is engaging in a strong exhortation. Notice the apodosis: "stop boasting and being false to the truth" (μὴ κατακαυχᾶσθε καὶ ψεύδεσθε κατὰ τῆς ἀληθείας). The exhortation is heightened by the adversative δὲ that introduces the protasis and contrasts so vividly with the "the gentleness that wisdom brings" at the

---

[195] R.A. Young, "A Classification of Conditional Sentences Based on Speech Act Theory," *Grace Theological Journal* 10.1 (1989): 29-49.

end of the previous clause.

Oftentimes great effort is taken to closely define the nuances of difference in these words. More valuable than seeking to define and contrast each of these negative terms is to see the total disorder and unstable characteristics that emerge from the words in 3:15 and 16. The word "disorder" (ἀκαταστασία) recalls the description of the double-minded man of 1:8 as "unstable" (ἀκατάστατος) and the tongue in 3:8 as "restless" (ἀκατάστατον). Notice also the verbal connections to other sections with the references to "bitter jealousy" (ζῆλον πικρὸν) as in 3:11 and 4:2. This vice list could be summed up as describing confusion and disorder.

The vivid contrast of the following virtue list in 3:17 can be seen in the emphasis on peace and harmony conveyed in the words that describe behavior derived from "above." The English reader cannot appreciate the rhetorical flourishes heard in the original oral reading of the book. There are six consecutive words beginning with epsilon: ἡ δὲ ἄνωθεν σοφία πρῶτον μὲν ἁγνή ἐστιν, ἔπειτα εἰρηνική, ἐπιεικής, εὐπειθής, μεστὴ ἐλέους. Then there are three words initiated by an alpha: καὶ καρπῶν ἀγαθῶν, ἀδιάκριτος, ἀνυπόκριτος. This careful alliteration contrasts graphically with the vice list which had no such alliteration. The contrast in the sound also sent a message of the difference between the behavioral disharmony from below and the harmonious order from above.

The final clause in 3:18 is close enough in sense to be properly placed but different enough to indicate its separate origin (note the unnecessary δὲ). It is used here as an aphorism which rounds off the effective argument and transitions in thought to the following passage. This can be seen in its reference to peace-making which is a fruit of the wisdom from above and is in contrast with the "wars" that characterize the admonition in 4:1ff. The participle τοῖς ποιοῦσιν most probably is a dative of agency.[196] "And a harvest of righteousness is sown in peace <u>by those who make</u> (or work for) peace." The appropriate intertext is undoubtedly the beatitude of Jesus in Mat. 5:9, "Blessed are the peacemakers, for they shall be called sons of God."

It is unnecessary, as we have done in previous paragraphs, to explain how this passage conveys the message of the book. This paragraph **is** the message of the book.

---

[196] Wallace, 163-166. See also James 3:7.

Chapter 4

ANALYSIS OF JAMES FOUR

17. Paragraph 17 (James 4:1-10)

4:1 Πόθεν πόλεμοι καὶ πόθεν μάχαι ἐν ὑμῖν; οὐκ ἐντεῦθεν, ἐκ τῶν ἡδονῶν ὑμῶν τῶν στρατευομένων ἐν τοῖς μέλεσιν ὑμῶν; ²ἐπιθυμεῖτε καὶ οὐκ ἔχετε, φονεύετε καὶ ζηλοῦτε καὶ οὐ δύνασθε ἐπιτυχεῖν, μάχεσθε καὶ πολεμεῖτε, οὐκ ἔχετε διὰ τὸ μὴ αἰτεῖσθαι ὑμᾶς, ³αἰτεῖτε καὶ οὐ λαμβάνετε διότι κακῶς αἰτεῖσθε, ἵνα ἐν ταῖς ἡδοναῖς ὑμῶν δαπανήσητε. ⁴μοιχαλίδες, οὐκ οἴδατε ὅτι ἡ φιλία τοῦ κόσμου ἔχθρα τοῦ θεοῦ ἐστιν; ὃς ἐὰν οὖν βουληθῇ φίλος εἶναι τοῦ κόσμου, ἐχθρὸς τοῦ θεοῦ καθίσταται. ⁵ἢ δοκεῖτε ὅτι κενῶς ἡ γραφὴ λέγει· πρὸς φθόνον ἐπιποθεῖ τὸ πνεῦμα ὃ κατῴκισεν ἐν ἡμῖν, ⁶μείζονα δὲ δίδωσιν χάριν; διὸ λέγει·

ὁ θεὸς ὑπερηφάνοις ἀντιτάσσεται, ταπεινοῖς δὲ δίδωσιν χάριν.

⁷ὑποτάγητε οὖν τῷ θεῷ, ἀντίστητε δὲ τῷ διαβόλῳ καὶ φεύξεται ἀφ᾽ ὑμῶν, ⁸ἐγγίσατε τῷ θεῷ καὶ ἐγγιεῖ ὑμῖν. καθαρίσατε χεῖρας, ἁμαρτωλοί, καὶ ἁγνίσατε καρδίας, δίψυχοι. ⁹ταλαιπωρήσατε καὶ πενθήσατε καὶ κλαύσατε. ὁ γέλως ὑμῶν εἰς πένθος μετατραπήτω καὶ ἡ χαρὰ εἰς κατήφειαν. ¹⁰ταπεινώθητε ἐνώπιον κυρίου καὶ ὑψώσει ὑμᾶς.

4 ¹What causes quarrels and what causes fights among you? Is it not from this, from your pleasures that are at war in your members? ²You desire and you do not have. You murder and you covet and are not able to obtain. You fight and quarrel. You do not have because you do not ask. ³You ask and do not receive, because you ask wrongly, to spend it on your pleasures. ⁴You adulteresses! Do you not know that friendship with the world means enmity with God? Therefore whoever wishes to be the world's friend becomes God's enemy. ⁵Or do you suppose that the Scripture speaks to no purpose? Does the spirit that he has caused to dwell in us long enviously? ⁶But he gives more grace. Therefore it says,

"God opposes the proud, but gives grace to the humble."

⁷Therefore submit yourselves to God and resist the devil, and then he will flee from you. ⁸Draw near to God and he will draw near to you. Cleanse your hands, you sinners, and purify your hearts, you double-minded. ⁹Be wretched and mourn and weep. Your laughter must be turned to mourning and your joy to gloom. ¹⁰Humble yourselves before the Lord, and he will exalt you.

The relationship between 4:1-10 and 3:13-18

This passage has features that both connect it closely with its co-text and that also distinguish it as the next discrete paragraph in the book. Linking it closely with 3:13-18 are the following features: 1) It also opens with a rhetorical question (4:1/3:13). 2) Its initial question also ends with the adjunct ἐν ὑμῖν. 3) The question about why peace is not present in the community is semantically tied, by contrast, with the reference to peace-making that ends 3:18. 4) The verb ζηλοῦτε in 4:2 echoes the noun ζῆλον in 3:14, as evidence that the behavior condemned in 4:1-3 comes not from above but from below. 5) A number of commentators see the vice φθόνος in 4:5 as sharing the same semantic field with a number of the vices condemned in 3:14-16, particularly the ζῆλος condemned in 3:14, 16. Indeed φθόνος and ζῆλος share the same semantic field in Louw and Nida ("Envy, Jealousy"; 88.160), while πικρὸς and ἐριθεία are in a closely related field ("Resentful, Hold a Grudge Against"; 88.167-170).[196] There are so many other lexical and semantic connections between the passages that some commentators view them as comprising one unit rather than two.[197]

While the links between 3:13-18 and 4:1-10 are simply too many to ignore, there are a number of ways in which each passage is distinct and which justify treating the latter as a separate paragraph with its own integrity and coherence: 1) Each of the sections begins with a rhetorical question and ends with an aphorism that looks very much like an adapted Jesus *logion*. 2) The topic introduced in 3:13 (wisdom) is different than the topic introduced in 4:1 (conflicts). 3) The way in which the topic of wisdom is handled in 3:14ff—with a comparison between wisdom that is not from above with wisdom from above—is different than the way the topic of personal conflicts is handled in 3:2ff. The first treatment is thematic while the second is strongly hortatory. 4) The tone of the two sections is quite different. While both passages describe behavior to be avoided, the latter passage is harsher and more hortatory in nature. There are three imperatives in 3:13-18 with no harsh accusations addressed to the implied readers. On the other hand, there are ten imperatives concentrated in 4:7-10 plus a series of severe

---

[196] *Louw and Nida,* 760-61.

[197] See the influential chapter by L.T. Johnson where he argues that 3:13-4:10 deals with the ethical topos of *envy.* "James 3:13-4:10 and the *Topos* περὶ φθόνου" in *Brother of Jesus Friend of God* (Grand Rapids: Eerdmans, 2004), 182-201. Johnson repeats this approach in his commentary, *The Letter of James,* 267-90.

indicative charges in 4:2, 3 as well as a series of direct questions that function rhetorically as condemnations of the reader's behavior (4:1, 2, 4-6). It could be observed that James functions as a sage in 3:13-18 while he functions as a prophet in 4:1-10.

Is there a way to bring together both the similarities and the differences between these two central paragraphs in James? As I have argued in the introduction, I believe that way is to view 3:13-18 as expressing the thematic peak of the discourse while viewing 4:1-10 as the hortatory peak of the discourse. While both passages convey the "two ways" approach to ethics so common in wisdom literature, 3:13-18 does that by describing the two ways of heavenly viewpoint versus earthly viewpoint. In 4:1-10 those two ways are elaborated as describing a person who is either God's friend and thus the world's enemy or who is God's enemy and thus the world's friend. In these two passages, James brings together the wisdom and prophetic traditions. While Baasland did call James *"the* wisdom writing of the NT," a more nuanced description of James would be that it is the NT writing that best exemplifies the concept of "prophetic wisdom."

Because 3:13-18 and 4:1-10 serve as the thematic and hortatory peaks of the book, both linguistically and semantically, their message is also stamped on each of the other discrete paragraphs in the discourse. James' call to reject human wisdom that makes one God's enemy in favor of Divine wisdom that makes one God's friend underlies the bipolar nature of each of his other paragraphs. This is true regardless of how specifically the manifestation of those behaviors are exemplified. Attempting to live one's life both ways will only result in being "double-souled" (4:8). On the other hand, to follow the Lord fully without yielding to competing loyalties will result in a whole, complete and "perfect" life. As we have attempted to point out how that is done in each of the preceding paragraphs, we will now briefly attempt to show how that is done in 4:1-10 and the succeeding paragraphs.

The Structure of 4:1-10

Three sub-sections develop this paragraph. The first is 4:1-3 where the plural of ἡδονή frames the charge as being both the source of the community's conflicts (4:1) and the reason for their unanswered prayers (4:3). The next two sections are transitioned by the conjunction οὖν (4:4, 7). The second section (4:4-6) opens, as in 4:1, with a rhetorical question and develops the bi-polar choices of the world versus God and centers the argument on one (possibly two) citations from scripture. The quotation in 4:6 also serves as something of a "structural lynchpin" for the entire paragraph.[198] The third section (4:7-10) introduced again by οὖν, consists of a concentrated catena of ten imperatives. The last of those commands (4:10) rounds off the exhortation framing the section with the same basic command with which it opens (4:7) and by utilizing a Jesus *logion*, as is often the author's style to end his paragraphs (e.g. 3:18).

4:1

A	S
Πόθεν	πόλεμοι

cj	A	S
καὶ	πόθεν	μάχαι ἐν ὑμῖν;

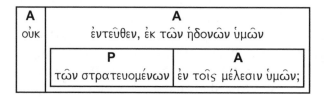

A	A	
οὐκ	ἐντεῦθεν, ἐκ τῶν ἡδονῶν ὑμῶν	
	P	A
	τῶν στρατευομένων	ἐν τοῖς μέλεσιν ὑμῶν;

4:2

P	cj	A	P
ἐπιθυμεῖτε	καὶ	οὐκ	ἔχετε,

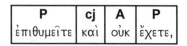

P	cj	P
φονεύετε	καὶ	ζηλοῦτε

cj	A	P	C/P
καὶ	οὐ	δύνασθε	ἐπιτυχεῖν,

P	cj	P
μάχεσθε	καὶ	πολεμεῖτε,

---

[198] Edgar, 187. This will be explained in the following comments.

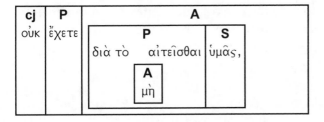

4:3

cj	A	P
ἵνα	ἐν ταῖς ἡδοναῖς ὑμῶν	δαπανήσητε.

(Note: For purposes of simplification, I have combined into one line the OpenText clausal display of each of the four compound clauses connected by καὶ in 4:2, 3)

This section opens with two rhetorical questions (4:1). The second question, however, functions as the answer to the first question. One could state the effect indicatively, "The outward conflicts that exist among you arise from the selfish pleasures that are at conflict inside of each one of you." The repetition of πόθεν, especially when it is not needed to ask the question, conveys the intensity of the inquisition. The entire rhetorical effect is heightened by both the triple alliteration (πόθεν πόλεμοι καὶ πόθεν) and the triple homoioteleuton (πόθεν, πόθεν, ἐντεῦθεν). James does not employ these rhetorical features simply for ornamentation, but to convey the intensity of his questions, which can only be appreciated fully by the oral culture in which the discourse was first heard. The familiar abrupt style continues in 4:2, 3 with a series of short, second person plural statements, which alternate between the negative (ἐπιθυμεῖτε, φονεύετε, ζηλοῦτε, μάχεσθε, πολεμεῖτε, οὐ λαμβάνετε) and the positive. The sense of the καὶ that connects these alternating experiences is better understood as adversative. For example, in 4:3: "You request but you do not receive" (αἰτεῖτε καὶ οὐ λαμβάνετε).

In attempting to untangle the convoluted syntax of these verses, it is also possible to detect a chiastic structure to them. If the three secondary clauses are removed, the primary clauses can be arranged as follows.

A ἐπιθυμεῖτε   καὶ οὐκ ἔχετε,
  B φονεύετε καὶ ζηλοῦτε   καὶ οὐ δύνασθε ἐπιτυχεῖν,
  B' μάχεσθε καὶ πολεμεῖτε   οὐκ ἔχετε
A' αἰτεῖτε   καὶ οὐ λαμβάνετε

The A clause parallels the A' clause and the B and B' compound clauses also are parallel, both structurally and semantically. While the author is hesitant to overly stress the role of chiasms (particularly the more complex they become), such an arrangement here can be helpful to discern the overall flow of the author's densely expressed thought. The addition of the secondary clauses in lines B' and A' completes the charge by explaining both the causes and the result of requests that are motivated by selfish desires.

Some commentators struggle with how such severe behavior, including "murder" (4:2) could ever be envisioned as part of the community's experience (ἐν ὑμῖν). Some have even posited a Zealot faction within the community.[199] When the rhetorical nature of the language is recognized, however, we must conclude that these are overstated expressions for effect. In his role as prophet, James is utilizing the hyperbolic language often witnessed in the canonical prophets and even in the hatred/murder statements by Jesus.[200] There is also a distinct possibility that he is echoing his brother's equating of hatred with murder (Matt. 5:21, 22)

A related issue is whether μέλεσιν ὑμῶν in 4:1 refers to bodily members or to metaphorical members of the Diaspora communities, as some commentators have advocated.[201] As has been noted, the parallelism with the ἐν ὑμῖν in the first question is only a formal one. More important is how James uses the word μέλος, which he clearly does in 3:5, 6 to refer to parts of the body. Parallels with Pauline metaphorical usage (e.g., Rom. 12:5; Eph. 4:25) miss the point if James' use of the word is not metaphorical. Furthermore, the cognate references to "desire" in 1:14,

---

[199] M.J. Townsend, "*James 4:1-4: A Warning against Zealotry?*" *ExpTim* 87 (1976), 211-13.
[200] See Isa. 1:15-17, 21-23; 3:14, 15; 5:8, 9; 22:12-14 for examples of such prophetic hyperbole.
[201] Davids, *James*, 157.

15 (see ἐπιθυμεῖτε in 4:2) clearly identify the problem addressed here as being inside their individual natures, not inside their individual communities. Of course we know that the whole people manifests these sinful urges, but that is not the point being made in 4:1-3. In using this term for members of the body, as his brother did (Matt. 5:29, 30), James reveals that as he wrote he had Jesus looking over his shoulder, not Paul.

As mentioned above, Johnson argues that James in 3:13-4:10 is discoursing on the *"Topos* περι φθόνου" due to its mention in 4:5 along with semantically related words for "envy." I suggest, however, that Johnson has too strictly limited the topos to envy and bases his argument too much on the use of that lexeme in a highly controversial "quotation" in that verse. James certainly is discoursing on a topos of concern to Jewish moralists, as well as Greco-Roman ones. If we must choose such a parallel, I suggest that it is the *"Topos* περι ἡδονῶν." This word, although it can refer to the legitimate pleasures of life, is used only in its evil meaning in the NT. James locates the source of these conflicts in these ἡδοναὶ in 4:1 and then puts the blame for unanswered prayer on selfish ἡδοναὶ in 4:3. Selfish pleasure appears to be the focus of his attack, rather than envy, which of course is a manifestation of selfish pleasure. While it is possible to identify this inner tendency with the "evil inclination" (*etser hara*) of Jewish tradition, the late documentation for that inclination in Jewish sources counsels caution in this regard.

One often overlooked matter is the shift in voice from the middle αἰτεῖσθαι in 4:2 to the active αἰτεῖτε in 4:3 and then back to αἰτεῖσθαι at the end of the verse. The change in voice has been difficult to adequately explain and a number of solutions have been offered. These range from seeing no significance difference in the voice[202] to Mayor's suggestion that the middle expresses the spirit of prayer while the active expresses only the words.[203] Perhaps another explanation is in the use of a negative adjunct accompanying the middle in the first and third occurrences and the absolute use of the active in the second verb. As can be seen in the above OpenText analysis of 4:2, 3, the middle voice is accompanied in both instances by a causal adjunct. This does not mean that the middle voice always expresses some negative aspect of prayer, but it may imply that when there is some significant accompanying action the subject's greater involvement in the predicator may

---

[202] Dibelius, 219.

[203] Mayor, 138. This is difficult to defend in the light of the use of the active voice in Matt. 7:7-10.

be expressed by the middle voice.[204] In any case, the switch to the active αἰτεῖτε probably indicates another use of the Jesus *logion* mentioned in Matt. 7:7-10. James is balancing Jesus' prayer promise by emphasizing that asking should be accompanied by the right motives, not with the goal of simply spending the answer to satisfy one's own pleasures.

4:4

add	A	P
μοιχαλίδες,	οὐκ	οἴδατε

cj	S	C	P
ὅτι	ἡ φιλία τοῦ κόσμου	ἔχθρα τοῦ θεου	ἐστιν;

cj	S				C	P
οὖν	**S** ὃς	**A** ἐὰν	**P** βουληθῇ	**C**	ἐχθρὸς τοῦ θεοῦ	καθίσταται.
				P εἶναι **C** φίλος τοῦ κόσμου		

4:5

cj	P
ἢ	δοκεῖτε

cj	A	S	P
ὅτι	κενῶς	ἡ γραφὴ	λέγει;

A	P	S		
πρὸς φθόνον	ἐπιποθεῖ	τὸ πνεῦμα		
		S ὃ	**P** κατῴκισεν	**A** ἐν ἡμῖν;

(The above differs from the OpenText display of 4:5, because I understand the last clause to be an interrogative primary clause, not a secondary clause.)

---

[204] Porter, *Idioms*, 67; Young, *Intermediate Greek*, 134.

4:6

C	cj	P
μείζονα χάριν	δὲ	δίδωσιν

cj	P
διὸ	λέγει·

S	C	P
ὁ θεὸς	ὑπερηφάνοις	ἀντιτάσσεται

C	cj	P	C
ταπεινοῖς	δὲ	δίδωσιν	χάριν.

In the second of three sections in 4:1-10, the serious charges brought by our author reach their apex. In a series of questions concluded by a scriptural citation, his diatribe embodies the essence of his argument, namely, that one must finally decide whose friend they are—the world's or God's. In keeping with the idea that 3:13-18 comprise the thematic peak of the book (follow wisdom from above and not from below), this passage equates choosing heavenly wisdom with being God's friend. Making the opposite choice will result in being opposed and resisted by God, who will become one's enemy. This charge leads to a series of imperatives in 4:7-10 that press even further for a decisive choice between two philosophies of life, one based on pleasing self and the other based on pleasing God.

The now familiar and tender nominative of address, ἀδελφοί μου, has been altered to the harsh μοιχαλίδες. Our author actually does not return to the regular use of the affectionate term until 5:7. The apparently inconsistent use of ἀδελφοί μου in 4:11 will be addressed in the comments on that verse. Before attempting to analyze 4:4-6, it would be good to note that we have now entered a section of this discourse that differs from both chapter one and from the three treatises that precede (2:1-12; 2:13-26; 3:1-12). Not only is the tone more severe in this section, but James has introduced the expression ἐν ὑμῖν (3:13 and 4:1), which he will continue to use in 5:13, 14, 19. He also begins to use the consequential conjunction οὖν at this very point (4:4, 7, 17; 5:7, 16). One conclusion that can be possibly drawn from these observations is that he is now dealing more with specific situations that he believes to exist within the communities he is addressing. While what he wrote in 1:2-3:12 still would have general application to his hearers/readers, it is in the last half of the book where he focuses in on what he believes are the specific behavior problems they are exhibiting. Even the use of the οὖν is for transitioning to the expected ethical application rather than for logical development of his argument—the way it often appears in Paul. This also could help to explain why he waits until 3:13-4:10 to expound the thematic and hortatory peaks of his discourse. Everything that precedes can be also viewed in light of the bi-polar opposite behaviors he presents, but from this section onward he exposes the wrong behavior even more closely and fervently. One can imagine a preacher initially discoursing about general issues but then becoming more fervent as he moves into problems that he knows are prevalent in his parishioners' lives.

The use of the feminine noun must have annoyed some literal minded scribes who added μοιχοὶ καὶ before μοιχαλίδες to add a reference to men as well. This adultery, however, is not the sexual act but is a figure often used by the prophets for spiritual unfaithfulness to the Lord (Isa. 54:5; Jer. 3:20; Eze. 16; Hos. 9:1) and was used by Jesus as well (Mat. 12:39; 16:4—another Jesus *logion*?). The Alexandrian and Western texts support this correct understanding of James' analogy.

This alarming address, followed by a rhetorical question in 4:4a and an amplification in 4:4b introduced by οὖν, lays out the stark cosmological opposition between friendship with God and friendship with the world. Then follows two more rhetorical questions in 4:5 (in my view the last clause is a question). These questions culminate in a scriptural quotation with citation formula from Prov. 3:34. For James the κόσμος is always a negative designation. It is the place where the lowly are held in dishonor (2:5) and is characterized by unrighteousness (3:6). The κόσμος is the opposite of God's order and is actively hostile to Him. Those who so engage in this world-order that is out of harmony with God's order become (καθίσταται) God's enemies rather than his friends. As also took place in 3:5, this verb takes a complement in the nominative case (ἐχθρὸς). This could be called the nominative of appellation, which is treated as a proper name.[205] Just as Abraham was called "Friend of God" (2:25), the friend of the world is called "Enemy of God (4:4)."

---

[205] Wallace, 61.

A second rhetorical question in 4:5a is introduced by the meta-comment ἣ δοκεῖτε.[206] Such questions are not meant to seek an answer but to function as a statement. That statement would be, "The scripture does not speak to no purpose." Some linguists call this a "queclarative"—a question that is intended to make a declaration.[207] This combination of meta-comment and queclarative heightens the prominence of the diatribe. It also leads into one of the most difficult interpretive challenges in the book. Are the following words a quotation? If they are, where in "the scripture" (ἡ γραφὴ are they to be found? Or should these words be taken in an entirely different way than a quotation from elsewhere? Needless to say, the answers provided by commentators are abundant.[208] Because of the scope and limits of this commentary, I refer the interested reader to the able discussions elsewhere and offer what I believe is the best approach to the verse. I will try to do this in light of both the grammar and the rhetoric of the passage. In other words, how is the discourse function best served by this statement?

I find the interpretation offered by Sophie Laws quite helpful with a slight variation that I believe strengthens her view. Laws' conclusion is that the "quotation" is best viewed as a question about the human spirit's longing toward envy:[209] "Does the spirit that he has caused to dwell in us long enviously?" Thus, the unmentioned God or the Spirit is not the subject of the verb ἐπιποθεῖ, a verb which never takes God or the Divine Spirit as its subject elsewhere in scripture. The only other reference to "the spirit" in James is to the human spirit (2:26). All commentators agree that the adjunct phrase πρὸς φθόνον functions adverbially. Finally, if we remove from our thinking that this is a quotation and read it as a question that expects a negative answer, the answer would be as follows. "No, the spirit which God has caused to dwell in us (κατῴκισεν) does not long enviously." God did not create man this way, since God is the source of only good (1:13-18).[210]

---

[206] A *meta-comment* is "when a speaker stops saying what they are saying in order to comment on what is being said." S. Runge, *Lexham Discourse Greek New Testament: Glossary* (Logos Research Systems, Inc., 2008).

[207] G. Thompson, *Introducing Functional Grammar*, 2nd ed. (London: Arnold, 2004), 80, 240-41.

[208] See Davids, 162-64 for a convenient summary of the alternatives.

[209] S. Laws, *The Epistle of James* (San Francisco: Harper & Row), 176-79. This view was also presented in an article by S. Laws, "Does Scripture speak in vain? A reconsideration of James iv.5," *NTS* 20 (1973-74): 210-15.

[210] An early understanding of this passage could also be reflected in *Shepherd of Hermas, Mandates* 3:1, 2. The author is urging his readers to love the truth "in order that

But what is the source of this "quotation"? What "scripture" is it? Laws suggests such passages as the LXX of Ps.83:3 or 40:2. I believe, however, that the best approach is that ἡ γραφὴ in 4:5 is not the immediately following words but anticipates the clear quotation in 4:6. Having disposed of the fact that scripture does not speak "vainly" in attributing envy to the created spirit within mankind, he now turns to what scripture does say. This would better explain the διὸ λέγει of 4:6a which is not "he says," but "it says." The sense would be as follows. While scripture does not say this in 4:5b, it does say this in 4:6b (Prov. 3:34). From a discourse perspective the additional rhetorical question or "queclarative" fits better with the thrust of the diatribe. He does away with any justification for the human conduct he is condemning and states that God offers not only an alternative to prideful self-seeking, but also the grace to enable the humble ones to choose Him as their friend.

The contrast between what he denies in 4:5 and what he affirms in 4:6 is strengthened by the δὲ that contrasts the promise of God with what he has just denied: "On the other hand, He gives all the more grace" (μείζονα δὲ δίδωσιν χάριν). The LXX quotation from Prov. 3:34 expands what he has affirmed and prepares the reader for what follows in 4:7-10. Previously, we mentioned that this quotation serves as a "structural lynchpin" for the entire paragraph of 4:1-10. Edgar perceptively explains both its anaphoric and cataphoric functions.

> The first line of the quotation 'God opposes the arrogant' looks back to the enemies of God, who stand over against God at the climax of vv. 1-4, while the second line of the quotation 'but to the lowly (ταπεινοῖς) he gives grace' anticipates the following verses, which culminate in the command: 'Humble yourselves (ταπεινώθητε) before the Lord and he will exalt you.'[211]

More will be said about the comparison and contrast between 4:1-3 and 4:7-10 in the following section. Thus far the message conveyed by both the inner texture and the intertexture of 4:4-6 is clearly delineated. The arrogant and proud do not acknowledge their dependence on God and live according to the order of the world as enemies of God. By contrast, God gives grace to the lowly (ταπεινοὶ) who are dependent on God.

---

the spirit which God caused to live (κατῴκισεν as in James 4:5) in this flesh may prove to be true." Later he states that we received in creation from the Lord an uncontaminated spirit (πνεῦμα). Both the thought and language of James is often reflected in *Hermas*.

[211] Edgar, 187.

Richard Bauckham observes that in his only clear citations of scripture (γραφὴ in 2:8 and 4:5, 6), James is revealing his hermeneutical keys to the OT literature. "Thus Leviticus 19:18b serves as James' hermeneutical key to the Torah and Proverbs 3:34 serves as James' hermeneutical key to the wisdom literature."[212] In the case of the Leviticus reference in 2:8, he follows Jesus in understanding this verse as the summary of the whole law. The Proverbs reference here in 4:6 expresses most neatly the theme of reversal of status that is also prominent in Jesus' teaching (e.g., Matt. 5:3-6; 10:23, 25, 31, 43-44).

4:7

P	cj	C
ὑποτάγητε	οὖν	τῷ θεω

P	cj	C
ἀντίστητε	δὲ	τῷ διαβόλω

cj	P	A
καὶ	φεύξεται	ἀφ ὑμῶν,

4:8

P	C
ἐγγίσατε	τῷ θεῷ

cj	P	C
καὶ	ἐγγιεῖ	ὑμῖν.

P	C	add
καθαρίσατε	χεῖρας,	ἁμαρτωλοί,

cj	P	C	add
καὶ	ἁγνίσατε	καρδίας,	δίψυχοι.

---

[212] Bauckham, 155.

4:9

P	cj	P	cj	P
ταλαιπωρήσατε	καὶ	πενθήσατε	καὶ	κλαύσατε.

S	A	P
ὁ γέλως ὑμῶν	εἰς πένθος	μετατραπήτω

cj	S	A
καὶ	ἡ χαρα	εἰς κατήφειαν.

4:10

P	A
ταπεινώθητε	ἐνώπιον κυρίου

cj	P	C
καὶ	ὑψώσει	ὑμᾶς.

This third section (4:7-10) of the larger paragraph contains some interesting stylistic links with the first section (4:1-3). These links underscore how the quotation in 4:6 looks both backward and forward, as previously noted. As can be seen in the clausal analysis above, there are eleven second person plural present indicative verbs in vv. 2, 3, while vv. 7-10 contain 9 second person plural aorist imperatives, 1 third person singular imperative, and 1 future indicative verb expressing the fulfillment of the preceding commands. These balanced sets of eleven clauses both compare and contrast the reproach of the beginning section with the call to repentance at its end. This evident contrast between the two passages contrast is underlined stylistically by the changes in tense and mood.

The sheer number of the clauses in 4:7-10 is not served best by an atomistic linguistic examination of each separate command. This is especially noted when we recognize that the clauses are not just eleven discrete elements to be seen in isolation from one another. This can be seen in the following analysis of their overall structure. Three couplets of imperatives (7b-9) are framed by two other imperatives dealing with submitting oneself to God (7a, 10), thus forming a five-fold structure.

1. ὑποτάγητε οὖν τῷ θεῷ,
2. ἀντίστητε δὲ τῷ διαβόλῳ καὶ φεύξεται ἀφ ὑμῶν,
   ἐγγίσατε τῷ θεῷ καὶ ἐγγιεῖ ὑμῖν.
3. καθαρίσατε χεῖρας, ἁμαρτωλοί,
   καὶ
   ἁγνίσατε καρδίας, δίψυχοι.
4. ταλαιπωρήσατε καὶ πενθήσατε καὶ κλαύσατε.
   ὁ γέλως ὑμῶν εἰς πένθος μετατραπήτω
   καὶ
   ἡ χαρὰ εἰς κατήφειαν.
5. ταπεινώθητε ἐνώπιον κυρίου καὶ ὑψώσει ὑμᾶς.

Many have noticed the inclusio framing the passage (numbers 1 and 5). Often overlooked, however, are the syntactic parallels in the three middle couplets. In the second one a command is issued with respect to the devil and to God with the response of movement expressed by both if the command is fulfilled (the Devil flees and God draws near). In the third the focus is directed toward body parts (hands and hearts) which obviously are meant to stand for actions and attitudes. "Sinners" and "double-minded" receive the commands. In number four the focus is on the inward repentance that should accompany such cleansing and purification. The imperatives mount up in rhetorical effect heightened by the homoioteleuton of 4:9a and the ellipsis of 4:9c. The final imperative with its intertextual echo of a Jesus *logion* concluding the parable of the Pharisee and the publican (Luke 18:14) affirms the eschatological reversal of status evident in the letter (1:12; 2:5; 5:1-6, 9) and in the many other Jesus *logia* (Mat. 5:3-10). The forgiveness of sins that results from such humble repentance and cleansing must also be viewed in the light of the "lynchpin quotation" from Prov. 3:34. Riesner observes, "So, perhaps, here 'grace' (4:6) may include not only the gift of wisdom, but also the forgiveness of sins."[213]

The thoroughness of this conversion invokes activity in each of the three zones of the human personality as it was viewed in the ancient world. Purposeful interaction is symbolized by the *hands* (4:8a) while emotion-fused thought is symbolized by the *heart* (4:8b) and self-expressive speech is symbolized by the *mouth* (laughter and crying in 4:9). This approach evidences the completeness of a person's turning to God which involves the whole person.

---

[213] Riesner, 1261.

The peak theme of James is so clearly expressed in 4:1-10 that it probably does not need to be pointed out. Perhaps that is why it should be called the hortatory peak of the discourse. In 4:8 we also see the second occurrence of the word invented by James to describe the dilemma of the double-souled person who wants things both ways (pl. δίψυχοι, see the s. in 1:8). It is obvious that the person who desires to be committed to both heavenly and earthly wisdom is in extreme spiritual danger from which only the thorough "conversion" described in 4:7-10 can rescue him.

18. Paragraph 18 (James 4:11, 12)

Μὴ καταλαλεῖτε ἀλλήλων, ἀδελφοί. ὁ καταλαλῶν ἀδελφοῦ ἢ κρίνων τὸν ἀδελφὸν αὐτοῦ καταλαλεῖ νόμου καὶ κρίνει νόμον· εἰ δὲ νόμον κρίνεις, οὐκ εἶ ποιητὴς νόμου ἀλλὰ κριτής. εἷς ἐστιν ὁ νομοθέτης καὶ κριτὴς ὁ δυνάμενος σῶσαι καὶ ἀπολέσαι· σὺ δὲ τίς εἶ ὁ κρίνων τὸν πλησίον;	Do not slander each other, brothers. The one who slanders a brother or condemns his brother, slanders the law and condemns the law. But if you condemn the law, you are not a doer of the law but a judge. The lawgiver and judge is one, the one who is able to save and to destroy. But who are you, you who are condemning your neighbor?

4:11

A	P	C	add
Μὴ	καταλαλεῖτε	ἀλλήλων	ἀδελφοί

S		P	C
P ὁ καταλαλῶν / **C** ἀδελφοῦ		καταλαλεῖ	νόμου
cj ἢ / **P** κρίνων / **C** τὸν ἀδελφὸν αὐτοῦ			

cj	P	C
καὶ	κρίνει	νόμον·

cj	cj	C	P
εἰ	δὲ	νόμον	κρίνεις,

A	P	C
οὐκ	εἶ	ποιητὴς νόμου

cj	C
ἀλλὰ	κριτής

4:12

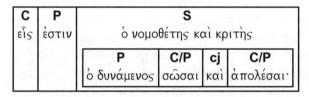

C	P	S			
εἷς	ἐστιν	ὁ νομοθέτης καὶ κριτὴς			
		P	**C/P**	**cj**	**C/P**
		ὁ δυνάμενος	σῶσαι	καὶ	ἀπολέσαι·

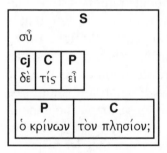

S		
σὺ		
cj	**C**	**P**
δὲ	τίς	εἶ
P	**C**	
ὁ κρίνων	τὸν πλησίον;	

The relationship between these two verses and the rest of the discourse has not always been evident. Many have despaired of seeing any real connection that the passage has with its co-text and describe it as a sort of free-floating admonition.[214] One of the main reasons for the apparent disconnect in these verses is the renewed address by the more tender ἀδελφοί (4:11), right in the middle of an otherwise condemnatory section (4:10-5:6) marked by the questioning about wars among you (4:1) and the strong condemnations of 4:13-17 and 5:1-6, each initiated by the challenging "come now" (ἄγε νῦν) imperatives. However, verbal and semantic connections with what precedes are not really absent. The nature of what is condemned, i.e., sinful slander, is really a manifestation of the selfish motives that are the causes of strife so strongly condemned in 4:1-3. Although the passage does commence with an address to the "brothers," the admonition is quite strong, even to the

---

[214] Peter Davids reaches a similar conclusion ("a free parenetic exhortation," 169). Davids, however, then attempts to show how the passage does connect with "the total context."

point of accusing the slanderer of placing himself above God and his law rather than submitting to both.

The collocation of a nominative of address with an imperative does indicate a new paragraph, but our author chooses the word ἀδελφοί for a very specific reason. He employs the singular of that word twice in the very next clause, thus heightening the seriousness of the brothers' slanderous talk, namely that the slander he condemns is not just against outsiders (which would be bad enough) but against other believers in the community of faith. Thus the paragraph connects both with its co-text and is distinct in its specific application within the community. Furthermore, the passage continues a stress on speech ethics, which has been a previous concern in the earlier paragraphs of the discourse (1:26; 3:1-12). What is unique is that he adds a specific concern about slander, the topic of the short paragraph.

Some commentators who depend on traditional grammars stress that a negated present imperative commands the ceasing of an action that is in progress. This approach is usually accompanied by the idea that a negated aorist imperative stresses that the action should never even start.[215] Recent thought on verbal aspect, however, reminds us that the ceasing of an action is not essential in this construction and should be determined only from the context. The present tense conveys a general rather than a specific prohibition. In this case it is the *practice* of slander that is forbidden.[216] A better approach is to recognize that when James uses an aorist imperative it is accompanied by an adjunct expression showing the time, result, or reason for the command (1:2; 21; 4:7-10; 5:1, 7, 8, 10). When he uses a present imperative, the command is general and specific examples may follow in subsequent comments on the command (2:1, 12; 4:11; 5:9, 12). This approach also prevents the interpreter from assuming through some sort of "mirror hermeneutic" that the author knows of a specific practice that is prevalent among the reading communities. Sadly, slander is present enough to merit a general warning at any time.

The verb καταλαλέω, which appears three times in 4:11, is best rendered as "slander" rather than the more generic "speak against" (ASV, NET, NAS)—an overly literal transference of the verb's component parts. The "speak evil" of some other translations (AV, ESV, NRS) is

---

[215] H.E. Dana and J.R. Mantey, *A Manual Grammar of the Greek New Testament* (Toronto: Macmillan, 1927), 301-2, is representative of this traditional view. See Wallace, 714-17 for a good critique.

[216] Porter, *Idioms*, 225.

better, but only the NIV and the New Jerusalem Bible convey the semantics of the word group by "do not slander."[217] One may speak against another and still speak the truth. James himself is certainly speaking against his readers by his admonitions! What is being condemned here is speech that is both inaccurate and damaging to the character and reputation of someone else. The usage of the noun elsewhere in the NT (1 Pet. 2:1) and in the Apostolic Fathers (1 Cl. 30:1-3; *Hermas* 2:2) also supports the translation of "slander" here.

By following the "topic/comment" method of analysis, we see in the following clauses how the topic of slander is expounded by relating it to the semantic field of κρίνω/κριτης which words appear no less than six times in 4:11b, 12. The semantics of this word group include the concept of "condemn" which fits here and also is required by the use of the verb in 5:9 and the noun in 5:12, where in both cases the context is one of eschatological condemnation.

As can be clearly seen in the OpenText analysis, the subject of the compound clause that ends 4:11 is: "The one who slanders (καταλαλῶν) a brother or condemns (κρίνων) his brother." It is that one who "slanders (καταλαλεῖ) the law and condemns (κρίνει) the law." The use of the noun κριτῆς in the apodosis of the conditional clause ending 4:11 may argue for rendering the verb as "to judge." Although there is no suitable English word like "condemner," that is only a problem in English. Greek hearers and readers would immediately connect the same semantic idea of "condemning" inherent in both verb and noun. The idea of "judging" here is not that of "rendering an opinion"—a legitimate meaning of "to judge." The more specific practice in the semantic field, "condemning," is the action condemned in this passage. The irony here is biting. We who are to be condemned by the law end up condemning the law by our slanderous speech. The conditional clause declares (a function of conditionals) that the one who condemns both his brother and the law is no longer a "doer" (ποιητὴς, echoing 1:25) of the law but a judge (κριτῆς)—a judge whose ironic role is to condemn the law!

Although the first clause of 4:12 is declarative and the second is interrogative, each contains an embedded clause in apposition to the subject of the sentence. These clauses are *right dislocated*, because they each appear at the end of their respective sentences. While this can be

---

[217] The word group includes the noun καταλαλία which expresses the more focused idea of "slander" (2 Cor. 12:20). Both Louw and Nida, 433, and BDAG, 519, indicate "slander" as a meaning of both verb and noun.

seen in the clause analysis above, a sentence flow display can better clarify this structure.

The lawgiver and judge is one,	he who is able to save and to destroy.
	ὁ δυνάμενος σῶσαι καὶ ἀπολέσαι
But who are you,	you who are condemning your neighbor
	ὁ κρίνων τὸν πλησίον;

The respective substantival participial clauses further define the subjects of each sentence. It is important to maintain the order of the Greek, where the numerical adjective εἷς fronts the copula ἐστιν. This not only brings to a prominent position the oneness of the lawgiver and judge, it also recalls the structure of Deut. 6:4, which this clearly echoes. "Hear O, Israel, the Lord our God, the Lord is one." The LXX also maintains this word order and would be readily recognizable to a Jewish reader (κύριος εἷς ἐστιν).

The switch to the word "neighbor" (πλησίον) at the end of 4:12 is a conscious echo of the love command in Lev. 19:18. The citation also evokes the entire context of Lev. 19:11-18 where the πλησίον is mentioned no less than six times. James, however, is filtering his use of Lev. 19 through the same love command issued by Jesus in Matt. 22:39. Therefore, his use of Lev. 19 here also echoes his use of this command in 2:8, where the context is showing partiality in one's synagogue. The context of 2:8 -13 shares many verbal affinities with 4:11, 12, especially its treatment of the law (νόμος in 2:8, 9, 10, 11, 12). This further supports the idea that the various references to the law in James are essentially the same, with each different descriptor conveying careful differences in nuance (law of liberty, royal law, etc.). It is the law given by Moses, but it is also the law as understood and expounded by Jesus. Therefore, it is appropriate to see in these references to slandering and condemning a brother another allusion to a Jesus saying found in Matt. 7:1, 2: "Judge (κρίνετε) not, that you be not judged (κριθῆτε). For with the judgment you judge you will be judged (κρίματι κρίνετε κριθήσεσθε), and with the measure you use it will be measured to you."

19. Paragraph 19 (James 4:13-17)

4:13 Ἄγε νῦν οἱ λέγοντες· σήμερον ἢ αὔριον πορευσόμεθα εἰς τήνδε τὴν πόλιν καὶ ποιήσομεν ἐκεῖ ἐνιαυτὸν καὶ ἐμπορευσόμεθα καὶ κερδήσομεν· ¹⁴οἵτινες οὐκ ἐπίστασθε τὸ τῆς αὔριον ποία ἡ ζωὴ ὑμῶν· ἀτμὶς γάρ ἐστε ἡ πρὸς ὀλίγον φαινομένη, ἔπειτα καὶ ἀφανιζομένη. ¹⁵ἀντὶ τοῦ λέγειν ὑμᾶς· ἐὰν ὁ κύριος θελήσῃ καὶ ζήσομεν καὶ ποιήσομεν τοῦτο ἢ ἐκεῖνο. ¹⁶νῦν δὲ καυχᾶσθε ἐν ταῖς ἀλαζονείαις ὑμῶν· πᾶσα καύχησις τοιαύτη πονηρά ἐστιν. ¹⁷εἰδότι οὖν καλὸν ποιεῖν καὶ μὴ ποιοῦντι, ἁμαρτία αὐτῷ ἐστιν.	4¹³Now listen, you who say, "Today or tomorrow we will go into such and such a town and spend a year there and trade and make a profit." ¹⁴You do not know what will happen tomorrow. What is your life? For you are a puff of smoke that appears for a little while and then vanishes. ¹⁵Instead you ought to say, "If the Lord wills, we will live and do this or that." ¹⁶But now you boast so arrogantly. All such boasting is evil. ¹⁷Therefore, whoever knows the right thing to do and fails to do it, for him it is sin.

4:13

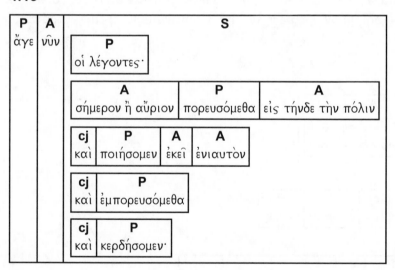

4:14

S	A	P	C	
οἵτινες	οὐκ	ἐπίστασθε	τὸ	
			A τῆς αὔριον	

C	S
ποία	ἡ ζωὴ ὑμῶν;

C ἀτμὶς		cj γάρ	P ἐστε
P ἡ φαινομένη, A πρὸς ὀλίγον			

A ἔπειτα	cj καὶ	P ἀφανιζομένη.

The above differs from the OpenText analysis of 4:14. I understand the verse to be composed of a relative clause, a primary interrogative clause and a final complex clause. The OpenText analysis considers ποία ἡ ζωὴ ὑμῶν as part of the Complement of the Predicator ἐπίστασθε.

4:15

A	
P ἀντὶ τοῦ λέγειν	S ὑμᾶς·

cj ἐὰν	S ὁ κύριος	P θελήσῃ

cj καὶ	P ζήσομεν	cj καὶ	C ποιήσομεν	P τοῦτο ἢ ἐκεῖνο.

4:16

A νῦν	cj δὲ	P καυχᾶσθε	A ἐν ταῖς ἀλαζονείαις ὑμῶν·

S	C	P
πᾶσα καύχησις τοιαύτη	πονηρά	ἐστιν.

4:17

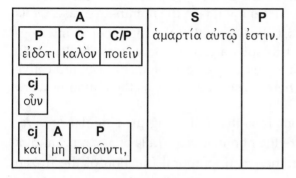

The greatest challenge in 4:13-17 is not interpreting its meaning. The topic of foolish planning apart from God's will is clear enough to all. The challenge is answering the question of how that topic is conveyed syntactically. A variety of answers has been offered by those who attempt to unravel its syntax. While the passage seems to burst onto the scene uninvited, there is a connection to the co-text. The thought of his own weakness and ignorance should deter a person from judging his fellows and finding fault with the law (4:11, 12). This concern should also prevent him from making confident assertions as to the future (4:13 ff.). The passage also clearly relates to the following paragraph due to their identical openings ("Αγε νῦν 4:13; 5:1). But even in this case there is a difference because after he addresses οἱ λέγοντες and mentions what they say (σήμερον ἢ αὔριον . . . κερδήσομεν·), he does not clearly issue a command like he does with οἱ πλούσιοι in 5:1 (κλαύσατε ὀλολύζοντες. . .). While "Αγε is an imperative, it is "frozen grammatically as a particle" that derives its meaning by whatever verb that follows, as is the case of the imperative κλαύσατε following it in 5:1.[218] But no such verb appears in the reported speech of 4:13b. The anacoluthon in 4:14 consists of a secondary relative clause (οἵτινες οὐκ ἐπίστασθε τὸ τῆς αὔριον), then a question (ποία ἡ ζωὴ ὑμῶν;), and finally a causal statement of why their boastful planning is wrong (ἀτμὶς γάρ ἐστε . . . ἀφανιζομένη).

---

[218] Dibelius, 231.

Compounding the problem is the fact that the critical texts (NA27/UBS4) punctuate 4:14 as an initial declarative clause, and it is translated this way by some versions as "You do not know what your life will be tomorrow."[219] This raises, however, some severe grammatical problems because it takes the interrogative pronoun as the object or complement of the verb even though it is in the nominative case. Of its 34 occurrences, ποῖος almost always is either the subject of an interrogative clause or the adjunct in such a clause. Only once (Matt. 24:42) does it appear in the nominative case as a complement to an indicative verb. Therefore, its usage here most probably is as the initiating word in a question.[220]

Another apparent anomaly is that following the singular imperative in both 4:13 and 5:1 are the nominative plurals οἱ λέγοντες and οἱ πλούσιοι. The rhetorical rather than temporal function of the frozen imperative Ἄγε νῦν, as mentioned above, explains the plurals and also the parenthetic nominatives in both verses.[221] The presence of the γάρ in the final statement concluding the verse seems a bit strange because we would not expect an answer to a question to begin this way. Perhaps we should understand the rhetorical force of the question "What is your life?" to convey the sarcasm of an implied answer. The sense would be "What is your life, really?" Then the explanation for the emptiness of such a life would be, "For your life is only a puff of smoke . . ." which makes a powerful rhetorical point.[222]

The complexity of the clauses, the anacoluthon, and the abrupt style that begs for additional conjunctions all combine to offer a serious challenge to anyone seeking to unpack their structure and meaning. As I have pondered over the rhetorical force of his language, I have come to the conclusion that James often utilizes the surface features of his language to communicate larger semantic messages. We saw this in the alliteration and rhyming used to emphasize the order of the heavenly virtues in 3:17 contrasted with language describing the vices that come from below in 3:14-16 which results in "disorder" (ἀκαταστασία). Perhaps the seeming disorder and lack of precision in the syntax of 4:13,

---

[219] NAS, NLT, CSB each translate 4:14a is this manner.

[220] As many versions take it (AV with a slight textual difference, NRS, NIV, ESV, NET).

[221] See BDF, 80, for explanations of both of these grammatical terms. For the "parenthetic nominative," see Wallace, 53-54.

[222] The word ἀτμὶς denotes a swirl of smoke arising from a fire (Gen. 19:28; Lev. 16:13; Ezek. 8:11). See Dibelius, 231-33, for an excellent defense of the above approach to the syntax of the verse.

14 is also intended to convey the resulting disorder of a life lived without God in its plans. All is uncertain despite our boastful planning because of our ignorance of the future, and even the language used to convey these ideas seems to be uncertain and in disorder. The contrast in the simple syntax of 4:15 may also be intended to convey the simplicity of a life that is lived consciously aware of the will of God.

Here, as elsewhere in James, the intertextual echoes abound for those with an ear sensitive enough to hear them. In this writer's opinion, too much attention has been paid to links between James and the Greco-Roman ethical traditions. While parallels can certainly be found, why should we think that they form the source when so many verbal and semantic links with the Jewish sapiential literature and the sayings of Jesus can also be found? One can hear in this passage, for example, the language of Prov. 27:1: "Don't boast (καυχῶ) about tomorrow (αὔριον) for you do not know (γινώσκεις) what the next day may bring forth." Consider also the saying of Jesus recorded in Lk. 12:18-21:

> "And he said, 'I will do this: I will tear down my barns and build larger ones, and there I will store all my grain and my goods. And I will say to my soul, 'Soul, you have ample goods laid up for many years; relax, eat, drink, be merry.' But God said to him, 'Fool! This night your soul is required of you, and the things you have prepared, whose will they be?' So is the one who lays up treasure for himself and is not rich toward God."

These and many other textual links with the ancient Jewish wisdom before him indicate that James is in the line of the Jewish sages as they were interpreted by Jesus the Sage.[223]

The contrasting character of the two ways tradition in James is effectively brought to the fore by the fronted articular infinitive construction in 4:15: ἀντὶ τοῦ λέγειν ὑμᾶς ("Instead, you ought to say"). Indeed, this is the "anti-language" that is so characteristic of the counter-cultural switch from earthly to heavenly behavior (3:13-18) that is impressed on every passage in this discourse. The reported speech that follows also continues the pattern of the imagined speech in 4:13. The four future tenses there are balanced here with two futures. Preceding

---

[223] Ben Witherington III, *Jesus the Sage: The Pilgrimage of Wisdom* (Minneapolis: Fortress Press, 1998. Witherington also draws on sapiential traditions in his commentary, *Letters and Homilies for Jewish Christians: A Socio-Rhetorical Commentary on Hebrews, James and Jude* (Downers Grove, IL: IVP Press, 2007).

them, however, is the conditional third class conditional protasis, "If (ἐὰν) the Lord is willing, then we will . . . ." The uncertainty of the condition contrasts with the boastful confidence expressed previously. But the condition is grounded in One who knows the future while we do not! This reflects the humility so commended in 3:17 that contrasts with the boastful pride condemned in 3:14-16. With a rhetorical flourish, James then repeats the νῦν he mentioned earlier but now turns it against the boaster. "But now (νῦν δὲ) you boast so arrogantly." Aware that the verb καυχάομαι can be used in a positive sense, James adds an adjunct phrase (ἐν ταῖς ἀλαζονείαις ὑμῶν) that should be understood adverbially, for how can you boast *in* your arrogances? This attitude cannot be excused as part of man's frailty. It is simply evil (πονηρά), only the second time James uses this word (see 2:4).

Not content with his condemnation of those who outwardly express their boastful arrogance in actual words (4:13, 14, 16), James rounds off his paragraph with a proverbial saying that goes even further. The οὖν appears here in the third of its five occasions (4:4, 7; 5:7, 16) and transitions to the application of the proverbial saying. "Therefore," it is not only wrong to openly disavow the Lord's control by one's boastful words. It is also wrong for "one in a state of knowing" (the perfect εἰδότι fronted for special emphasis) to do the right thing (acknowledging dependence on God's will) and then does not acknowledge it, to him it is sin. Theologians would call these two faults the "sin of commission" (doing the wrong thing) and the "sin of omission" (not doing the right thing).

We must be careful, however, not to over-theologize these statements by anachronistic parallels from later dogmaticians. It is better to recognize that James is probably drawing again on the wisdom of his brother. This closing aphorism reminds one of Jesus' parable of the watchful servants. "And that servant who knew his master's will but did not get ready or act according to his will, will receive a severe beating" (Lk. 12:47).

Chapter 5

ANALYSIS OF JAMES FIVE

19. Paragraph 19 (James 5:1-6)

5:1 Ἄγε νῦν οἱ πλούσιοι, κλαύσατε ὀλολύζοντες ἐπὶ ταῖς ταλαιπωρίαις ὑμῶν ταῖς ἐπερχομέναις. ²ὁ πλοῦτος ὑμῶν σέσηπεν καὶ τὰ ἱμάτια ὑμῶν σητόβρωτα γέγονεν, ³ὁ χρυσὸς ὑμῶν καὶ ὁ ἄργυρος κατίωται καὶ ὁ ἰὸς αὐτῶν εἰς μαρτύριον ὑμῖν ἔσται καὶ φάγεται τὰς σάρκας ὑμῶν ὡς πῦρ. ἐθησαυρίσατε ἐν ἐσχάταις ἡμέραις. ⁴ἰδοὺ ὁ μισθὸς τῶν ἐργατῶν τῶν ἀμησάντων τὰς χώρας ὑμῶν ὁ ἀπεστερημένος ἀφ᾽ ὑμῶν κράζει, καὶ αἱ βοαὶ τῶν θερισάντων εἰς τὰ ὦτα κυρίου σαβαὼθ εἰσεληλύθασιν. ⁵ἐτρυφήσατε ἐπὶ τῆς γῆς καὶ ἐσπαταλήσατε, ἐθρέψατε τὰς καρδίας ὑμῶν ἐν ἡμέρᾳ σφαγῆς, ⁶κατεδικάσατε, ἐφονεύσατε τὸν δίκαιον. οὐκ ἀντιτάσσεται ὑμῖν;	Jas 5 ¹Now listen, you rich people, weep and wail because of the misery that is coming upon you. ²Your wealth is rotten, and your clothes are moths-eaten. ³Your gold and silver are corroded, and their corrosion will testify against you and eat your flesh like fire. It is in the last days that you have hoarded your wealth. ⁴Look! The wages which you defrauded from the laborers who mowed your fields are crying out against you, and the cries of the harvesters have reached the ears of the Lord of Sabaoth. ⁵You have lived on earth in luxury and self-indulgence. You have fattened your hearts for the day of slaughter. ⁶You have condemned; you have murdered the righteous person. Does He not oppose you?

This paragraph has characteristics that justify both its discrete role with its own internal cohesion/coherence and its literary connections with the near and far co-text. It begins with the "frozen imperative" Ἄγε, which again performs more of a rhetorical role than a specific command. The nominative of address οἱ πλούσιοι, although not the familiar ἀδελφοί that initiates other paragraphs, is followed by a regular imperative κλαύσατε. This collocation of address plus imperative appears at the beginning of many other paragraphs. The paragraph ends with a challenging rhetorical question in 6b as is often the case elsewhere in the discourse. We will defend our calling this a question in the following analysis. A new paragraph begins in 5:7 with the transitional οὖν accompanied by the repeated collocation of ἀδελφοί with the imperative μακροθυμήσατε.

While these characteristics affirm that 5:1-6 is a unit, the paragraph also shares a number of connections with what precedes. The most obvious is the initial Ἄγε νῦν which initiated the previous paragraph (4:13). The thematic content of both paragraphs involves the existence of a group of people who place too much emphasis on material possessions, although the specific condemnation of each group differs. Furthermore, 5:1-6 shares many connections with 4:1-10, where the condemnation of selfish pleasures that divide fellow believers (4:1-3) ends with a call to repentance (4:7-10) that is strikingly similar to the same thrust of 5:1, 2. This is particularly true in the case of the following shared words: φονεύετε/ ἐφονεύσατε; ταλαιπωρήσατε/ ταλαιπωρίαις; κλαύσατε/ κλαύσατε; πένθος, πενθήσατε/ ὀλολύζοντες. This is even more evident when the semantic fields of the words, rather than simply the same cognates, are examined by tracing these similar fields in a work like the Louw and Nida lexicon. The difference between these two passages, however, is that a hope of forgiveness is offered to those addressed in 4:7-10, while in 5:1-6 the crying and weeping of the oppressing rich is because of their certain judgment to come (5:1).

The final verbal link between these passages is the rare verb ἀντιτάσσεται which appeared earlier (4:6) with God as the subject in the Prov. 3:34 quotation. The same form of that verb in 5:6 is what I take as a question with God also as the implied subject. While more will be said about that verb later, one must agree that its use at this point clearly rounds off the strong attack begun in 4:1 that reaches its apex at 5:6. Thus 5:1-6, while maintaining its own integrity, ends a sub-division in the discourse that many see as the main body of the letter. This leads directly, with the use of the rare οὖν, to the concluding remarks of the letter (5:7-20).

We will consider 5:1-3 and 5:4-6 separately, because the orienter ἰδού at 5:4 signifies a slight transition in the thought progression at that point.

5:1

P	A	add
Ἄγε	νῦν	οἱ πλούσιοι,

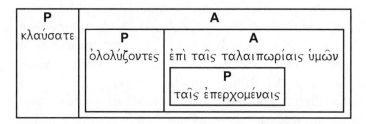

P	A		
κλαύσατε	**P** ὀλολύζοντες	**A** ἐπὶ ταῖς ταλαιπωρίαις ὑμῶν	
		P ταῖς ἐπερχομέναις	

5:2

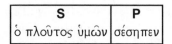

S	P
ὁ πλοῦτος ὑμῶν	σέσηπεν

cj	S	C	P
καὶ	τὰ ἱμάτια ὑμῶν	σητόβρωτα	γέγονεν,

5:3

S	P
ὁ χρυσὸς ὑμῶν καὶ ὁ ἄργυρος	κατίωται

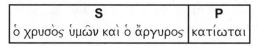

cj	S	A	P
καὶ	ὁ ἰὸς αὐτῶν	εἰς μαρτύριον ὑμῖν	ἔσται

cj	P	C	A
καὶ	φάγεται	τὰς σάρκας ὑμῶν	ὡς πῦρ.

P	A
ἐθησαυρίσατε	ἐν ἐσχάταις ἡμέραις.

As is the case in the previous paragraph (4:13-17), 5:1 also opens with Ἄγε νῦν, a second person imperative plus adverb. Most English translations render it as "Come now... ." This overly literal translation ignores what is obvious in Greek: the imperative is singular in form but the ones being addressed are plural in form (οἱ πλούσιοι) and the following imperative is plural (κλαύσατε). This pattern is the same as in 4:13 except there the plural group addressed (οἱ λέγοντες) are quoted but issued no command, and the sentence is not really completed. This disjunct between the singular and plural imperatives underscores the fact that it is the rhetorical function of Ἄγε νῦν that is in view, not the literal command of "come," which is only one of the meanings of ἄγω.[224] It is an orienter, a word used to direct the reader to the importance of what follows. It is also called a "meta-comment," a comment by the speaker/writer that is not necessary to the structure of the following clause, but is an added expression that calls attention to the importance of what is about to be said.[225] The NIV/TNIV are two of the few English versions that recognize this rhetorical function of Ἄγε νῦν and render it "Now listen!"—the translation that I have used as well.

The following clause commands the rich to "cry by wailing," an imperative followed by a participle of manner (κλαύσατε ὀλολύζοντες), due to the miseries that are coming upon them. The vivid present tense form of the adjunct participle (ταῖς ἐπερχομέναις) places the judgment clearly in an eschatological context. This is not, however, because of the tense form but because of the context which is clearly eschatological (5:3b: ἐν ἐσχάταις ἡμέραις). The prominent vividness of the present tense is then compounded by the series of perfects that follow in 5:2, 3, raising to an even higher level the prominence of the condemnation being issued. The following six primary clauses in these two verses contain three perfect verbs (σέσηπεν, γέγονεν, κατίωται) which stress the present state of the rich person's possessions. Their wealth is in a state of rottenness; their clothes are in the state of being moth-eaten; and their precious money lies in a state of corrosion. The traditional explanation of the perfect as describing an event taking place in the past with present effects does not offer an adequate picture of James' vivid language. Only an aspectual approach to the perfect tense does.[226]

These perfects are followed in 5:3 by two future tense forms as the silver and gold are personified. Their corrosion will be (ἔσται) a witness

---

[224] BDAG, 16. In the entry on ἄγε, BDAG states that this form is used as an "interjection" (9).

[225] Other linguists refer to this as a "meta-lingual comment," Brown and Yule, 132.

[226] Porter, 79, 267. See also Porter, *Idioms*, 41, "It can be no accident that the author uses the semantically strongest tense form available."

against the rich, and their money will turn on them and will eat
(φάγεται) their flesh like fire. The theme of an eschatological reversal,
mentioned briefly before in 1:11, 12, is now elevated to the prominent
context of the entire paragraph. This is dramatically portrayed in the
aorist condemnation that ends 5:3: "You have hoarded (ἐθησαυρίσατε)
your wealth in the last days." Perhaps the impact of this closing
statement is best conveyed in English by switching the order of the
components. The sense would be: "Although you have amassed all this
wealth (and have not adequately shared it as the following passage
states), what you *have* hoarded so selfishly for the future will all be lost
because 'it is in the last days that you *have* hoarded it'!" This clear
eschatological reference prepares the reader for the following specific condemnation issued against the fraudulent employers who have deprived
their day-laborers of their pay (5:4) and face, not a present day of feasting,
but a future day of slaughter (5:5) because God himself resists them (5:6).

The problem concerning the rusting of a metal (gold) which does not
rust is a problem only if one wishes to make it so. In their discussion of
the noun ἰός, Louw and Nida have the following insightful comment.

> Pure gold is not affected significantly by oxidation, but much of the gold
> of the ancient world was not pure, and therefore oxidation and resulting
> tarnish did take place. However, in most languages it is inappropriate to
> speak of 'rust' as occurring with gold and silver. If there is no satisfacto-
> ry term to indicate the deterioration in gold and silver resulting in
> extreme tarnish, it may be possible to translate Jas 5.3 as 'your gold and
> silver will be ruined and this will serve as a witness against you.'[227]

Old Testament echoes again resound through the intertexture of this
passage. Isaiah's fierce condemnation of Babylon, which also included
economic aspects, utilizes similar language. "Wail (ὀλολύζετε) for the
day of the Lord is near and a destruction will come from God" echoes
a prophetic oracle like Isa. 13:6. Judgment for their abuse of silver and
gold is also mentioned in Isa. 13:12, 17. In the next section (5:4), James
clearly recalls the "the Lord of Sabaoth" of Isa. 13:4, 13. When NT
authors cite isolated OT texts like James does here they often invoke
the larger context of those OT passages. More will be mentioned about
this reference to the "Lord of Sabaoth" in our treatment of Jas. 5:4.

Jas. 5:2, 3 sound like an abbreviation of Jesus' words in Lk. 6:24, 25:
"But woe to you who are rich (πλουσίοις), for you have received your

---

[227] Louw and Nida, 27.

consolation. Woe to you who are full now, for you shall be hungry. Woe to you who laugh now, for you shall mourn and weep (κλαύσετε)." Both direct verbal connections and semantic similarities abound. Jesus also condemned the hoarding of treasures in Mt. 6:19-20: "Do not *lay up for yourselves treasures* (θησαυρίζετε ὑμῖν θησαυροὺς) on earth, where *moth* (σὴς) and *rust* destroy and where thieves break in and steal, but lay up for yourselves *treasures* in heaven, where neither moth nor *rust* destroys and where thieves do not break in and steal." James now condemns the rich for practicing the very thing Jesus warned against.

The eschatological thrust of these sections should caution against confidently asserting that James is *the* wisdom writing of the NT. While James is closer to OT wisdom literature than any other NT writing, his wisdom has a unique apocalyptic thrust. This "apocalyptic wisdom" has been noted by a number of writers.[228] In this wisdom rooted in an apocalyptic context we hear the voice of Jesus as well. While there is much in Jesus' teaching that could characterize him as a "sage" in the Israelite tradition, his apocalyptic thrust leads us to situate his role as an "eschatological sage." This approach is more consistent when we consider the entire corpus of his teaching. A severe form critical analysis forces us to choose between his wisdom teachings and his apocalyptic teachings. However, it is too simplistic to think that James' brother was either a sage or a prophet. He uniquely combined the two roles, and James is obviously following closely in his sandals.

5:4

S		P
ὁ μισθὸς τῶν ἐργατῶν		κράζει

P	C
τῶν ἀμησάντων	τὰς χώρας ὑμῶν

P	A
ὁ ἀπεστερημένος	ἀφ᾽ ὑμῶν

---

[228] T.C. Penner, *The Epistle of James and Eschatology: Rereading an Ancient Christian Letter* (Sheffield: Sheffield Academic Press, 1996); P.J. Hartin, " 'Come Now, You Rich, Weep and Wail . . .' (James 5:1-6)," *JTSA* 84: 57-63.

cj	S	A	P
καὶ	αἱ βοαὶ	εἰς τὰ ὦτα κυρίου σαβαὼθ	εἰσεληλύθασιν
	P τῶν θερισάντων		

5:5

P	A
ἐτρυφήσατε	ἐπὶ τῆς γῆς

cj	P
καὶ	ἐσπαταλήσατε

P	C	A
ἐθρέψατε	τὰς καρδίας ὑμῶν	ἐν ἡμέρᾳ σφαγῆς

5:6

P
κατεδικάσατε

P	C
ἐφονεύσατε	τὸν δίκαιον

A	P	C
οὐκ	ἀντιτάσσεται	ὑμῖν;

Many of the characteristics of 5:1-3 described above apply also to 5:4-6, but in a more intensive manner. Just as 5:1 opened with the "meta-comment" Ἄγε νῦν, 5:4 opens with a similar "orienter" (ἰδοὺ) that points the reader to the words that follow. The accusatory tone against the rich in 5:1-3 is brought to an even greater level in 5:4-6 with specifics of the accusation brought forth. The personification of the cor-roded riches both "testifying" and "eating" flesh in 5:3 is developed further by the defrauded wages of the day laborers crying out against their employers (5:4). The eschatological themes expressed by the future tenses (5:3); the allusions to *Isaiah* (5:1, 3); and the reference to the "last days" in 5:3b are stressed in the same ways in 5:4-6 by references to a future judgment and a clear allusion to *Jeremiah's* "day of slaughter." Therefore, in approaching the unique features in this section, we will briefly: 1) survey its clause and tense usage; 2) mention a textual variant; 3) examine two OT allusions; and 4) justify viewing the final clause in 5:6c as a question rather than a statement.

As can be seen in the Open Text clausal analysis above, after the initial orienter ἰδού, 5:4-6 conveys its message through eight primary clauses marked by asyndeton. Only two of those clauses contain brief secondary participial clauses (5:4). In both of these, the subject of the clause is fronted, calling our attention to the cries of the defrauded laborers (present κράζει) and how those cries have entered (perfect εἰσεληλύθασιν) God's ears. This three-fold combination of the imperative orienter plus the initial placement of the subjects plus the present/perfect tenses convey a high degree of prominence for these cries to God and His willingness to hear them.

The five consecutive clauses in 5:5-6b convey the accusations against the rich defrauders. Not only have they engaged in gross self-enrichment, which James conveys by the colorful alliteration of the aorist verbs (ἐτρυφήσατε, ἐσπαταλήσατε, ἐθρέψατε), but their actions also include judicial acts of condemnation (κατεδικάσατε) and even murder (ἐφονεύσατε). The judicial actions may recall another vividly described court scene in 2:1-4. While the murder accusation may be hyperbolic, one cannot discount that this is meant to be taken literally. If day laborers are defrauded, who depend on receiving their pay at the end of the day (Mt. 20:1-16), their lack of daily bread may lead to the deaths of family members. The heartless employers, therefore, are indirectly to blame.

There is an impressive amount of evidence that the substantive τὸν δίκαιον, serving as the complement to the predicate ἐφονεύσατε, could refer to the Righteous One, the Messiah. This was an early title applied to Jesus by Peter (Acts 3:14), Stephen (Acts 7:52) and Paul (Acts 22:14). OT roots for this Messianic title can also be found in such texts as Isaiah 3:10 and 53:11. If *Wisdom of Solomon* 2:10-20 influences the language used here, however, it is best to view the substantive adjective as a collective term for the righteous poor who are the subjects of oppression in the co-text.[229] The final clause in 5:6c suddenly returns to

[229] The *Wisdom* passage shares many unique verbal connections with James. The substantive δίκαιος appears three times in that passage as the object of attacks by

a present tense in making a statement about opposition (ἀντιτάσσεται) to the oppressors. We take this as a question instead of a declaration but we will defer our defense of that translation to the end of the analysis of this paragraph.

The syntax of the first clause in 5:4 is a bit complex and translators have struggled to express the thought clearly while not straying too far from its form and word order. The attributive participle clause ὁ ἀπεστερημένος ἀφ ὑμῶν ("which is kept back by you") clearly refers back to the wages (μισθὸς τῶν ἐργατῶν) since both are in the nominative case. The intervening attributive participle clause τῶν ἀμησάντων τὰς χώρας ὑμῶν ("who have mowed your fields") provides a challenge for rendering a faithful but smooth translation since the predicate is at the end of the sentence and the subject is at the beginning. It is probably best to avoid the passive voice and express it as two coordinate clauses: "You have defrauded the workers who mow your fields and their missing wages are crying out to the Lord Sabaoth." The word translated as "kept back" by a number of translations, the participle ἀπεστερημένος, is not in the two fourth century uncials Aleph and B, which have the similar participle ἀφυστερημένος. Although the Westcott and Hort text contained this last word, a majority of the editors of NA27 and UBS4 preferred the first word. It appears that Metzger was part of the minority decision because he writes the following. "The earliest reading appears to be the rare word ἀφυστερημένος, which copyists emended to a more familiar word."[230] I agree with Metzger, although the final meaning conveyed by the expression is not seriously affected by whatever word choice is made.[231]

Two clear OT allusions occur at the end of both 5:4 and 5:5, and these are indicated by the italicized form of those words in NA27 and the footnote in UBS4. The first describes how the cries of the defrauded workers "have entered into the ears of the Lord of Sabaoth" (εἰς τὰ ὦτα κυρίου σαβαὼθ εἰσεληλύθασιν). I have chosen to use the English transliteration of the Hebrew *tsevaot* because the James text chose to use the Greek transliteration as it is found in the LXX. The allusion to either

---

wicked people (2:10, 12, 18) and is identified clearly as a poor person (2:10). Two verbs in the passage are also used in James to describe mistreatment of the poor (καταδυναστεύσωμεν in 2:10/Jas. 2:6; καταδικάσωμεν in 2:20/Jas. 5:6). The righteous person is not a Messianic term in *Wisdom*, since he is paired with a "widow" (χήρας) in 2:10, another victim mentioned by James (1:27).

[230] Metzger, 614.
[231] Louw and Nida, 563, 576.

Isaiah 5:9 or 22:14 (in the LXX) is obvious when we recognize that these are the only other places where the expression "the ears of the Lord of hosts" is used. The co-text of Isa. 5:9 concerns oppression of the poor and that of 22:14 describes the extravagant living of the rich in language similar to that in James. The personification of the defrauded wages "crying out" is similar also to the figure of Abel's blood crying out to God (Gen. 4:10).

It remains to justify why we take Jas. 4:6c (οὐκ ἀντιτάσσεται ὑμῖν) as a question and further explain who is the subject of the verb ἀντιτάσσεται. The commentaries list the various views about this clause and offer the reasons for each view. I will limit myself to explaining, from discourse considerations, why God should be considered as the subject of this rhetorical question: "Does He (God) not oppose you?" When Luis Alonso Schokel suggested this interpretation of Jas. 5:6c in 1973, he listed fifty previous authors who had not recognized the connection between Jas 5:6 and Jas. 4:6. The consequence of this connection is that 5:6c becomes a question with God doing the opposing.[232] Schockel's simple argument is that ἀντιτάσσεται has appeared earlier only in 4:6 where it is part of the quotation from Prov. 3:34: "God opposes (ἀντιτάσσεται) the proud, but gives grace to the humble." Jas. 5:6c, therefore, concludes the commentary on that quotation. "This explains the surprising present ἀντιτάσσεται and the lack of a specific subject."[233] The call to repentance in 4:7-10 expounds the latter part of Prov. 3:34—He gives grace to the humble. The role of God as judge, beginning in 4:11 and continuing through the harsh words of 4:13-17 and 5:1-6, develops the first half of the quotation—He opposes the proud. The conclusion to our author's prophetic attack comes in the final clause: "God opposes the arrogant. You have behaved arrogantly. **Should He not oppose you?**"[234]

---

[232] L.A. Schokel, "James 5, 2 [sic] and 4, 6," *Bib* 54:73-76. His list of authors is on 75. A dozen or more post-1973 authors could now be added to his list. See Adamson (1976), Laws (1980), Davids (1982), and Witherington (2007). On the other hand, Westcott and Hort punctuated 5:6c as a question.

[233] Schokel, 74. It also explains the lack of a conjunction that would connect the clause to what precedes. For example: "You murdered the righteous one, *but* he does not oppose you." The asyndeton, however, supports the idea that someone other than the righteous one is the subject of ἀντιτάσσεται.

[234] While other authors have recognized the clause as a question, they either take the subject to be the righteous poor or Jesus. As far as I can discern, L.T. Johnson was the first major commentator who espoused Schokel's view (*Letter of James*, 305). Some recent monographs have recognized the wisdom of his view (Penner, 155-58; Edgar,

We regretfully do not have the space to develop the relevance of 5:1-6 to the current issues of poverty, riches, and wealth accumulation. For a thorough discussion of these implications, the reader is referred to the insightful monograph mentioned in previous chapters, *Has God Not Chosen the Poor?* by David Edgar. Edgar applies insights from Bruce Malina and others writing from a social-science perspective to effectively apply the social message of James to both ancient and modern contexts.

20. Paragraph 20 (James 5:7-11)

5:7 Μακροθυμήσατε οὖν, ἀδελφοί, ἕως τῆς παρουσίας τοῦ κυρίου. ἰδοὺ ὁ γεωργὸς ἐκδέχεται τὸν τίμιον καρπὸν τῆς γῆς μακροθυμῶν ἐπ᾽ αὐτῷ ἕως λάβῃ πρόϊμον καὶ ὄψιμον. ⁸μακροθυμήσατε καὶ ὑμεῖς, στηρίξατε τὰς καρδίας ὑμῶν, ὅτι ἡ παρουσία τοῦ κυρίου ἤγγικεν. ⁹μὴ στενάζετε, ἀδελφοί, κατ᾽ ἀλλήλων ἵνα μὴ κριθῆτε· ἰδοὺ ὁ κριτὴς πρὸ τῶν θυρῶν ἕστηκεν. ¹⁰ὑπόδειγμα λάβετε, ἀδελφοί, τῆς κακοπαθίας καὶ τῆς μακροθυμίας τοὺς προφήτας οἳ ἐλάλησαν ἐν τῷ ὀνόματι κυρίου. ¹¹ἰδοὺ μακαρίζομεν τοὺς ὑπομείναντας· τὴν ὑπομονὴν Ἰὼβ ἠκούσατε καὶ τὸ τέλος κυρίου εἴδετε, ὅτι πολύσπλαγχνός ἐστιν ὁ κύριος καὶ οἰκτίρμων.	5 ⁷Be patient, therefore, brothers, until the coming of the Lord. Look! The farmer waits for the precious fruit of the earth, being patient about it, until it receives the early and the late rains. ⁸You also, be patient. Establish your hearts, for the coming of the Lord is at hand. ⁹Do not grumble against one another, brothers, so that you may not be judged. Look! The Judge stands before the gates. ¹⁰As an example of patient suffering, brothers, take the prophets who spoke in the name of the Lord. ¹¹Look! We consider those blessed who endure. You have heard of the endurance of Job, and you have seen the outcome from the Lord, because the Lord is compassionate and merciful.

James 5:7-11 shares lexical and thematic connections with its co-text while maintaining its own discrete role as a separate paragraph in the discourse. The οὖν in 5:7, making one of its few appearances (see 4:4, 7, 17; 5:16), indicates the transition from describing the suffering of the laborers in 5:1-6 to the exhortation given to them in 5:7-11, which

---

203; Taylor, 67, 68). While it is attractive to see a messianic reference here ("the Righteous One"), by taking the verb as an indicative statement with the righteous person as the subject, the following should be noted. Assuming that Wisdom 2 is the source for Jas. 5:6, it is interesting that when the righteous person is said to "oppose" those oppressing and condemning him, the verb is ἐναντιοῦται—not a NT word and definitely not the verb ἀντιτάσσεται of 4:6 and 5:6.

could be summarized as follows. "Be patient in your sufferings because the Lord will recompense both you and your unfair employers." While those condemned in 5:5 were described as feeding their hearts for a *day of slaughter*, the brethren are exhorted in 5:8 to establish their hearts for the *day of the Lord*. On the other hand, the particle οὖν collocated with the imperative μακροθυμήσατε and the nominative of address ἀδελφοι, plus the introduction of a new semantic topic (μακροθυμία/ὑπομονή) combine to indicate a new paragraph. There is discussion among commentators about whether 5:12 concludes this paragraph or starts a new one or even stands alone. Evidence will be provided by means of a semantic chain in 5:7-11 that these verses form a stand-alone unit. Furthermore, the repetition of ἀδελφοί in 5:9, 10 does not indicate new paragraphs at those points but they serve to span the topic introduced in 5:7. By discerning that same semantic chain we will justify this observation as well.

The internal structure (the inner texture) of the paragraph reveals that a slight transition occurs between 5:7-9 and 5:10, 11. The passage is introduced by the topic imperatival clause in 7a: Μακροθυμήσατε οὖν, ἀδελφοί, ἕως τῆς παρουσίας τοῦ κυρίου. The two following sub-sections share the following features. Each utilizes the imperative ἰδοὺ (5:7b, 9b/5:11), as was the case in the previous paragraph (5:4). There the word called attention to the cries of the day laborers. Here attention is called to the patience of the farmer, the role of the judge, and the blessedness of the prophets. The example of patience in the first section is the farmer, while two examples of patience in the second section are the prophets and Job. Finally, two similar statements are made about the Lord's coming in the first section (His coming is near and He is at the door), while in the second section two statements are made about the Lord's character (He has a purpose and He is compassionate and merciful).

We first examine the paragraph as a whole to justify the above conclusions about its limits and topic/theme. Two concepts of *patience* represented by the word groups μακροθυμέω/μακροθυμία and ὑπομονέω/ὑπομονή dominate the paragraph. Some older writers, probably influenced by a Classical Greek training, have attempted to see fine distinctions between these two words, with μακροθυμία describing *forbearance* with people and ὑπομονή describing *patience* with circumstances.[235]

---

[235] "This distinction will hold good wherever the words occur, namely, that μακρο- θυμία will be found to express patience in respect of persons, ὑπομονή in respect of things." R.C. Trench, *Synonyms of the New Testament* (London: James Clarke, 1961), 185.

While this may occasionally be the case, the two words have such a semantic overlap in their usage that it is unwise to maintain such a fine difference.[236] A better approach is to view these along with similar words as part of a "semantic chain."[237] The Louw and Nida lexicon, by grouping words according to their semantic domains, is a useful tool in this regard. When 5:7-11 is analyzed in this way, we see that in addition to the six occurrences of the two words, the passage contains four additional words that can also be included in the same semantic domain. Following is a table with the bolding of the chained words and the number of its semantic domain below each word.

Semantic Chain of "Field 25" Words in James 5:7-11

μακροθυμήσατε οὖν, ἀδελφοί, ἕως τῆς παρουσίας τοῦ κυρίου. ἰδοὺ ὁ γεωργὸς
25.168

ἐκδέχεται τὸν τίμιον καρπὸν τῆς γῆς **μακροθυμῶν** ἐπ᾽ αὐτῷ ἕως λάβῃ πρόϊμον
25.168

καὶ ὄψιμον. **μακροθυμήσατε** καὶ ὑμεῖς, στηρίξατε τὰς καρδίας ὑμῶν, ὅτι ἡ
25.168

παρουσία τοῦ κυρίου ἤγγικεν. μὴ **στενάζετε**, ἀδελφοί, κατ᾽ ἀλλήλων ἵνα μὴ
33.384/25

κριθῆτε· ἰδοὺ ὁ κριτὴς πρὸ τῶν θυρῶν ἔστηκεν. ὑπόδειγμα λάβετε, ἀδελφοί, τῆς

κακοπαθίας καὶ τῆς **μακροθυμίας** τοὺς προφήτας οἳ ἐλάλησαν ἐν τῷ ὀνόματι
24.89/25   25.167

κυρίου. ἰδοὺ **μακαρίζομεν** τοὺς **ὑπομείναντας**· τὴν **ὑπομονὴν** Ἰὼβ ἠκούσατε καὶ τὸ
25.120   25.175   25.174

τέλος κυρίου εἴδετε, ὅτι **πολύσπλαγχνός** ἐστιν ὁ κύριος καὶ **οἰκτίρμων**.
                    25.52   88.81/25

---

[236] It is difficult to see this fine distinction in such passages as Heb. 6:12 and even in the current passage, Jas. 5:10: ὑπόδειγμα λάβετε, ἀδελφοί, τῆς κακοπαθίας καὶ τῆς μακροθυμίας τοὺς προφήτας. In Trench's view, ὑπομονὴ would be the more appropriate word in 5:10.

[237] Reed, *Philippians*, 296-330.

There are two examples needing disambiguation because Louw and Nida's classification of the words κακοπαθίας (5:10) and οἰκτίρμων (5:11) place them in different domains. In each case the word is paired with another word in domain 25: κακοπαθίας with μακροθυμίας and οἰκτίρμων with πολύσπλαγχνός.

Discerning this semantic chain helps to justify two observations previously made. The first is that 5:7-11 is a self-contained and discrete section with the *topos* "patience" as its theme. The second is that this analysis justifies viewing both 5:1-6 and 5:12 as separate paragraphs because the semantic chain is contained within 5:7-11.

Due to the length of this macro-analysis of 5:7-11, the micro-analysis of the clausal structure in 5:7-9 and 10-11 will be brief.

5:7

P	cj	add	A
μακροθυμήσατε	οὖν	ἀδελφοί	ἕως τῆς παρουσίας τοῦ κυρίου

P
ἰδοὺ

S	P	C	A		
ὁ γεωργὸς	ἐκδέχεται	τὸν τίμιον καρπὸν τῆς γῆς	**P** μακροθυμῶν		**A** ἐπ᾽ αὐτῷ
			cj ἕως	**P** λάβῃ	**C** πρόϊμον καὶ ὄψιμον

5:8

P	cj	S
μακροθυμήσατε	καὶ	ὑμεῖς

P	C
στηρίξατε	τὰς καρδίας ὑμῶν

cj	S	P
ὅτι	ἡ παρουσία τοῦ κυρίου	ἤγγικεν

5:9

A	P	add	A
μὴ	στενάζετε	ἀδελφοί	κατ᾿ ἀλλήλων

cj	A	P
ἵνα	μὴ	κριθῆτε

P
ἰδοὺ

S	A	P
ὁ κριτὴς	πρὸ τῶν θυρῶν	ἔστηκεν

Of the ten clauses in 5:7-8, eight are primary and two are secondary (5:8c and 5:9b). The two embedded clauses (5:7c) contain a participle of manner and a temporal subjunctive, each modifying the verb ἐκδέχεται in the primary clause. The fronted imperative μακροθυμήσατε in 5:7 and 5:8 is exemplified by the farmer's patience in waiting for the early and later rains of the autumn and spring seasons. This agricultural touch is consistent with a Palestinian provenance for the letter.[238] Further imperatives call for the readers to "establish their hearts" (in contrast with the rich who fatten their hearts, 5:4), and to not grumble against one another. The temptation to grumble may initially appear out of place, but as the farmer may grumble when the rains delay, so the brothers may grumble impatiently with each other when the Lord delays his coming. An echo of the Dominical saying about judging in Matt. 7:1 may be appropriate here, especially with its use of the verb κρίνω in 5:9c.

The eschatological tone, already negatively announced in the preceding paragraph (5:1-6), is repeated as a positive reason to establish the hearts of the patient sufferers in 5:8c (ὅτι ἡ παρουσία τοῦ κυρίου ἤγγικεν). The reminder of the judge standing at the door in 5:9d (ὁ κριτὴς πρὸ τῶν θυρῶν ἔστηκεν) is stressed because of the danger

---

[238] D.Y. Hadidian, "Palestinian Pictures in the Epistle of James," *ExpTim* 63 (1952): 227-28; P.H. Davids, "Palestinian Traditions in the Epistle of James," in *James the Just and Christian Origins*, eds. Bruce Chilton and Craig A. Evans (Leiden: Brill, 1999), 47-48.

that believers face if they wrongly judge and condemn each other. The stative aspect of the perfect tense is employed in both these expressions to express the state of the Lord's presence—His coming is at hand and He stands before the gates.[239] The urgency of all this is stressed by calling the reader's attention (ἰδοὺ) to the presence of the judge.

5:10

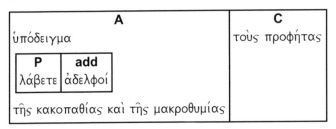

A		C
ὑπόδειγμα		τοὺς προφήτας

P	add
λάβετε	ἀδελφοί

τῆς κακοπαθίας καὶ τῆς μακροθυμίας

S	P	A
οἳ	ἐλάλησαν	ἐν τῷ ὀνόματι κυρίου

5:11

P
ἰδοὺ

P	C
μακαρίζομεν	P
	τοὺς ὑπομείναντας

C	P
τὴν ὑπομονὴν Ἰὼβ	ἠκούσατε

cj	C	P
καὶ	τὸ τέλος κυρίου	εἴδετε

---

[239] Porter, *Verbal Aspect*, 358-59.

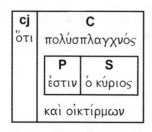

cj	C		
ὅτι	πολύσπλαγχνός		
	P	**S**	
	ἐστιν	ὁ κύριος	
	καὶ οἰκτίρμων		

James continues his asyndetic style with five primary clauses, two of which are supported by a relative clause (5:10b) and a causal clause (5:11e). The imperative beginning 5:10a is collocated with the familiar address ἀδελφοί, as was the case in 5:9. This collocation, however, does not justify the beginning of a new paragraph because the following clauses continue the same semantic topic introduced in 5:7. The Open Text analysis displays a "double accusative" following the command to "take" (λάβετε). The initial ὑπόδειγμα functions as an adjunct to the "prophets" and is in an especially prominent position preceding the predicator, something that James rarely does in this type of sentence (see 1:2). The reader's attention, therefore, is drawn to the prominent "exemplars" that follow—both the prophets and also Job. The prophets are examples of two characteristics that serve the purpose of the discussion: τῆς κακοπαθίας καὶ τῆς μακροθυμίας. It is best to translate these two genitives as a *hendiadys* ("patient suffering"). Both canonical and non-canonical Second Temple literature stressed the suffering of the prophets (Ez. 20:4, 5; 1 Mac. 2:59-64; Sir. 44-50; Mt. 5:12; 23:34; Acts 7:52). Therefore, the readers were not only to look to the prophets' word spoken in the name of the Lord (5:10b), they were also to look to their example of patient suffering, for they also had experienced the same things described in 5:1-6.

James then commands his readers to "look" at how we bless those who endure (5:11). We have noted that the attempt to maintain a distinction between the word groups μακροθυμία and ὑπομονή is doomed to failure because of their semantic overlap. In this instance, however, it is important to notice that James uses the latter word for the first time in this passage in describing Job. James appeals to the reader's knowledge of this patriarch and his ὑπομονή. Contemporary readers of Job may be pardoned if they do not always find Job patient in his dialogues with the friends in Job 3-37! If a careful nuance is placed on the "endurance" (ὑπομονὴν) of Job throughout his trials rather than on his "patience" (μακροθυμίας), the problem of Job's less than stellar response at times is better understood.[240] Job was not always patient with his interlocutors, but he began (1-2) and ended (42) well. While struggling with the why of God's dealings with him, he never cursed God. He struggled but he endured until the final outcome.[241] That word *outcome* is the best meaning of the word τέλος, which the readers have "seen." Rather than "purpose" or "end," the translation of τέλος as "outcome" better focuses on the events of Job 42. Finally, the ὅτι clause concluding the paragraph provides the reason that leads to the outcome of the suffering, not only of Job, but of the readers as well: "because the Lord is compassionate and merciful." This is preferred to its introducing a substantival clause and translated as "that," for James elsewhere uses ὅτι substantival clauses closely following verbs, which is not the case here.[242]

The message for James' readers, therefore, is to focus on the ultimate outcome of their own trials in light of the Lord's coming. As He was compassionate and merciful to Job, He will be the same to them at the outcome of their own trials.

21. Paragraph 21 (James 5:12)

Πρὸ πάντων δέ, ἀδελφοί μου, μὴ ὀμνύετε, μήτε τὸν οὐρανὸν μήτε τὴν γῆν μήτε ἄλλον τινὰ ὅρκον· ἤτω δὲ ὑμῶν τὸ Ναὶ ναὶ καὶ τὸ Οὒ οὔ, ἵνα μὴ ὑπὸ κρίσιν πέσητε.	But above all, my brothers, do not swear an oath, neither by heaven nor by earth nor by any other oath. Your "yes" should be yes and your "no" should be no, so that you not fall under judgment.

---

[240] This is preferred over appeals to the *Testament of Job*, because of the lack of real parallels to that work and its questionable dating. Patrick Gray, "Points and Lines: Parallelism in the Letter of James and the *Testament of Job*," NTS 50 (2004): 406-24. Thanks are extended to Craig Blomberg and Mariam Kamell for alerting me to this article and to Zondervan for providing me with an advance copy of their commentary. Craig Blomberg and Mariam Kamell, James, in *Zondervan Exegetical Commentary on the New Testament*, ed. Clinton Arnold (Grand Rapids: Zondervan, 2008), 230.

[241] C.R. Seitz, "The Patience of Job in the Epistle of James," in *Konsequente Traditionsgeschichte*, ed. Rudiger Bartelmus, Thomas Kruger, and Helmut Utschneider (Gottingen: Vandenbrock & Ruprecht, 1993), 373-82.

[242] The conjunction ὅτι appears sixteen times in James. Ten times it follows closely a verb and introduces a Complement (1:3, 7, 13; 2:19, 20, 22, 24; 4:4, 5; 5:20). Six times it introduces an adverbial clause and is translated "because" (1:10, 12, 23; 3:1; 5:8, 11). Jas. 5:11 follows the second pattern.

5:12

A	cj	add	A	P	A
πρὸ πάντων	δέ	ἀδελφοί μου	μὴ	ὀμνύετε	μήτε τὸν οὐρανὸν μήτε τὴν γῆν μήτε ἄλλον τινὰ ὅρκον·

P	cj	S	C
ἤτω	δὲ	ὑμῶν τὸ Ναὶ	ναὶ

cj	S	C
καὶ	τὸ Οὒ	οὔ

cj	A	A	P
ἵνα	μὴ	ὑπὸ κρίσιν	πέσητε

I have chosen to focus on this passage as standing alone rather than attach it to its preceding or subsequent co-text. This is due not only to its special discourse markers, but also to its unique semantic content which is not linked directly to its surrounding paragraphs. The closing purpose clause does echo the coming of the judge in 5:9, which counsels against viewing it as a free floating piece of advice inserted here for no particular reason.[243] However, the great diversity among commentators as to whether it ends one section or initiates the next is reason to stress its unique role in the discourse.

The verse consists of three primary clauses—each of which is imperatival. The second person plural predicator in the first clause, collocated with the nominative ἀδελφοί, is the way so many other paragraphs open. In the second clause, there is a shift to the third person, which does not lessen the imperatival force, but is consistent with the Jesus *logion*, which will be examined shortly. The ellipsis in the coordinated third clause suppresses the predicator, which is also consistent with the *logion*. A secondary result clause concludes the verse and relates the exhortation to the coming of the judge mentioned in the previous paragraph (5:9).

The verse opens with πρὸ πάντων δέ with the postpositive conjunction clearly relating the exhortation to the preceding paragraph.

---

[243] Contra Dibelius, 248.

There is a distinctly new note sounded by the Adjunct πρὸ πάντων which appears only here in the letter. An influential article by Francis has argued that this is one of the indications that this verse begins the official closing of the letter.[244] While there is not space to adequately interact with Francis' arguments, it should be noted that introducing-the-conclusion is not the function of the expression either in its other NT occurrence (1 Peter 4:8) or in its only use in the Apostolic Fathers (*Didache* 10:4).[245] Furthermore, we have seen that this verse shares affinities more with the preceding than the subsequent paragraph. BDAG's explanation of it as a "marker of precedence in importance or rank," translated as *above all*, is quite accurate.[246] L.T. Johnson has effectively argued that Lev. 19:12-18 is ever present in James' mind, especially in this chapter. He suggests that since Lev. 19:12 is behind the command in 5:12, James refers to it as the *first* of those commands in Leviticus 19. According to Johnson the sense would be: "And the first of all (these commands), brothers, is not to swear."[247] While Johnson's suggestion is creative, the use of πρὸ as first in a succession is not its meaning when used elsewhere with πάντων (e.g., Col. 1:17).

Then why does our author consider this command to be of such ultimate importance? It is not necessary to think that James has placed this command above the royal law which he has enunciated in 2:12. Perhaps James uses this expression because this command sums up all that he has said about speech ethics, a major theme in this letter. Furthermore, the importance that he attaches to this command may be related to the fact that this is the most explicit reference to a Jesus *logion* anywhere in his letter. In our previous comments on 2:5, we explored the use of the sayings of Jesus in James. We have noted that 5:12 has striking verbal similarities to Matt. 5:33-37, yet there are still differences between the sayings. While the differences are real, they are mostly in adjunct expressions or secondary clauses that explain or expand on the primary clauses. When we strip those adjuncts away, some striking verbal similarities emerge.

---

[244] F.O. Francis, "The Form and Function of the Opening and Closing Paragraphs of James and I John," *ZNW* 61 (1970), 125.

[245] *Polycarp to the Philippians* 5:3 uses the singular πρὸ πάντος not to conclude the letter, but rather to alert young men to be concerned with purity.

[246] BDAG, 864. L&N: a "marker of prime importance" tr. *more important than all else* (627).

[247] Johnson, "Use of Leviticus 19," 133.

James 5:12	Matt. 5:34-37
μὴ ὀμνύετε μήτε τὸν οὐρανὸν μήτε τὴν γῆν μήτε ἄλλον τινὰ ὅρκον· ἤτω δὲ ὑμῶν τὸ ναὶ ναὶ καὶ τὸ οὒ οὔ	μὴ ὀμόσαι μήτε ἐν τῷ οὐρανῷ μήτε ἐν τῇ γη μήτε ἐν τῇ κεφαλῇ σου ὀμόσῃς ἔστω δὲ ὁ λόγος ὑμῶν ναὶ ναί, οὒ οὔ·

Commentators have noted that while oaths were not condemned in the OT, both Philo and the Essenes limited them. Jesus himself responded to a legal call to an oath in Mt. 26:63, 64. Consistent with James' over- all emphasis on wholeness, the command counsels against a two–level speech on the part of Jesus followers. If one is given to the use of oaths to defend his statements, how can others recognize the truthfulness of those statements not accompanied by an oath? Followers of Jesus are not to be *double*. They are to be *single* in everything they do, and above all (πρὸ πάντων) in their speech.

22. Paragraph 22 (James 5:13-18)

¹³Κακοπαθεῖ τις ἐν ὑμῖν, προσευχέσθω· εὐθυμεῖ τις, ψαλλέτω· ¹⁴ἀσθενεῖ τις ἐν ὑμῖν, προσκαλεσάσθω τοὺς πρεσβυτέρους τῆς ἐκκλησίας καὶ προσευξάσθωσαν ἐπ᾽ αὐτὸν ἀλείψαντες αὐτὸν ἐλαίῳ ἐν τῷ ὀνόματι τοῦ κυρίου. ¹⁵καὶ ἡ εὐχὴ τῆς πίστεως σώσει τὸν κάμνοντα καὶ ἐγερεῖ αὐτὸν ὁ κύριος· κἂν ἁμαρτίας ᾖ πεποιηκώς, ἀφεθήσεται αὐτῷ. ¹⁶ἐξομολογεῖσθε οὖν ἀλλήλοις τὰς ἁμαρτίας καὶ εὔχεσθε ὑπὲρ ἀλλήλων ὅπως ἰαθῆτε. Πολὺ ἰσχύει δέησις δικαίου ἐνεργουμένη. ¹⁷Ἠλίας ἄνθρωπος ἦν ὁμοιοπαθὴς ἡμῖν, καὶ προσευχῇ προσηύξατο τοῦ μὴ βρέξαι, καὶ οὐκ ἔβρεξεν ἐπὶ τῆς γῆς ἐνιαυτοὺς τρεῖς καὶ μῆνας ἕξ· ¹⁸καὶ πάλιν προσηύξατο, καὶ ὁ οὐρανὸς ὑετὸν ἔδωκεν καὶ ἡ γῆ ἐβλάστησεν τὸν καρπὸν αὐτῆς.	¹³Is anyone among you suffering? He should pray. Is anyone cheerful? He should sing praise. ¹⁴Is anyone among you sick? He should call for the elders of the church, and let them pray over him, anointing him with oil in the name of the Lord. ¹⁵And the prayer of faith will save the one who is sick, and the Lord will raise him up. And if he has committed sins, he will be forgiv- en. ¹⁶ Therefore, confess your sins to one another and pray for one another, that you may be healed. The prayer of a righteous person has great power as it is working. ¹⁷Elijah was a person with a nature like ours, and he prayed fervently that it might not rain, and for three years and six months it did not rain on the earth. ¹⁸Then he prayed again, and heaven gave rain, and the earth bore its fruit.

We have previously argued that the conclusion of this *Diaspora encyclical* begins with 5:13. That the conclusions of ancient letters often mentioned the recipients' health and a prayer is certainly consistent with the references to health and prayer in this paragraph. Our author, however, does not conform exactly to the way in which those matters are usually treated.[248] He is concerned more with communal matters as evidenced by the three occurrences of ἐν ὑμῖν in 5:13, 14, 19 and the ἀλλήλοις and ἀλλήλων in 5:16. The topic of prayer is introduced in 5:13 and is commented on in the paragraph through 5:18. There is a semantic chain of twelve Field 33 (Communication/Prayer) words in the paragraph. There are the eight verbs—προσεύχομαι (5:13, 14, 17, 18), εὔχομαι (5:16), ψαλλέω (5:13), προσκαλέω (5:14), and ἐξομολογέομαι (5:16)—and four nouns—ὄνομα (5:14), εὐχή (5:15), δέησις (5:16), and προσεύχη (5:17) in this chain. The paragraph first describes prayer in the community (5:13-16) and then describes the prayers of Elijah as an exemplar (5:17, 18).

5:13

P	S	A
κακοπαθεῖ	τις	ἐν ὑμῖν

P
προσευχέσθω

P	S
εὐθυμεῖ	τις

P
ψαλλέτω

---

[248] Francis' observations (see footnote 20) about the ancient letter form as applied to James are hampered by the unique form of James as a *Diaspora encyclical*. We should not expect this type of *letter* to conform to ancient epistolography.

5:14

P	S
ἀσθενεῖ	τις ἐν ὑμῖν

P	C
προσκαλεσάσθω	τοὺς πρεσβυτέρους τῆς ἐκκλησίας

cj	P	A	A			
καὶ	προσευξάσθωσαν	ἐπ᾽ αὐτὸν	**P**	**C**	**A**	**A**
			ἀλείψαντες	αὐτὸν	ἐλαίῳ	ἐν τῷ ὀνόματι τοῦ κυρίου

5:15

cj	S	P	C
καὶ	ἡ εὐχὴ τῆς πίστεως	σώσει	**P**
			τὸν κάμνοντα

cj	P	C	S
καὶ	ἐγερεῖ	αὐτὸν	ὁ κύριος

cj	C		
κἂν	**C**	**P**	**P**
	ἁμαρτίας	ᾖ	πεποιηκώς

P	C
ἀφεθήσεται	αὐτῷ

5:16

P	cj	C	C
ἐξομολογεῖσθε	οὖν	ἀλλήλοις	τὰς ἁμαρτίας

cj	P	A
καὶ	εὔχεσθε	ὑπὲρ ἀλλήλων

189

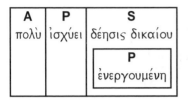

This sub-paragraph opens with three rhetorical questions, each inquiring if there is any (τις) individual in the community with a special situation. Those found are then commanded to do certain acts in accord with their situations (5:13, 14a). How the elders are to pray over a sick one is described (5:14b) with the results of such a prayer (5:15). A direct command is then issued to the entire community to confess their sins to one another (5:16a). The section is finally rounded off by an aphorism about the effectiveness of a righteous person's prayer (5:16b). How can the language used help to answer some of the questions raised in this simple description?

In 2:2 the spiritual center of these communities is a building called a synagogue. Here the term used refers to a local worshipping community, an *ecclesia* (ἐκκλησία). The reference here is not to a building, but to the communal gathering of believers. It is difficult to know if these elders were appointed/elected and if they were synonymous with the functioning overseers/bishops (ἐπίσκοποι), which is the case at a later period in Acts 20 and in some of the Pauline letters (Phil. 1:1; 1 Tim. 3; Titus 1). They most probably were respected communal spiritual leaders, like the "elders" in Jewish synagogues of the Second Temple Period.

Much discussion has taken place over the use of oil to anoint the sick, with Roman Catholicism drawing from this passage the sacrament of *extreme unction* (now called "the sacrament of the sick").[249] It is important to note that the reference to the anointing is part of a secondary adjunct clause, with the primary clause describing the praying of the elders (see the OpenText analysis of 5:14). While this does not answer the remaining questions about the use of oil, it places the subject in the

---

[249] This use of the passage by the Roman church was another reason why Luther disliked the epistle.

larger context of prayer. It is a subsidiary practice accompanying the most prominent action, namely the praying over the suffering one. Was the oil intended to play a sacramental role (Mark 6:13) or a medicinal role (Lk. 10:34)? Perhaps the medicinal role was primary with the sacramental functioning in a secondary role.[250]

The implications for practice in the modern church would lie in favoring one method to the neglect of the other one. The reference in 5:15 to the prayer arising from "the faith" (the subjective genitive τῆς πίστεως) that "will save" (σώσει) the sickly one, should be taken not in a spiritual but in a physical sense. This is illustrated by the next action, i.e., that "the Lord will raise him up," with the addendum, "And if he has committed sins, he will be forgiven." In other words, the order is first physical healing and then spiritual healing.

The transitional particle in 5:16 leads to the overall lesson to be gained from this instruction: the command to confess sins to one another. Since the entire context is that of the worshipping community, this is intended to be a communal command, not limited to private confession to each other. Other early Christian communities understood this in a communal sense. *Didache* 4:14 commands the young convert to "confess (same verb as in James) your sins in an assembly (ἐν ἐκκλησίᾳ)." Such practice is rarely witnessed today and is usually limited to the general confession in the liturgical churches.

5:17

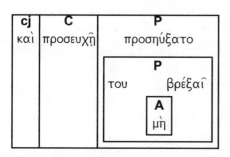

---

[250] Moo suggests the attractive idea that since the function of anointing with oil was to "consecrate" someone, the anointing here was to "consecrate" or "set apart" the sick one for concentrated prayer. Moo, 241.

cj	A	P	A	A
καὶ	οὐκ	ἔβρεξεν	ἐπὶ τῆς γῆς	ἐνιαυτοὺς τρεῖς καὶ μῆνας ἕξ

5:18

cj	A	P
καὶ	πάλιν	προσηύξατο

cj	S	C	P
καὶ	ὁ οὐρανὸς	ὑετὸν	ἔδωκεν

cj	S	P	C
καὶ	ἡ γῆ	ἐβλάστησεν	τὸν καρπὸν αὐτῆς

The previous verse ends with the general aphorism, "The prayer of a righteous person has great power as it is working." This rounds off the discussion of prayer in 5:13-16 and also leads into the next sub-paragraph. James holds up before his readers the one who is the prime exemplar of a righteous man whose prayers worked powerfully—Elijah the prophet. The non-typical (for James) parataxis of these six clauses, with the five consecutive uses of καὶ, is the most prominent linguistic feature of this compact sub-paragraph. It recalls the narrative context of this exemplar, drawn from the text of 1 Kings. And yet it is the source for these actions that is often called into question. It is common among commentators to posit a non-canonical source such as *4 Ezra* or *The Lives of the Prophets* as influencing our author in the details of his description. The problem is two-fold. First, the text of 1 Kings does not mention that Elijah prayed for the rain to be withheld nor that he prayed that it commence. Second, the OT does not mention that three and a half years was the length of the drought, only generally referring to the "third year" (1 Kings 18:1). What can be said about these issues?

This commentator has no problem with the possibility of James using a non-canonical source in his arguments, since other NT authors like Jude did as much. Suggesting that James used *4 Ezra* or *The Lives of the Prophets*, however, raises more questions than it answers. The current scholarly consensus is that both of these works are no earlier than the late first century.[251]

---

[251] D.R.A. Hare, "Lives of the Prophets," *ABD*, ed. D.N. Freedman (New York, 1992): 5:502; M.E. Stone, "Second Book of Esdras," *ABD*: 2:611-14.

Furthermore, there is no reference to Elijah's first prayer in either of these sources. Finally, neither of them refers to the three and a half year period of drought.

Perhaps we should look closer at the most logical source for this information—within the text of 1 Kings. The language of Elijah in 1 Kings 17:1 at least implies a prayer: "As the LORD, the God of Israel, lives, **before whom I stand**, there shall be neither dew nor rain these years, except by my word." Also, the language used to describe the prelude to the long-awaited deluge in 1 Kings 18:42 also implies a prayer: "And he bowed himself down on the earth and put his face between his knees." With this language so evident before us in the canonical text, why should we look elsewhere?

The three and a half year drought is also found in the words of Jesus in Lk. 4:25. A suggested source for this drought length usually is some unknown haggadic tradition, or it is explained as a supposed eschatological/apocalyptic reference (Daniel or Revelation), the latter being quite anachronistic even with a later date for James and Luke. The author's familiarity with Palestinian traditions, which seems to permeate the writing, offers a better explanation. Earlier in the chapter James displays his knowledge of Palestinian agriculture with his reference to the early and later rains (5:7). After the later rains in the Spring, there is a six month drought before the early rains in the Autumn commence. If the announcement of the drought was at the end of the dry season, the additional three years of drought would then provide the total length mentioned by James and Jesus. This explanation, also offered by a long time Palestinian resident, E.F.F. Bishop, has been overlooked by most commentators.[252]

Why would James choose these two incidents of prayer in Elijah's ministry, even if the account in 1Kings does not clearly mention them as prayers? There are other prayers by Elijah that are clearly mentioned (1Kings 17:20-21; 18:36-37; 2Kings 1:12). With an eye to the previous context of the paragraph (5:14-16), perhaps James utilized these two instances of prayer because the rain prayed for brought refreshment to the parched earth (5:18), just as the prayer of faith will bring refreshment to the sick person (5:15).

The message of this exemplar passage is that the great prophet was made of the "same stuff" of which both the readers and the author (ἡμῖν) were made. The difference is that Elijah prayed with faith and

---

[252] E.F. Bishop, "Three and a Half Years," *ExpTim* 61 (1949-50): 126-27.

was not of a double mind (1:6-8). Furthermore, he "prayed with prayer" a cognate dative expression (προσευχῇ προσηύξατο) recalling the Hebrew Infinitive Absolute and conveyed by "he prayed fervently."[253] The praying of the great, although still human, prophet was held up as an example of what the readers' prayers could accomplish if they prayed in faith from the background of a righteous life. It is this type of single minded praying that is inspired by wisdom from above.

23. Paragraph 23 (James 5:19, 20)

᾽Αδελφοί μου, ἐάν τις ἐν ὑμῖν πλανηθῇ ἀπὸ τῆς ἀληθείας καὶ ἐπιστρέψῃ τις αὐτόν," γινωσκέτω ὅτι ὁ ἐπιστρέψας ἁμαρτωλὸν ἐκ πλάνης ὁδοῦ αὐτοῦ σώσει ψυχὴν αὐτοῦ ἐκ θανάτου *καὶ καλύψει πλῆθος ἁμαρτιῶν*.	Jas 5 [19]My brothers, if anyone among you wanders from the truth and someone brings him back, [20]let him know that whoever brings back a sinner from his wandering will save his soul from death and will cover a multitude of sins.

5:19

add	cj	S	P	A
αδελφοί μου	ἐάν	τις ἐν ὑμῖν	πλανηθῇ	ἀπὸ τῆς ἀληθείας

cj	P	S	C
καὶ	ἐπιστρέψῃ	τις	αὐτόν

5:20

P
γινωσκέτω

cj	S			P	C	A
ὅτι	P	C	A	σώσει	ψυχὴν αὐτοῦ	ἐκ θανάτου
	ὁ ἐπιστρέψας	ἁμαρτωλὸν	ἐκ πλάνης ὁδοῦ αὐτοῦ			

---

[253] To intensify the action of the verb is the function of cognate datives (Wallace, 168).

cj	P	C
καὶ	*καλύψει*	*πλῆθος ἁμαρτιῶν*

This final paragraph opens with αδελφοί—the fifteenth occurrence of this nominative of address and the tenth time that it inaugurates a new paragraph (1:2, 16, 19; 2:1, 14; 3:1; 4:11; 5:9, 12, 19). This address preceding the protasis of a conditional clause is collocated with an imperative (γινωσκέτω) preceding the apodosis of the clause in 5:20. The imperative is not demanded in the syntax so its function is as another "meta-comment" that calls attention to the prominent ὅτι content clause concluding the sentence and the book. Commentators have generally overlooked that this is only the second time that James fronts the αδελφοί μου, which normally is preceded by the imperative command. The placing of the address here and in 2:1 may serve as an inclusio for the two paragraphs that open and close what many commentators view as the body of the letter with chapter one serving as "something of a table of contents."[254]

There are also some interesting verbal connections with chapter one. The imperative γινωσκέτω echoes the appeal to γινώσκοντες in 1:3. The subjunctive πλανηθῇ describes the erring that was warned against by the μὴ πλανᾶσθε command in 1:16. Larger semantic parallels with the entire work are also plain. The "two ways" tradition is the basis of the entire paranetic appeal and is evidenced by the peak paragraph in 3:13-18 with its comparison of the wisdom from above and that from below. This finds a clear illustration with the reference to the "erroneous way" in 5:20 and the "truthful way" in 5:19. In addition to its connections at the macro-level of discourse, the paragraph's connection at the micro-level is evidenced by the τις ἐν ὑμῖν which ties this paragraph with the preceding one which also opens with the repetition of the same expression three times (once implied) in 5:13, 14. This expression also focuses the instruction on the internal life of the community rather than the general warnings to the faithless planners and the greedy rich in 4:13-5:6. The rather abrupt ending is absent of the typically Pauline greetings to particular churches. This is consistent with the *catholic* or general nature of this encyclical and is quite similar to the end of First John where the author abruptly ends with a warning against idolatry and an exhortation about a sinning brother (1 John 5:16-21). It is also no more abrupt than the conclusions in two other

---

[254] Johnson, *Letter of James*, 15; Bauckham, *James*, 63.

wisdom writings, *Sirach* 51:30 and *Wisdom of Solomon* 19:22.[255]

There still remain the questions of whose soul is saved and whose sins are covered. While there are text critical issues in these verses, the variant readings point to later scribes who desired to clarify a possible misunderstanding and the critical text probably does reflect the earliest and best readings. I doubt if anyone would read it other than referring to the converted sinner unless commentators had suggested differently. At first blush that seems to be the sense. Syntactical as well as theological reasons also support this interpretation. There is a distinct parallel construction between the following two clauses which is apparent when we re-arrange the elements of the clauses.

Subject	Predicator	Adjunct
ὁ ἐπιστρέψας	ἁμαρτωλὸν	ἐκ πλάνης ὁδοῦ αὐτοῦ
σώσει	ψυχὴν αὐτοῦ	ἐκ θανάτου

It is clear from the construction that the soul that is saved in the second clause is that of the sinner in the first clause. If that is true, the parallelism of the final two clauses makes it clear that the sins that will be covered are also those of the sinner.

Predicator	Complement	Adjunct
σώσει	ψυχὴν αὐτοῦ	ἐκ θανάτου
καὶ καλύψει	πλῆθος	ἁμαρτιῶν.

The future tense of καλύψει may have in mind future sins. Thus, the sense would be that the action of converting the erring brother will also affect his future sins. This is consistent with its usage both in *Prov.* 10:12 and in *1 Peter* 4:8.

---

[255] *Sirach*: "Do your work in good time, and in his own time God will give you your reward." *Wisdom*: "For in everything, O Lord, you have exalted and glorified your people, and you have not neglected to help them at all times and in all places."

It is appropriate that the final comment on this paragraph and on the discourse as a whole concerns the intertext of these thoughts. In a book that has so often utilized the *logia* of Jesus as well as the canonical writings of the OT, those two sources again inform James' closing counsel about the communal restoration of sinners. While this could be an allusion to the parable of the lost sheep in *Mt.* 18:12-14, the theme of restoring a sinning brother is also prominent in *Lk.* 17:3, 4. While the last expression about the covering of sins could allude to *Prov.* 10:12, the LXX there differs in wording, sharing only the common verb. The saying was later known in Jewish-Christian tradition (*1 Clem.* 49:4; *2 Clem.* 16:4). This formulation was also regarded by Clement of Alexandria and others as an *agraphon* of Jesus (Clement, *Paed.* 3.91.3; *Didascalia* 4).

Riesner's concise conclusion to his own commentary can serve as a fitting conclusion to our own comments on this paragraph and also on the entire discourse. "In any case, the last words of a sometimes stern letter remind the readers of the chances of repentance, forgiveness, and reconciliation."[256]

---

[256] Riesner, 1262.

A NEW PERSPECTIVE ON JAMES
WHY HAVE WE BEEN UNJUST TO JAMES THE JUST?

After four hundred years of languishing in a backwater of neglect largely due to the opinions of two German Martins, James is finally emerging into the light of serious scholarly attention. The remarks on James by Martin Luther are well known in lay circles. The magisterial commentary on James by Martin Dibelius has been the work to be consulted in academic circles. Whether it be Luther's "strawy epistle" or Dibelius' disjointed "ethical paranesis," the opinions of these German giants have influenced negatively generations of commentators. The last twenty five years, however, have witnessed both James and the writing attributed to him emerging into the brightness of a new day in Jacobean scholarship. Serious works on the epistle that are bold enough to attribute the work to James, the brother of Jesus and to date it before his death in 62 A.D., continue to appear.[257] Furthermore, monographs on James the man, while not rivaling the plethora of works on Paul, exhibit almost as many perspectives as authors.[258] A new appreciation of James has been emerging, although no consensus on questions relating to the man and his letter has yet emerged. My own research on James as part of writing a linguistic commentary on the letter has caused me to re-think and re-read both

---

[257] Such commentaries are those by L.T. Johnson, Peter Davids, Douglas Moo, Craig Blomberg and Dan McCartney. Their bibliographical information is listed in the following Bibliography.

[258] Good treatments of James the man are done by Adamson, Painter, and Witherington and are also listed in the Bibliography. The eccentric treatment by Robert Eisenman in his two volumes on James is quite radical in its conclusions, linking James with the "Teacher of Righteousness" in the Dead Sea Scrolls. While Eisenman's work deserves a fuller answer, I cite here the observation of McCartney (2009): "The suggestion that James was the central figure of the Qumran community caused a brief sensation in the popular media, but virtually all other scholars have rightly rejected it because it is built on too many speculative leaps and historical improbabilities." See Painter 1999: 230-34, 277-88.

the letter and the sparse references to the man in Acts, Galatians and 1 Corinthians. The result of that research has caused me to develop a new perspective on James the leader and also on James the letter. I firmly believe that there is still a need to do a fresh reading of the James materials, and to that end I offer the results of my own fresh reading.

A New Perspective on James the Leader

I offer no new proposals on the role that James played in the immediate family of Jesus prior to the cross and resurrection. The only debate in this regard is whether James shared in the apparent unbelief or disbelief attributed to Jesus' brothers in John 7:5, and hinted at in Mark 3:21 and 31-35. I also have no wish to engage again the oft-repeated discussion about the meaning of the word "brother." I accept the accuracy of John 7:5 and I am comfortable with the view that James along with his sisters and brothers were the uterine siblings of Jesus. It is important to note that the Greek Orthodox and Roman Catholic views about James being either a child of a previous marriage or a cousin are driven by a desire to maintain the perpetual virginity of Mary.[259]

What I do want to address is the role that James performed in the early church. My proposal is simple. I believe that a careful reading of Luke's account in Acts and Paul's comments in Galatians fully support the idea that James was not just a significant leader in the early church, nor was he just the leader of the Jerusalem church, but that he was *the leader of the church*. The implications of this fact are significant not only for the Roman Catholic attitude toward Peter, but also for the Protestant Evangelical attitude toward Paul.

Ironically it was a chapter written by still another German Martin (Martin Hengel) that first alerted me to this new perspective on James. That chapter, published in German, has been largely neglected by British and American scholars.[260] With my discovery of an even more neglected article by Richard Bauckham in an obscure European journal which reviews much of the same evidence, I undertook my own

---

[259] Some readers may desire a more thorough treatment of the "brother" issue. I refer them to the classic study by J.B. Lightfoot, Dissertations on the Apostolic Age: Reprinted from Editions of Paul's Epistles (1892) 3-44. McCartney summarizes well the evidence for the natural reading of "brother." McCartney, 7-12.

[260] Martin Hengel, "Jakobus der Herrenbruder—der erste 'Papst'?" in *Glaube und Eschatologie*, ed. Grasser and Merk (Tubingen: JCB Mohr, 1985) 71-104. I am grateful to Joanna Chou for her accurate translation.

renewed investigation and came to similar conclusions.[261] I mentioned these scholars, not to enlist their support of my particular views, but to inform skeptics that I have not lost my senses when I make the following claims.

After the Pentecostal effusion, James rose quickly to a parity of leadership with the traditional apostles and by the early forties was *the* leader, although as a *primus inter pares*, not only of the Jerusalem church (a point usually recognized) but of the entire "Jesus Movement." My argument is that if a stranger arrived in Jerusalem or in Antioch or even in Rome itself between the years of 40-62 and asked the question, "Who is in charge of this movement?", any knowledgeable Christian, even Peter or John or Paul, would have answered without any hesitation, "James." And he would not have needed to add "the brother of Jesus" because everyone would have known that there was only one person who would be instantly recognized by that single name without any additional description or qualifier. "James" was the one known in his lifetime as "the brother of Jesus" and by later generations by the title "James the Just." Again I believe that such is the clear implication of canonical statements and that it is also supported by a large number of writers from the second through the fifth centuries.

The evidence for James' rise to leadership in the church is found not only in Acts but also in Galatians and 1 Corinthians. Paul mentions that James received a special appearance of the risen Lord, which would have led to a radical reassessment of his brother's person and role (1 Cor. 15:7). Some even believe that he had already come to recognize Jesus and that this was an appearance to commission James as a leader, but the evidence is too scant to be dogmatic about that. James is simply mentioned as being with the apostles and Mary in Acts 1:14, where he is probably processing the new information that the one whom he thought was beside himself was actually the Son of God and Lord of creation! Paul mentions that during his first visit to Jerusalem after his conversion he saw only two of the "apostles"—Peter and James! (Gal. 1:19). From his statement about James in 1 Cor. 15 and Gal. 1:19, it appears that Paul classed James with the apostles. This is an important fact to note about James' rise to leadership.

---

[261] Richard Bauckham, "James at the Centre." *EPTA Bulletin* (1995): 23-33. Bauckham elaborated his ideas in "James and the Jerusalem Church," *The Book of Acts in its First Century Setting*, vol. 4, (1995), 415-480.

JAMES, THE LEADER OF THE JERUSALEM CHURCH

Galatians 2:9—the *first* of the pillars (Acts 11-42AD)

Acts 12:17—Peter: "tell James and the brothers" (44AD)

Acts 15:13-21—*the* leader at the Jerusalem Council διὸ ἐγὼ κρίνω—dio ego krino (15:19) (49AD)

Acts 21:18-26—tells Paul what to do; he obeys (57AD)

The information in the above box is crucial for the argument that James became the leader of the entire church. When Paul and Barnabas visited Jerusalem as described in Galatians 2:1-10 (most probably the famine relief visit of Acts 11-12), they met privately with the Big Three—James, Peter, and John (Gal. 2:9). The order of these "pillars" should not be overlooked. James was first in order and his "primacy" is illustrated in Peter's attitude toward James from at least this point onward. After "the pillars" affirm Paul's Gentile ministry they remind him only to remember the poor. Paul was eager to add that he had done that and would continue to do so. **Paul did what James told him to do.** In that dramatic episode in Acts 12 when Peter was released miraculously from prison, he made a special effort to ask the people in John Marks' mother's prayer meeting to inform James and the brothers about his release. Peter here acknowledges the leadership role of James as he also does later at the Jerusalem Council.

The events in Acts 15 surrounding what is sometimes called the Apostolic Council make it obvious that James has by then risen to be THE leader of the church. The crucial decision about whether or not believing Gentiles would have to convert to Judaism was clearly made. NO, circumcision would not be required of them, even if there was a vocal group (not including James) that pushed for it. The text is clear that James rendered the final decision as the head of the church, to which the apostles and brethren agreed as being the guidance of the Holy Spirit! Peter had first related his experience with Cornelius accompanied by the Spirit's work. Then Paul and Barnabas related their experience with Gentile conversions accompanied by signs (15:7-12). James, however, does not base his argument on experience but on how the prophets affirm this Gentile conversion with a citation from Amos 9:11, 12 and Isa. 45:21. These prophets agree with the experiences of Paul and Peter in that when Gentiles come into the kingdom, they will come in as Gentiles, not as converts to Judaism. Note the crucial language attributed to James as he introduces his concluding decision in 15:19a: (διὸ ἐγὼ κρίνω)—(*dio ego krino*). Many translations blunt the force of these words which to any Greek reader would mean, "**Therefore, I decide**... The transitional conjunction διὸ introduces the conclusion to the argument. This is followed by the pronoun ἐγὼ which is not needed in Greek so it must be added for particular prominence and emphasis (Therefore, I...). Then the verb κρίνω describes James' action in rendering the verdict. Any good Greek lexicon informs that this verb carries the sense of a judicial verdict or decision and should not be blunted by an idea like, "Well, let me sum up our discussion." James makes the final decision and everyone agrees with it! He is not a pope. He is the "first among equals" (*primus inter pares*). Peter and Paul acknowledge that authority and then they proceed to do what he tells them! When James added that certain practices particularly offensive to Jews be observed by the Gentile believers and composes a letter (a diaspora encyclical?) requesting such, Paul delivered the letter as he was instructed to do so (see Acts 16:4). For the second time, **Paul did what James told him to do**.

In Acts 21:18-26 Paul exemplified what he calls elsewhere "becoming all things to all men" (1 Cor. 9:22), by again doing what James asks him to do in regard to ending the Nazirite vows of four young men. Paul probably thought that such an action was not necessary, but out of deference to James, he does it. He perhaps even used some of the offerings from the Gentile believers that he had brought with him to pay for this action in the Temple (see 2 Cor. 8, 9; Rom. 15:25-29). For at least the third time, **Paul did what James told him to do**.

"In Jerusalem 49 AD James appears to have been the world head of Christianity."[262] I believe that this bold statement by Barnett is quite accurate. This is not an overstatement, but is in accord with the facts as they emerge from Acts and Galatians. Bauckham's article in an obscure European journal also rehearses some of the same material as well as his larger chapter, "James and the Jerusalem Church."

An important question also arises. If this leadership role of James was the real situation reflected in the NT writings, did the early church in later centuries recognize James' primacy? The answer is "yes" and it is witnessed by writers, Jewish and Christian, from the second through the early fifth centuries.

---

[262] Paul Barnett, *Jesus and the Rise of Early Christianity*, (IVP, 1999) 314.

The martyr death of James took place in 62 AD and is vividly described by the Jewish historian Josephus.[263] The passage has been thoroughly discussed and does not need to be further elaborated here since it is widely accepted as an essentially genuine description of the demise of James. I would prefer to raise another important issue. I have never heard anyone comment on the significance of the fact that Josephus never mentions Peter, John or Paul. Apart from a statement about "the tribe of Christians" in the controversial "Testimonium Falvianum" about Jesus, the only early Christian that Josephus mentions is James! Could it be because of his leading role that was recognized even outside the movement?

Clement of Alexandria reproduced a tradition that the risen Jesus had actually appointed James to the leader of the apostles, something affirmed by Eusebius' citation of the Jewish-Christian historian, Hegessipus, and even attested by Jerome. Statements by such orthodox leaders as these are also echoed in a number of pseudepigraphal "gospels" such as *The Gospel of Thomas*, Saying 12: "The disciples said to Jesus, 'We know that you will depart from us. Who is to be our leader?' Jesus said to them, 'Wherever you are, you are to go to James the Just, for whose sake heaven and earth came into being'." I mention this, not because I have any confidence that Jesus actually said that, but because these and many other sayings about James' role reflect an attitude that actually prevailed in the early church, despite the growing authority of Peter's so-called successors in Rome! How did this universal recognition of James develop if it did not reflect the actual state of events? While no one claimed a continuing primacy for the bishop in Jerusalem in succeeding centuries, everyone acknowledged James' original role!

Hesychius of Jerusalem in the fifth century preached in the church founded by James on Mt Zion, where the episcopal seat supposedly used by James was still displayed. In a sermon on Acts 15, he said the following about his predecessor: "How shall I praise the servant and brother of Christ, the commander in chief of the new Jerusalem, the prince of the presbyters, the leader of the apostles, among the heads the highest, among the shining lights the one who shines brightest, among the stars the most illustrious? Peter speaks, but James makes the law. (*here he cites Acts 15:19*). 'I judge, whose judgment neither the law of custom nor the decree of an assembly can challenge. For in me

---

[263] Flavius Josephus, *Antiquities of the Jews*, 20: 200.

speaks the one who is judge of all, the living and the dead'."[264] Even after acknowledging some measure of rhetorical hyperbole by Hesychius, this description must indicate something about the position that James held, at least in the minds of Christians, for four centuries after his death.

If James was THE leader of the early church, there are some serious implications of this fact both for Roman Catholicism and also for Protestant Evangelicalism. In other words, Peter was not the primate of the church. He was behind James and he even yielded to his leadership. I will leave to my reader to conclude why James the brother of our Lord has been marginalized by Rome and written out of the history of the early church. It is interesting that among the so-called "saints" in Romanism, "St. James" refers to the "James the Less" among the apostles, not the James we have been studying! This is a clear indication of his marginalization and is most probably intentional so as to blunt the role of James the brother of Jesus in favor of the imagined role of Peter.

It is easy to find fault with Rome, but there are also some implications for those in Protestant circles as well. In Protestant evangelical circles we have often exalted Paul above the role that he actually played in the early church. Although none of us will acknowledge it, we have an un-mitred "pope" and he is Paul. While we have a NT canon of 27 books, the 13 epistles of Paul are our unspoken "canon within a canon." I affirm very strongly that I am not trying to "put down" or criticize Paul or reconstruct the description about him in the NT. I only desire to portray him and his role as is indicated in the NT and **also by his own words**. We should be reminded that Paul himself told us something about the level of his role when he called himself "the least of the apostles" (1 Cor. 15:9). Bauckham reminds us: "If for once we displace Paul from the central position he occupies not only in the New Testament contents page but also in the perceptions of early Christian history, and instead place James at the centre, the exercise will not diminish Paul's stature but will expand our horizons."[265]

A New Perspective on James the Letter

Someone once asked me what influence my new perspective on James the Leader had for our study of the letter attributed to him, especially

---

[264] Cited by Bauckham, "James at the Centre," (1995), 23.
[265] Bauckham, "James at the Centre," 25.

among those who already acknowledge the canonicity and consequent authority of the book. Again I would ask you consider the attitude of the earliest Christians to this letter vis-à-vis the other letters of the NT.

In the body of the commentary I referred to Luther's infamous statement about the book of James. In his Preface to the NT of 1522, Luther says of James that it is "really an epistle of straw," for "it has nothing of the nature of the gospel about it." In his Preface to the Epistle itself he writes: "James throws things together in such disorderly fashion that it seems to me he must have been some good, pious man, who took some sayings of the Apostles' disciples and threw them thus on paper."

Luther's frustration over James' lack of order (at least to him!) further demeaned the epistle in his eyes. I must add that John Calvin did not share this pessimism about the Letter of James, but expounded the book at length and published a commentary on it. What can a new perspective on the letter offer us? First we must look at the position of James in our current New Testaments, which is following the Pauline epistles and Hebrews, heading what is often called the "General" or "Catholic" Epistles. And then we must ask if that has always been the order.

In other words, pride of place has gone to Paul's epistles after the Book of Acts and heading the other writings of the apostles. However, this was not the case for over 1000 years of church history. The oldest complete copy of the NT that we posses (Codex Vaticanus) has James, the two Peters, the three Johns and Jude immediately after Acts. Then follow the Pauline Epistles. Codex Alexandrinus also has this order. Furthermore, the Eastern Orthodox Church still has maintained this order in their Bibles and the earliest editions of the Greek NT (Tischendorf, Tregelles and Westcott/Hort) also adopted this ancient order. English versions in the west and the current critical Greek texts (NA27; UBS4) changed the ancient order to the order in the Vulgate, which has been reflected in our New Testaments since the 16th century. The ancient recognition of the three "pillars" (Gal. 2:9) can also be seen in the order of the General Epistles: James' letter is followed by those of Peter and John. Throughout the Middle Ages, Greek New Testaments listed James and the General Epistles after Acts. There are hundreds of manuscripts referred to as *Praxapostolos*, which are comprised of Acts and the General Epistles, with James as the first of the epistles after Acts. The ancient manuscripts witnessed to James at the head with Paul always included, but in his proper place—after the pillars. I am convinced that Paul would have agreed with this order as well.

To return to the question asked of me that I previously referenced. Why does this matter? Well, if we recognize that James wrote to the whole church (as did Peter and John) while Paul wrote to individual churches and individuals, this does not diminish Paul's significance. It enhances the role of the diaspora encyclical written by the number one man in Jerusalem. To put it in lay terms, this recognition adds a bit of *octane to* our reading of this little letter. **As James the Leader should not be marginalized, so James the Letter should not be marginalized either.**

One final word about Luther's slur that James borrowed a few ideas from the apostles and thus "threw them on paper." Luther thought that the doctrine of the book was bad and also that the organization of the book was equally bad. My exploration of the discourse structure of the epistle, formed around the call to be "whole" and not divided, with the positing of 3:13-18 as its "peak" and its call to follow wisdom from above and not below, followed by the segments introduced with "brothers" plus an imperative or question have suggested that there is a structure to this epistle that Luther somehow missed. Perhaps his vision was clouded by his love for Paul and by his own deliverance from a works-righteousness, which he (wrongly) supposed James to be advocating.

HOMILETICAL SUGGESTIONS FOR EXPOSITORS

T he following could serve as an introductory message to a series on James. Rather than just preaching a sermon divorced from a text, the expositor could base such a message on James 1:1, and develop the life of James in the following way:

"James the Man" (James 1:1)

1. Blinded by the Light

    Mark 6:3; John 7:5

2. Brought to the Light

    1 Corinthians 15:7; Acts 1:14

3. Bearing the Light

    Gal. 1:18, 2:9; Acts 15; James 1:1 ("a slave")

"Responding to Trials" (James 1:2-12)

1. By Rejoicing at the Maturity Trials Can Bring (2-4)

2. By Asking God for Wisdom to Face the Trials (5-8)

3. By Viewing Trials As Leveling Experiences (9-11)

4. By Looking Beyond Trials to the Reward (12)

It may be difficult to cover all of 1:2-12 in one message. Perhaps two to four messages could be given, but each should be viewed as part of the entire message of the paragraph, and not preached as messages isolated from the context.

"Does God Care About Our Trials?" (James 1:12-15)

1. Believers Should Acknowledge God's Goodness in Their Trials (1:12)

   a. God wants us to pass His test
   b. God rewards us when we do pass His test

2. Believers Should Not Blame God for Their Temptations (1:13-15)

   a. God is not the problem because He cannot be tempted and therefore cannot tempt others. (1:13)
   b. We are the problem because we give into temptation through our own evil desires. 1:14, 15

"Is God Really Good?" (James 1:16-18)

Introduction: Recent books by atheists ("God is Not Great")

1. We must guard against being deceived on this subject 1:16

2. All good gifts come from a God who does not change 1:17

3. God's greatest gift is his birthing of Christians 1:18

"How to Listen to a Sermon" (James 1:19-27)

1. Before the Sermon—Prepare 1:19-21a

   "Put Off" "lay aside all sin"
   "Put On" "be swift to hear"

2. During the Sermon—Persevere 1:21b

   Receive the Word "with meekness receive the Word"
   Retain the Word ""engrafted"

3. After the Sermon—Practice 1:22-25; 26-27

   Negatively—"not hearers only"
   Positively—"be doers"
   An example of "doing": 1:26, 27
   　　　　False religion: He controls his tongue
   　　　　True religion: He cares for the poor
   　　　　　　　　　He is concerned about purity

"Fingerprints of a Real Religion" (James 1:26, 27)

1. Real Religion is Characterized by SOBRIETY 1:26
(the inward mark)

2. Real Religion is Characterized by CHARITY 1:27a
(the outward mark)

3. Real Religion is Characterized by PURITY 1:27b
(the upward mark)

"The Case of the Near-Sighted Usher" (James 2:1-13)

1. Showing Favoritism is Inconsistent with the Faith of Jesus (2:1)

2. Showing Favoritism is Especially Harmful to the Poor (2:2-4)

3. Showing Favoritism is Forbidden by Jesus and the Law (2:5-13)

   a. The teaching of Jesus (2:5-7)
   b. The teaching of the "royal law" (2:8-12)

Concluding Aphorism (2:13)

"A Demonic Orthodoxy" (James 2:14-26)

1. Real Faith is Accompanied by Actions (2:14-17)

   Faith Does Not Survive without Acts

2. Real Faith is Shown by Actions (2:18-19)

   Faith is Shown by Acts of Love

3. Real Faith Should be Shown by Actions of Trust (2:20-26)

   Faith is Illustrated by Acts of Trust

Abraham (2:21-23)

Rahab (2:25)   The "problem" of Paul and 2:24

Conclusion: "Whole" people have both faith and actions—a faith that acts! Both orthodoxy and orthopraxy are important.

"A Subject in Everyone's Mouth" (James 3:1-12)
"How to Prevent Foot in Mouth Disease"

Introduction: Speech is a main theme in James—1:19, 26; 2:12; 4:11; 5:12

1. The Tongue is a Small member (3:3-5)

   The Bit 3
   The Rudder 4

2. The Tongue is a Savage Monster (3:6-8)

   Fire 6
   Beasts 7
   Poison 8

3. The Tongue is a Subtle Mixture (3:9-12)

   Fountain 11
   Tree 12

Conclusion: No "doubleness"—be whole.

"Wise and Otherwise" (James 3:13-18)

Introduction: The crucial role of this passage as the "peak" of this epistle (two ways—choose wisdom)

1. True Wisdom Shows Itself in Actions (3:13) [The Truly Wise]

2. False Wisdom Shows Itself in Disorder (3:14-16) [The Worldly Wise]

3. Divine Wisdom Shows Itself in Peace (3:17,18) [The "Other Wise"]

"Ever Present Enemies" (James 4:1-6)

Introduction: Note contrast with end of chapter 3 (peace/war)

I. The War Which We Fight (4:1-3)

   Outward problems traced to inward causes

II. The World Which We Face (4:4, 5)

   More spiritual than physical

III. The Way Which We Follow (4:6)

> Grace from beginning to end. Who receives it?
> The way up is down (cf. 4:7-10 "humble yourselves")

"Six Steps to Success" (James 4:7-10)

Introduction: "How to be Successful"   "Steps to Success"

Note contrasts with the "steps to success" in the message of the possibility preachers.

    I.   Submit Yourselves 4:7
    II. Resist the Devil 4:7
    III. Draw Near to God 4:8
    IV. Cleanse Hands and Heart 4:8
    V. Repent of Your Sins 4:9
    VI. Humble Yourselves 4:10

You end where you began (v. 7). The paradoxes of the Christian life: last/first; slave/free; die/live; humbled/exalted; the way down is the way up!

"When Planning Becomes Presumption" (James 4:13-17)

Introduction: James puts aside a shepherd's staff ("brothers") & puts on a prophet's mantle ("you who say"). He exhorts us about …

1. OUR DIARY (4:13)

"Today or tomorrow …."

    1. He chooses his time
    2. He picks his place
    3. He limits his stay
    4. He plans his method
    5. He calculates his profit

Luke 14:28-31 — (The parable of the rich fool.)

2. OUR DAY (4:14)

Proverbs 27:1 Do not boast about tomorrow, for you do not know what a day may bring.

Luke 12:18-20 "I will tear down my barns and build larger ones . . ." But God said to him, "Fool! This night your soul is required of you."

3. OUR DUTY (4:15-17)

a. We should *refer* to God's will. [Paul: Acts 18:21; 1 Cor. 4:19]

b. We should *defer* to God's will. [Matt. 6:10 "May your will be done…"]

c. We should *prefer* God's will. [Romans 12:2 Do not be conformed to this world, but . . . discern the **will of God**.]

*To know God's will and **not** do it … is **sin**! (4:17)*

Conclusion: John 14:6 "I am the way, and the truth, and the life. No one comes to the Father except through me."

"Being a Christian in Your Values" (James 5:1-12)

I. Be Aware of Placing Your Value in Things (5:1-6)

The rich often oppress the poor
(always exceptions: Letourneau)
"It doesn't apply to me" (but anyone can place inordinate value in *things*)

II. Be *Patient* Until the Lord's Coming (5:7, 8)

Continue trusting, sewing, waiting

III. Be *Content* in the Lord's Providence (5:9-12)

"grumble" ("grudge" meant grumble in 1611)
Look at the prophets (Jeremiah, e.g.)
Look to your tongue (v. 12)

"Being a Christian in Caring" (James 5:13-20)

Introduction: The "One Anothers" of the New Testament

I. Be Sympathetic to One Another 5:13-15

"among you" (2)

II. Be Honest with One Another 5:16-18
   "one another" (2)

III. Be Supportive of One Another 5:19-20
   "among you" (1)

NOTE: Although not usually listed as important commentaries, I have found the following works on James quite helpful for providing some stimulating sermonic ideas: (1) Anglican vicar Guy King's messages on the book titled *A Belief That Behaves*, Christian Literature Crusade, 1967; and (2) Scottish professor William Barclay's brief expositions titled *The Letters of James and Jude*, Westminster Press, 1976.

A SAMPLE EXEGETICAL OUTLINE
By Raymond G. Matlock

I. **Introduction (1:1)**
   A. The writer (1a)
      1. His given name
      2. His glorious identification
         a. A slave of God
         b. A slave of the Lord Jesus Christ
   B. The readers (1b)
      1. Who they were—the twelve tribes
      2. Where they were—in the dispersion
   C. The requisite greeting (1c)

II. **Heavenly wisdom concerning trials (1:2-15)**
   A. Be joyful in trials (2-4)
      1. Plan on seeing trials as an opportunity for joy (2)
      2. Ponder on what you know to be true (3)
      3. Prize the ultimate goal (4)
   B. Be asking God for wisdom (5-8)
      1. The primacy of wisdom (5a)
      2. The pursuit of wisdom (5b)
      3. The progenitor of wisdom (5c)
      4. The pleasure of God in granting wisdom (5d)
         a. He gives to all generously
         b. He gives to all without finding fault
      5. The prerequisite for obtaining wisdom (6-8)
         a. Asking in unwavering faith (6a)
         b. A commentary on faithlessness (6b)
            i. It is never steady
            ii. It cannot expect an answer
            iii. It demonstrates a divided mind
   C. Be boasting in how God views you (9-11)
      1. The poor man's boast (9)

        a. His earthly position (9a)
        b. His heavenly position (9b)
    2. The prosperous man's boast (10-11)
        a. His earthly position (10a)
        b. His heavenly position (10b)
        c. His end—as all men, he will pass away (10c-11)
  D. Be speaking what is true about trials (12-15)
    1. The promise to those who persevere (12)
    2. The prohibition against blaming God for our temptation to sin (13)
    3. The personal responsibility for succumbing to temptation (14)
    4. The process that follows succumbing to temptation (15)
        a. Lust conceives sin (15a)
        b. Sin is born (15b)
        c. Sin leads to death (15c)

III. Heavenly wisdom concerning God's goodness (1:16-18)
  A. God is good—don't be deceived (16)
  B. God is the unchanging source of everything that is good (17)
    1. What—every good thing/every perfect gift (17a)
    2. Where from—from above (17b)
    3. Who from—the unchanging Father (17c)
  C. God has proven His goodness through salvation (18)
    1. He alone is the cause of it (18a)
    2. He accomplishes it by His Word (18b)
    3. He acts on our behalf for His own good purpose (18c)

IV. Heavenly wisdom concerning our response to the Word (1:19-27)
  A. Receiving the word restrains anger (1:19-21)
    1. The command for all "to know" (19a)
    2. The command for each person "to be" (19b-20)
    3. The call to "put off" and to "receive" (21)
  B. Remaining in the word results in blessing (22-25)
    1. The command for practical obedience to intellectual knowledge (22)
    2. The forgetful hearer (23-24)
    3. The faithful doer (25)
  C. Recognizing the requirements of the word represents true religion (26-27)
    1. Controlling the tongue (26)
    2. Caring for the helpless (27a)

3. Continuing in purity (27b)

V. Heavenly wisdom concerning favoritism (2:1-13)
A. It is incompatible with faith in Christ (1-4)
   1. It evaluates another based on human standards rather than Christ's (1-3)
   2. It exposes thinking that is inconsistent with Christ's (4)
B. It is incompatible with God's choice (5-7)
   1. God chooses to esteem the poor and honor His Son (5)
   2. The rich choose to exploit the poor and dishonor God's Son (6-7)
C. It is incompatible with the king of laws and the lawgiving King (8-13)
   1. It transgresses the king of laws (8-10)
   2. It transgresses the lawgiving King (11-13)

VI. Heavenly wisdom concerning living faith (2:14-26)
A. Faith without works is dead (14-17)
   1. The question proffered (14)
   2. The portrait painted (15-16)
   3. The parallel explained (17)
B. Faith is more than mere orthodoxy (18-19)
   1. The challenge to demonstrate faith (18)
   2. The incompleteness of orthodoxy alone (19)
C. Faith is vindicated by works (20-26)
   1. The entreaty to recognize uselessness of dead faith (20)
   2. The example of Abraham (21-24)
      a. The question proffered (21)
      b. The relationship between faith and works explained (22)
         i. Faith works together with works (22a)
         ii. Works perfect faith (22b)
      c. The results of faith working with works (23-24)
         i. Faith reaches its ultimate significance (23a)
         ii. Faith results in fellowship with God (23b-24)
   3. The example of Rahab (25-26)
      a. The question proffered (25)
      b. The example explained (26)

VII. Heavenly wisdom concerning our speech (3:1-12)
A. The prohibition against many seeking to be authoritative speakers (1)

B. The power of speech to direct (2-5a)
1. The principle stated (2)
2. The portraits that illustrate the principle (3-4)
    a. Small bits directing large horses (3)
    b. Small rudders directing large ships (4)
3. The principle applied (5a)
C. The power of speech to destroy (5b-8)
1. The portrait of its destructive power (5b)
2. The pernicious nature of speech described (6)
    a. Speech is fire (6a)
    b. Speech commands the world of iniquity (6b)
    c. Speech is set in a position to infect the whole body (6c)
    d. Speech is set in a position to inflame the course of life (6d)
    e. Speech is set on fire hell (6e)
D. The powerlessness of man to tame his speech (7-8)
1. Men posses the power to tame every species of wild beasts (7)
2. Men do not possess the power to tame their speech (8)
E. The paradox of inconsistent speech is proof of its pernicious nature (9-12)
1. It is used to both bless and to curse others (9-10)
2. It is like a fountain that sends forth two kinds of water (11)
3. It is like a tree that bears two kinds of fruit (12a)
4. It is like salt water producing fresh water (12b)

VIII. Heavenly wisdom concerning wisdom (3:13-18)
A. True wisdom is demonstrated through our deeds (3:13)
1. Good deeds are demonstrated out of good behavior (13a)
2. Good deeds are done in gentleness (13b)
B. The traits of false wisdom have their source in hell (14-16)
1. False wisdom is betrayed by selfishness (14)
2. False wisdom is foreign to heaven, the Spirit (Word), and God (15)
3. False wisdom defiles every place it exists (16)
C. The traits of true wisdom have their source in heaven (17-18)
1. True wisdom is from heaven (17a)
2. True wisdom is first pure (17b)
3. True wisdom produces mature believers (17c)
    a. It produces quiet teachableness (peaceable, gentle, and reasonable)
    b. It produces compassion in heart and actions (full of mercy and good fruits)

     c. It produces sincere loyalty to God and others
       (Unwavering and without hypocrisy)
    4. True wisdom is propagated by true peacemakers (18)

IX. Heavenly wisdom concerning conflict (4:1-10)
A. The source of conflict (1)
B. The shocking results of conflict (2-6)
    1. Murder (2a)
    2. Fights and quarrels (2b)
    3. Unanswered prayer (2c-3)
    4. Hostility with God (4-6)
C. The solution to conflict (7-10)
    1. Submission and self-abasement [humility] (7a, 10a)
    2. Submission and self-abasement explained (7b-9)
       a. Stand against the devil and stand near to God (7b)
       b. Seek personal sanctification (8b)
       c. Sorrow (9)
    3. The sublime satisfaction that results from submission and self-abasement (10b)

X. Heavenly wisdom concerning slander (4:11-12)**
A. The slanderer substitutes himself in the place of the Law (11)
    1. By making himself his brother's judge (11a)
    2. By making himself the law's judge (11b)
B. The slanderer substitutes himself in the place of God (12)
    1. By making himself equal to God (12a)
    2. By making himself the judge of his neighbor (12b)

XI. Heavenly wisdom concerning arrogance (4:13-17)
A. The arrogant substitute themselves in the place of the Sovereign Lord (13-15)
    1. By depending on themselves (13)
    2. By failing to depend upon the Lord (14-15)
B. The arrogant substitute their own glory in the place of God's glory (16-17)
    1. By actively pursuing their own glory (16)
    2. By failing to act upon what is right in God's sight (17)

XII. Heavenly wisdom concerning trusting in riches (5:1-6)
A. Those who trust in riches substitute earthly riches in the

place of heavenly treasure (1-3)
  1. By failing to properly utilize earthly riches (1-3a)
  2. By attempting to store up treasure on earth rather than heaven (3b)
B. Those who trust in riches substitute self-indulgence in the place of justice (4-6)
  1. By holding back the worker's wages (4)
  2. By hoarding riches through injustice (5-6)

XIII. Heavenly wisdom concerning patiently enduring poverty and persecution (5:7-11)

A. Patiently wait upon the Lord—He is returning soon (7-9)
  1. Wait and anticipate the future fruit (7-8)
       a. Emulate the farmer's patience (7-8a)
       b. Establish your hearts because the Lord's coming is near (8b)
  2. Wait and avoid frustrated speech (9)
       a. Escape the judgment incurred by frustrated speech (9a)
       b. Expect the Judge's entrance at any moment (9b)
B. Patiently wait upon the Lord—His purpose and character demand it (10-11)
  1. Our suffering has a purpose (10-11a)
       a. The example of the prophets (10)
       b. The example of Job (11a)
  2. Our suffering provokes Him to action (11bc)
       a. Based on His many compassions (11b)
       b. Based on His mercy (11c)

XIV. Heavenly wisdom concerning prayer (5:12-18)

A. Faithful promises exhibit righteous conduct (12)
  1. Promises are not to be secured by external entities (12a)
  2. Promises are to be secured by personal integrity (12b)
B. Faithful prayer exhibits dependence upon God (13-16a)
  1. Be faithful to pray when suffering (13a)
  2. Be faithful to praise when cheerful (13b)
  3. Be faithful to pursue the prayers of others when without strength (14-16a)
       a. Enlist the prayers of church leaders (14a)
       b. Enlist the physical aid of church leaders (14b)
       c. Expect that faithful prayer provides rescue (15)
  4. Be faithful to pray for others (16a)

C. Faithful prayer of the righteous is powerful to effect
   miraculous results (16b-18)
   1. The prayers of the righteous have great power (16b)
   2. The example of the power of a righteous man's prayers
      (17-18)
      a. Elijah was a mere man (17a)
      b. Elijah's prayer brought dearth (17b)
      c. Elijah's prayer brought plenty (18)

XV. Heavenly wisdom concerning he who turns a sinner from the error of his way (5:19-20)

A. A soul will be saved from eternal separation (19-20a)
B. A multitude of sins will be covered (20b)

---

*Raymond Matlock, a teacher at Grace Community Bible Church (www.gcbiblechurch.org), developed this outline for his adult Sunday School class, based upon Dr. Varner's analysis of the Epistle of James. It is offered as an example of how one expositor employed the information in this commentary to communicate how the distinct units within the text fit within the larger theme and flow of thought that the text itself reveals.

** See the alternate outline on page 224 that treats 4:11-5:6 as one discourse, dealing with self-sufficiency. Based on:

—The overarching attitude of self-sufficiency that leads to slander, boasting, and trusting in riches.

—Segmenting the book on the vocative noun "brothers" (ἀδελφοί) rather than the nominative of address (cf. vv. 4:13—"You who say" (οἱ λέγοντες) and 5:1—"You rich" (οἱ πλούσιοι)

ALTERNATE OUTLINE FOR JAMES 4:11-5:6

Treats 4:11-5:6 as one discourse on self-sufficiency. Based on:

—The overarching attitude of self-sufficiency that leads to slander, boasting, and trusting in riches
—Segmenting the book on the vocative noun "brothers" (ἀδελφοί) rather than the nominative of address [cf. vv. 4:13—"You who say" (οἱ λέγοντες) and 5:1—"You rich" (οἱ πλούσιοι)]

X. Heavenly wisdom concerning self-sufficiency (4:11-5:6)
   A. Self-sufficiency leads to slander (4:11-12)
      1. It substitutes self in the place of the Law (11)
         a. By making himself his brother's judge (11a)
         b. By making himself the law's judge (11b)
      2. It substitutes self in the place of God (12)
         a. By making himself equal to God (12a)
         b. By making himself the judge of his neighbor (12b)
   B. Self-sufficiency leads to boasting (4:13-17)
      1. It substitutes autonomy in the place dependence (13-15)
         a. By depending on one's self (13)
         b. By failing to depend upon the Lord (14-15)
      2. It substitutes arrogance in the place of God's glory (16-17)
         a. By actively pursuing his own glory (16)
         b. By failing to act upon what is right in God's sight (17)
   C. Self-sufficiency leads to trusting in riches (5:1-6)
      1. It substitutes earthly riches in the place of heavenly treasure (1-3)
         a. By failing to properly utilize earthly riches (1-3a)
         b. By attempting to store up treasure on earth rather than heaven (3b)
      2. It substitutes self-indulgence in the place of justice (4-6)
         a. By withholding the worker's wages (4)
         b. By hoarding riches through injustice (5-6)

ORIGINAL OUTLINE FOR JAMES 4:11-5:6

X. Heavenly wisdom concerning slander (4:11-12)
  A. The slanderer substitutes himself in the place of the Law (11)
     1. By making himself his brother's judge (11a)
     2. By making himself the law's judge (11b)
  B. The slanderer substitutes himself in the place of God (12)
     1. By making himself equal to God (12a)
     2. By making himself the judge of his neighbor (12b)

XI. Heavenly wisdom concerning arrogance (4:13-17)
  A. The arrogant substitute themselves in the place of the Sovereign Lord (13-15)
     1. By depending on themselves (13)
     2. By failing to depend upon the Lord (14-15)
  B. The arrogant substitute their own glory in the place of God's glory (16-17)
     1. By actively pursuing their own glory (16)
     2. By failing to act upon what is right in God's sight (17)

XII. Heavenly wisdom concerning trusting in riches (5:1-6)
  A. Those who trust in riches substitute earthly riches in the place of heavenly treasure (1-3)
     1. By failing to properly utilize earthly riches (1-3a)
     2. By attempting to store up treasure on earth rather than heaven (3b)
  B. Those who trust in riches substitute self-indulgence in the place of justice (4-6)
     1. By holding back the worker's wages (4)
     2. By hoarding riches through injustice (5-6)

BIBLIOGRAPHY

Those most useful books and articles for teaching and preaching James are marked by an asterisk and then briefly annotated.

COMMENTARIES

*Adamson, James B. *The Epistle of James*. New International Commentary on the New Testament. Grand Rapids, MI: Eerdmans, 1976.
  A valuable contribution to a noted commentary series, Adamson's volume will soon be replaced by one written by Scot McKnight.

*Bauckham, Richard. "James." Pages 1483-92. *Eerdmans Bible Commentary*. James D.G. Dunn and John W. Rogerson, eds. Grand Rapids: Eerdmans, 2003.
  Bauckham is one of the most respected authors on James and this commentary, although brief, gets directly to the heart of what James is saying.

Bengel, J. A. *Bengel's New Testament Commentary*. Tr. by C. Lewis and M. Vincent. 2 vols. Grand Rapids, MI: Kregel, 1887.

*Blomberg, Craig L. and Kamell, Mariam J. *James*. Zondervan Exegetical Commentary on the NT. Grand Rapids: Zondervan, 2008.
  The initial volume in what looks to be a valuable series, Blomberg and Kamell offer excellent exegetical and applicational analysis.

Bray, Gerald, ed. *Ancient Christian Commentary on Scripture*. Vol. 11, *James, 1-2 Peter, 1-3 John, Jude*. Downers Grove, IL:IVP, 2000.

*Brosend II, William F. *James and Jude*. New Cambridge Bible Commentary. Cambridge: CUP, 2004.
  Brosend is often overlooked, but his analysis stressing the inner-texture, intertexture, sociological texture, and homiletical texture of the text is often helpful.

*Davids, Peter. *The Epistle of James*. New International Greek Testament Commentary. Grand Rapids, MI: Eerdmans, 1982. *Viewed by some as the standard work on the Greek text of James, Davids sometimes yields too much to critical views. Still a valuable work.*

Dibelius, Martin. *Commentary on James*. Hermeneia. Translated by Michael Williams. Philadelphia, PA: Fortress Press, 1976.

Doriani, Daniel M. *James*. Reformed Expository Commentary. Phillipsburg, NJ: Presbyterian & Reformed, 2007.

*Hartin, Patrick J. *James*. S.P. Collegeville: Liturgical, 2003. *Hartin has written much about James. This commentary is the culmination of his many monographs and articles, although not always appealing to Protestant evangelicals.*

Hiebert, D. Edmond. *James*. Rev. ed. Chicago, IL: Moody, 1992.

Hodges, Zane C. *The Epistle of James: Proven Character through Testing*. Irving, TX: Grace Evangelical Society, 1994.

Hort, F. J. A. *The Epistle of James*. London: Macmillan, 1909.

Huther, J. E. *Critical and Exegetical Handbook to the General Epistles of James, Peter, John, and Jude*. New York, NY: Funk & Wagnalls, 1887.

*Johnson, Luke Timothy. *The Letter of James*. Anchor Bible. New York: Doubleday, 1995. *One of the better volumes in what is an uneven series. Protestant readers may find it difficult to even discern the author's Roman Catholic background.*

Kistemaker, Simon. *Exposition of the Epistle of James and the Epistles of John*. New Testament Commentary. Grand Rapids, MI: Baker, 1986.

Knowling, R. J. *The Epistle of James*. 2nd ed. London: Meuthen, 1910.

*Laws, Sophie. *A Commentary on the Epistle of James*. Harper's New Testament Commentaries. San Francisco, CA: Harper & Row, 1980. *An unassuming commentary that offers a very insightful and creative analysis.*

Martin, Ralph. *The Epistle of James*. Word Biblical Commentary. Waco, TX: Word Books, 1988.

*Mayor, Joseph B. *The Epistle of St. James: The Greek Text with Introduction, Notes, and Comments*. 3rd ed. London: MacMillan & Co., 1910.
The old standard on the Greek text, with a very thorough introduction that argues for traditional positions on James and its reception in the early church.

*McCartney, Dan G. *James*. Baker Exegetical Commentary on the NT. Grand Rapids. MI: Baker Academic, 2009.
One of the best recent treatments of James. McCartney thoroughly covers all the subjects touching on James research.

Mitton, C. L. *The Epistle of James*. Grand Rapids, MI: Eerdmans, 1966.

Moffatt, James. *The General Epistles James, Peter, and Judas*. Moffatt New Testament Commentary. London: Hodder and Stoughton, 1928.

*Moo, Douglas J. *The Letter of James*. Pillar New Testament Commentary. Grand Rapids, MI: Eerdmans, 2000.
An enlargement of his contribution to the Tyndale Commentary. In my opinion, Moo's balanced treatment is probably the best all around commentary for the expositor.

Mussner, Franz. *Der Jakobusbrief*. Herders Theologischer Kommentar zum Neuen Testament. Freiburg: Herder, 1981.

*Nystrom, David. *NIV Application Commentary on James*. Grand Rapids, MI: Zondervan, 1997.
While some of his efforts at application seem a bit forced at times, Nystrom still delivers a helpful exposition.

Plumptre, E. H. *The General Epistle of St. James with Notes and Introduction*. Cambridge Bible for Schools and Colleges. Cambridge, MA: Cambridge University Press, 1890.

Richardson, Kurt. *James*. New American Commentary. Nashville, TN: B&H, 1997.

Riesner, Rainer. "James." Pages 1255-63. *Oxford Bible Commentary*. John Barton and John Muddiman, eds. New York: Oxford University Press, 2001.

Ropes, James H. *A Critical and Exegetical Commentary on the Epistle of St. James*. International Critical Commentary. New York: Charles Scribner's Sons, 1916.

Scaer, David P. *James: The Apostle of Faith*. St. Louis: Concordia, 1993.

Wall, Robert W. *The Community of the Wise: The Letter of James*. Valley Forge, PA: Trinity Press International, 1997.

*Witherington, Ben. *Letters and Homilies to Jewish Christians*. Downers Grove: IL: IVP, 2007.
> *Witherington writes more books than most of us read, but his commentaries are remarakably thorough, helpful, and sensitive to language issues.*

MONOGRAPHS AND ESSAYS

*Adamson, James B. *James: The Man and His Message*. Grand Rapids: Eerdmans, 1989. *Now out of print, this is one of the best books on James the man.*

Aune, D. E. *Westminster Dictionary of New Testament and Early Christian Literature and Rhetoric*. Westminster John Knox Press, 2003.

Baker, William R. *Personal Speech-Ethics in the Epistle of James*. Tubingen: Mohr, 1995.

*Bauckham, Richard. *James: Wisdom of James, Disciple of Jesus the Sage*. London: Routledge, 1999.
> *Although not a commentary in the strict sense, this work is invaluable and an essential one to be consulted for a number of issues related to the study of James and his book.*

Beale, G.K. and D.A. Carson (eds). *Commentary on the New Testament Use of the Old Testament*. Grand Rapids: Baker Academic, 2007.

Beekman, John, and John Callow. *The Semantic Structure of Written Communication*. Dallas, TX: Summer Institute of Linguistics, 1981.

Black, David Alan (ed.). *Linguistics and New Testament Interpretation: Essays on Discourse Analysis*. Nashville, TN: Broadman, 1992.

Blomberg, Craig. *Neither Poverty Nor Riches: A Biblical Theology of Material Possessions*. New Studies in Biblical Theology. Grand Rapids: Eerdmans, 1999.

Callow, Kathleen. *Discourse Considerations in Translating the Word of God*. Grand Rapids: Zondervan, 1974.

Cargal, Timothy. *Restoring the Diaspora: Discursive Structure and Purpose in the Epistle of James*. SBL Dissertation Series. Atlanta, GA: Scholar's Press, 1993.

Chester, Andrew, and Ralph P. Martin, eds. *The Theology of the Letters of James, Peter, and Jude.* Cambridge: CUP, 1994.

Cheung, Luke L. *The Genre, Composition, and Hermeneutics of James.* London: Paternoster, 2003.

Chilton, Bruce, and Craig A. Evans (eds.). *James the Just and Christian Origins.* Supplements to Novum Testamentum. Leiden: Brill, 1999.

_____, eds. *The Missions of James, Peter and Paul: Tensions in Early Christianity.* Boston: Brill, 2005.

Cotterell, Peter, and Max Turner. *Linguistics and Biblical Interpretation.* Downers Grove, IL: InterVarsity Press, 1989.

Davids, Peter. "Tradition and Citation in the Epistle of James." Pages 113-26 in *Scripture, Tradition and Interpretation: Festschrift for E. F. Harrison.* Ed. by W. Ward Gasque and William S. LaSor. Grand Rapids: Eerdmans, 1978.

_____. "James and Jesus." Pages 63-84 in *The Jesus Tradition Outside the Gospels.* Ed. by David Wenham. Sheffield: JSOT Press, 1984.

_____. "The Epistle of James in Modern Discussion." Pages 3621-45 in *Aufstieg und Niedergang der römischen Welt: Geschichte und Kultur Roms Im Spiegel der neuern Forschung.* Edited by Hildegard Temporini and Wolfgang Haase. Vol. 25.5. Berlin: Walter de Gruyter, 1988.

_____. "Palestinian Traditions in the Epistle of James." Pages 33-57 in *James the Just and Christian Origins.* Edited by Bruce Chilton and Craig A. Evans. Leiden: Brill, 1999.

Deppe, Dean B. *The Sayings of Jesus in the Epistle of James.* Chelsea, MI: Bookcrafters, 1989.

*Edgar, David H. *Has God not Chosen the Poor? The Social Setting of the Epistle of James.* JSNT Supplement Series. Sheffield: Sheffield Academic Press, 2001.
This often overlooked monograph offers some helpful and creative comments on many passages in James.

Egger, Wilhelm. *How to Read the New Testament: An Introduction to Linguistics and Historical-Critical Methodology.* Peabody, MA: Hendrickson, 1996.

Eisenman, Robert. *James the Brother of Jesus.* New York: Viking, 1996.

Fanning, Buist. *Verbal Aspect in New Testament Greek.* New York, NY: Oxford University Press, 1990.

Green, Joel B. (ed.). *Hearing the New Testament: Strategies for Interpretation.* Grand Rapids: Eerdmans, 1995.

Grimes, J. E. *The Thread of Discourse.* The Hague: Mouton, 1975.

Guthrie, George H. *"James."* Pages 197-273 in The Expositor's Bible Commentary, Revised Edition, ed. Tremper Longman III and David E. Garland, vol. 13. Grand Rapids: Zondervan, 2006.

Halliday, M. A. K. *Explorations in the Functions of Language.* New York, NY: Elsevier North-Holland, 1997.

_____. *Language as Social Semiotic: The Social Interpretation of Language and Meaning.* Baltimore, MD: University Park Press, 1978.

_____. *Language, Context, and Text: Aspects of Language in a Social-Semiotic Perspective.* Oxford: Oxford University Press, 1989.

Halliday, M. A. K. and Ruqaiya Hasan. *Cohesion in English.* London: Longman 1976.

_____. *An Introduction to Functional Grammar.* London: Edwin Arnold, 1985.

Hartin, Patrick. *James and the Q Sayings of Jesus.* JSNT Supplement Series. Sheffield: JSOT Press, 1991.

_____. *A Spirituality of Perfection: Faith in Action in the Letter of James.* Collegeville, MN: Liturgical Press, 1999.

Hengel, Martin. "Jakobus der Herrenbruder—der erste 'Papst'?" in *Glaube und Eschatologie,* ed. Grasser and Merk. Tubingen: JCB Mohr, 1985, 71-104.

*Johnson, Luke Timothy. *Brother of Jesus, Friend of God: Studies in the Letter of James.* Grand Rapids, MI: Eerdmans, 2004.
After writing his excellent commentary, Johnson published his many articles on James which cover in a more in-depth way many issues related to the book.

*Levinsohn, Stephen H. *Discourse Features of NT Greek.* 2nd ed. Dallas: SIL, 2000.
One of the best treatments of discourse analysis with many examples from the NT.

Longacre, Robert E. *The Grammar of Discourse.* 2nd ed. New York, NY: Plenum, 1996.

_____. "Towards an Exegesis of 1 John Based on the Discourse Analysis of the Greek Text." Pages 271-86 in *Linguistics and New Testament Interpretation.* Edited by David Alan Black. Nashville, TN: Broadman, 1992.

Louw, Johannes P. *A Semantic Discourse Analysis of Romans.* Pretoria: University of Pretoria, 1979.

_____."Reading Texts as Discourse." Pages 17-30 in *Linguistics and New Testament Interpretation.* Edited by David Alan Black. Nashville, TN: Broadman, 1992.

Louw, J.P., and Eugene A. Nida. *Greek-English Lexicon of the New Testament: Based on Semantic Domains.* 2 vols. New York: United Bible Societies, 1998.

*MacArthur, John F., Jr. *The Gospel According to the Apostles.* Nashville: Word, 2000.
Although not limited to James, MacArthur's volume effectively utilizes James 2 to undergird his presentation of the Gospel.

Maynard-Reid, Pedrito U. *Poverty and Wealth in James.* Maryknoll, NY: Orbis Books, 1987.

Metzger, Bruce M. *A Textual Commentary on the Greek New Testament.* 2nd ed. New York: United Bible Societies, 1994.

Painter, John. *Just James: The Brother of Jesus in History and Tradition.* Rev. ed. Columbia: University of South Carolina Press, 2004.

Penner, Todd C. *The Epistle of James and Eschatology: Re-Reading an Ancient Christian.* JSNTSup. Sheffield: Sheffield Academic Press, 1996.

Pike, K. L. *Language in Relation to a Unified Theory of the Structure of Human Behavior.* The Hague: Mouton, 1967.

Porter, Stanley E. *Verbal Aspect in the Greek of the New Testament with Reference to Tense and Mood.* New York: Lang, 1989.

*_____. *Idioms of the Greek New Testament.* Sheffield: JSOT Press, 1992.
Porter has pioneered a more linguistic approach to Greek and the analysis of the New Testament. His work is both seminal and helpful.

_____."Jesus and the Use of Greek in Galilee." Pages 123-54 in *Studying the Historical Jesus: Evaluations of the State of Current*

..

Research. Edited by Bruce D. Chilton and Craig A. Evans. Leiden: Brill, 1994.

_____."Discourse Analysis and New Testament Studies: An Introductory Survey." Pages 14-35 in *Discourse Analysis and Other Topics in Biblical Greek.* Edited by Stanley E. Porter and D. A. Carson. Sheffield: Sheffield Academic Press, 1995.

_____ (ed). *Handbook to Exegesis of the New Testament.* Leiden: Brill, 1997.

Porter, Stanley E. and David Tombs (eds). *Approaches to New Testament Study.* Sheffield: Sheffield Academic Press, 1995.

Porter, Stanley E. and Craig A. Evans (eds). *New Testament Interpretation and Methods: A Sheffield Reader.* Sheffield: Sheffield Academic Press, 1997.

_____. *Linguistics and the New Testament: Critical Junctures.* JSNT Supplement Series. Sheffield: Sheffield Academic Press, 1999.

Porter, Stanley E. and Jeffrey T. Reed (eds). *Discourse Analysis and the New Testament.* JSNT Supplement Series. Sheffield: Sheffield Academic Press, 1999.

Reed, Jeffrey T. "Modern Linguistics and the New Testament: A Basic Guide to Theory, Terminology, and Literature." In *Approaches to New Testament Study.* Edited by Stanley E. Porter and David Tombs. Sheffield: Sheffield Academic Press, 1995.

_____. *A Discourse Analysis of Philippians: Method and Rhetoric in the Debate Over Literary Integrity.* Sheffield: Sheffield Academic Press, 1997.

*_____."Discourse Analysis." Pages 189-217 in *Handbook to Exegesis of the New Testament.* Edited by Stanley E. Porter. Leiden: Brill, 1997 *Along with Porter, Reed has been at the vanguard of developing a discourse analysis model that is applicable to all Biblical texts.*

*Runge, Steven E. *Discourse Grammar of the Greek New Testament.* Peabody, MA: Hendrickson Publishers, 2010. *Although this work was published too late for me to utilize it much, Runge has provided a pioneering study in a discourse approach to Greek grammar, plowing some fresh ground. Helpful.*

Sevenster, J. N. *Do You Know Greek? How Much Greek Could the First Jewish Christians Have Known?* Novum Testamentum Supplements. Leiden: Brill, 1968.

Silva, Moisés. *Biblical Words and Their Meanings: An Introduction to Lexical Semantics*. Grand Rapids, MI: Zondervan, 1983.

Tamez, Elsa. *The Scandalous Message of James: Faith Without Works is Dead*. Rev. ed. New York: Crossroad, 2002.

*Taylor, Mark E. *A Text-Linguistic Investigation into the Discourse Structure of James*. London: T&T Clark, 2006.
While Taylor's approach is not the discourse analysis method I prefer, his pioneering work is to be commended and is often quite insightful.

Stowers, Stanley K. *Letter Writing in the Greco-Roman Antiquity*. Philadelphia, PA: Westminster, 1986.

Wachob, Wesley Hiram. *The Voice of Jesus in the Social Rhetoric of James*. Society for New Testament Studies Monograph Series. Cambridge, MA: Cambridge University Press, 2000.

Wallace, Daniel B. *Greek Grammar beyond the Basics*. Grand Rapids: Zondervan, 1996.

Webb, Robert L., and John S. Kloppenberg, eds. *Reading James with New Eyes: Methodological Reassessments of the Letter of James*. London: T&T Clark, 2007.

JOURNAL ARTICLES

Amphoux, Christian B. "Vers une Déscription Linguistique de L'Épître de Jacques." *NTS* 25 (1978): 58-92.

Baasland, Ernst. "Der Jakobusbrief als Neutestamentliche Weisheitsschrift." *ST* 36 (1982): 199-39.

Cladder, Hermann J. "Die Anfang des Jakobusbriefes." *ZKT* 28 (1904): 37-57.

*Cranfield, C. E. B. "The Message of James." *SJT* 18 (1965): 192-93, 338-45.
Helpful summary with material that can be easily taught to others.

Elliot, John H. "The Epistle of James in Social Scientific Perspective: Holiness-Wholeness and Patterns of Replication." *BTB* 23 (1997): 71-72.

Francis, Fred O. "The Form and Function of the Opening and Closing Paragraphs of James and 1 John." *ZNW* 61 (1970): 110-26.

Jacob, I. "The Midrashic Background for James II, 21-23." *NTS* 22 (1975): 457-64.

*Kirk, J. A. "The Meaning of Wisdom in James: Examination of a Hypothesis." *NTS* 16 (1969-70): 24-38.
Explores the idea that wisdom in James is a reference to the Holy Spirit.

Laws, Sophie. "Does Scripture Speak in Vain? A Reconsideration of James IV. 5." *NTS* 20 (1973-74): 210-15.

Louw, Johannes P. "Discourse Analysis and the Greek New Testament." *BT* 24 (1973): 101-18.

McKnight, Scot. "James 2.18a: The Unidentifiable Interlocutor." *WTJ* 52 (1990): 355-64.

Perdue, Leo G. "Paraenesis and the Epistle of James." *ZNW* 72 (1981): 241-56.

Popkes, Wiard. "James and Scripture: An Exercise in Intertextuality." *NTS* 45 (1999): 213-29.

Reed, Jeffrey T. "Cohesive Ties in 1 Timothy: In Defense of the Epistle's Unity." *Neot* 26 (1992): 131-47.

_____."Discourse Analysis as New Testament Hermeneutic: A Retrospective and Prospective Appraisal." *JETS* 39 (1996): 223-40.

*Reese, James M. "The Exegete as Sage: Hearing the Message of James." *BTB* 12:82-85.
Excellent article stressing the wisdom theme and the significance of 3:13-18.

Schokel, L. Alonzo. "James 5, 2 (sic) and 4,6." *Biblia* 54:73-76.
An overlooked article that develops an argument and interpretation of James 5:6 that is based on discourse analysis, although the author does not call it that.

Shepherd, Massey H. "The Epistle of James and the Gospel of Matthew." *JBL* 75(1976): 40-51.

Terry, Ralph Bruce. "Some Aspects of the Discourse Structure of the Book of James." *Journal of Translation and Text-Linguistics* 5 (1992): 106-25.

Tollefson, Kenneth D. "The Epistle of James as Dialectical Discourse." *BTB* 21 (1997): 66-69.
An overlooked article that is very sensitive to the linguistic features of James. Tollefson also sees the importance of 3:13-18 in the overall structure of the book.

Varner, Wm. "A Discourse Analysis of Matthew's Nativity Narrative," *TB* 58.2 (2007): 98-120.

Wall, Robert W. "James as Apocalyptic Paraenesis." *ResQ* 32 (1990): 11-22.
Ward, Roy B. "Partiality in the Assembly: James 2:2-4." *HTR* 62: 87-97.

Watson, Duane F. "James 2 in Light of Greco-Roman Schemes of Argumentation." *NTS* 39 (1993): 94-121.

_____. "The Rhetoric of James 3.1-12 and a Classical Pattern of Argumentation." *NovT* 35 (1993):48-64.

Wifstrand, A. "Stylistic Problems in the Epistles of James & Peter." *ST* 1 (1948): 170-82.